Secrets of
Question

How the Most Powerful Tool in Business

Based

Can Double Your Sales Results

Selling

Thomas A. Freese

SOURCEBOOKS, INC.®
NAPERVILLE, ILLINOIS

This publication is designed to provide accurate and authoritative information in regard to the subject matter covered. It is sold with the understanding that the publisher is not engaged in rendering legal, accounting, or other professional service. If legal advice or other expert assistance is required, the services of a competent professional person should be sought. — *From a Declaration of Principles Jointly Adopted by a Committee of the American Bar Association and a Committee of Publishers and Associations*

QBS™, Question Based Selling™, The Herd Theory™, The Conversational Layering Model™, and The Mutual Agenda™ are all trademarks of QBS Research, Inc. All other brand names and product names used in this book are trademarks, registered trademarks, or trade names of their respective holders. Sourcebooks, Inc., is not associated with any product or vendor in this book.

Published by Sourcebooks, Inc.
P.O. Box 4410, Naperville, Illinois 60567-4410
(630) 961-3900
FAX: (630)961-2168

Library of Congress Cataloging-in-Publication Data

Freese, Thomas A.
    Secrets of question based selling: how the most powerful tool in business can double your sales results / Thomas A. Freese.
        p.cm.
    Includes index.
        ISBN 1-57071-658-7 (alk. paper).—ISBN 1-57071-588-2 (pbk.: alk. paper)
        1. Selling I. Title.

HF5438.F753 2000
658.85—dc21   00-044041

Printed and bound in the United States of America
BG   10   9   8   7   6   5   4   3   2   1

This book is dedicated to
my three miracles: My wife Laura,
and our daughters Sarah and Mary Claire.

Acknowledgments

Three long and wonderful years were invested in bringing this book to fruition. At the beginning of the project, it was easy to fill pages with words. Ideas were just flying onto the paper. As the project matured, however, it became clear that crafting my ideas about selling into a comprehensive and cohesive message was going to be an enormous challenge. But somehow it happened—and I could not have done it without the encouragement, loyalty, and support of a tremendous team of professionals and friends, whom I would like to thank, acknowledge, and congratulate.

Much appreciation goes out to Dr. Ross West who helped me to get the book started and point it in the right direction. As the project took off, Bobbie Christmas and Lee Kuck, both world-class editors, made significant contributions for which I am grateful. I wish to thank Emily Gilreath for her contribution in making this material more readable by removing my wayward commas and undangling my participles. I also wish to thank Ken Lucas for helping to create the QBS cover and Jill Dible whose book design experience and talents were able to transform my text and graphics into a work of art. Lastly, I wish to thank my good friend and fellow strategist, Dr. Michael Myers, Ph.D., for his publishing experience—but even more importantly, for helping me keep this project in perspective and on track.

I am grateful also to Scott Whitney for his contributions. In addition to creating a "killer" website for QBS Research, Inc., Scott's input was integral to the organization and development the QBS sales training programs that are now being delivered all over the world. He is a true professional.

Special thanks go out to my sales mentors whom I have had the privilege to work with and learn from over the years. In no particular order, I wish to acknowledge Barry Gillman, Chris Andrews, Rob Van Naarden, Paul Hoyt, Tom Mulstay, Jeff Hudson, John Van Siclen, Jim Jones, and Enzo Torresi.

Emotional support played a far greater role in the creation of this book than I could have imagined, and I can honestly say that this project would not have succeeded without the motivation and encouragement from the following talented and caring people: Richard Sites, Joe Monday, Judy Schwarz,

Harry Lockhart, Leslie Fletcher, Chip Graddy, Ruth Todd, Vivian Golub, Jim Elliott, Steve Johnson, Judy Feeley, David Averett, Steve Huey, David Reddaway, Jim Quigley, Greg Jones, and Matt Ure. I would like to add a special note of thanks to the men in my Bible study group who offered encouragement on a weekly basis since this project began.

I must also thank my clients as well as all the people who recommended Question Based Selling to their sales organizations, especially those people who were willing to take a chance on the QBS methodology before it took off.

Last but certainly not least, I wish to thank my wife and daughters for keeping the noise down to a dull roar while dad was upstairs writing.

Table of Contents

THE BEST SALES EXPERIENCE...I HOPE YOU NEVER HAVE.

On Monday, August 22, 1994, our dreams were shattered when my wife Laura was diagnosed with cancer. Sensing the gravity of the situation, Dr. George Cierny carefully placed a box of Kleenex on the adjoining table before telling us that a grapefruit-sized tumor had been discovered in Laura's hip. She had lymphoma, and we were both devastated.

In the blink of an eye, life as we knew it had changed. With a bouncing baby girl, two thriving professional careers, and a nice home in the suburbs, we had been living out the American Dream. Now, we were faced with the challenge of chemotherapy, the loss of Laura's mobility, and a 60/40 chance of survival. Laura's career was halted and she would probably lose fertility. On top of that, Dr. Cierny, as if he was looking down the barrel of a loaded gun, added, "We probably won't have to amputate...but we'll see."

Unless you have actually been there, it's hard to imagine the emotional impact of this news. It was like being hit in the face with a brick. The grief on my wife's face was daunting. I remember thinking, "This can't be happening!"

Success in my business life suddenly seemed unimportant. The fact that sales were booming was insignificant. Though I had achieved top sales honors for several consecutive years, these accomplishments now paled in comparison to the new challenges that lay ahead. It was a helpless feeling. After all, what difference does success make when everything else is falling apart?

After grieving over this news for several days, life found a way to slap us back into reality. The daily routine took over. There were chores to do and mouths to feed, and our two-year-old daughter needed our love and attention now more than ever. Self-pity was fruitless. Instead, we dug in—knowing that we were engaged in a battle that would yield only one winner.

Laura underwent chemotherapy treatments for six long months. When she wasn't in the hospital with complications, she was at home—struggling to maintain her strength. I continued to work, but mostly for therapeutic reasons. Selling was a release of sorts, one that helped distance me from the uncertainty of her medical condition. The usual seventy-hour work week shrank dramatically, and it was safe to assume that my sales would suffer as a result. Selling was still a passion, but it was no longer a priority.

This adversity caused my perspective to change dramatically. With respect to my selling career, it was as if a great burden had been lifted, where all the stress, anxiety, and pressures that usually exist in a competitive business situation were suddenly gone. No more nervous butterflies before key presentations. No more agonizing over things that were out of my control. While I still wanted to do a good job, I didn't have the time or the emotional energy to worry. As a result, I relaxed and focused on those things that were most important.

Ironically, this change in perspective placed me in a unique position of strength. Because I was no longer intimidated by the threat of losing a sale, it was easy to ask the "hard" questions without fearing how customers might respond. It was also easy to differentiate important action items from other things that were unnecessary. Those action items that were beneficial for the customer, my company, and me, got done. Anything that was unreasonable, superfluous, or unnecessary, didn't. It was that simple.

Everyone (including me) expected my sales results to drop off considerably, but that didn't happen. Devastation gave way to new resolve, and any lingering trepidation regarding a sale was quickly replaced by a new sense of clarity and purpose. In fact, during the six-month period that Laura was sick, I worked less and sold more. But not just a little more. I sold *twice as much* as I ever had. Twice as much! I couldn't believe it. The significance of this eclipsed anything else that I had ever accomplished.

Through a strange twist of fate, Laura's illness had actually created an opportunity. It had given me a chance to view the sales process from a completely different perspective. When new priorities took over, I no longer had anything to lose, and when the traditional risks of failure disappeared, my effectiveness soared. It was horrifying and enlightening at the same time—which is why I call it, *"The best sales experience...I hope you never have."*

With the efforts, prayers, and support of countless people, Laura's cancer was reversed into full remission. She had been to the edge and back—and when the battle was over, she emerged the winner. Laura reclaimed her energy, but she never lost her spirit. Several months later, thanks to the miracle of modern medicine, her hip was replaced and her mobility was fully restored. She was back.

Almost two years after Laura was diagnosed, tears flowed once again as the city of Atlanta was getting ready to host the Twenty-Sixth Summer Olympic Games. When the organizers for the Olympics heard about Laura's story, they recognized that she had faced the ultimate personal challenge and had won. Because it was clear that her victory over cancer was as great as anything that would be achieved on the athletic field, she was given the honor of carrying the Olympic Torch.

On July 19, 1996, friends and family joined an enthusiastic crowd of 50,000 people who lined the streets of Atlanta to cheer the Olympic torch relay as it passed by on the way to the opening ceremonies. Whether they knew it or not, they were cheering for Laura too as she hoisted the Olympic Flame—a symbol that reflected her own personal accomplishment. In fact, if you look closely, you can see the gold medal in her eyes.

While adversity didn't actually teach me how to sell, it did inspire me to complete my dream, which you are now holding in your hands. *Secrets of Question Based Selling* is the result of many years of extensive research, coupled with some good old-fashioned trial and error. As a sales methodology, QBS has already endured the test of time, and it has also proven itself under pressure.

My sincere hope is that this book will inspire you as much as it has me and the many others whom I have had the opportunity to instruct. Life is short, and success is *definitely* within reach. May your own experiences in sales, and in life, build on the premise that faith, commitment, and hard work will always persevere. Always!

Introduction

Have you ever noticed that companies all over the world spend millions of dollars telling salespeople *what to say*, but they spend almost nothing teaching them *what to ask*? It's true. Sales organizations invest in training salespeople how to position the value of their product or service, but they just assume salespeople already know how to ask the right questions.

In sales, questions are important. You have to ask questions to identify new opportunities, qualify accounts, and uncover needs. You have to ask questions to find out who will make the decision within your accounts, and to know how best to position your solution. You also have to ask questions to smoke out any objections and to find out what else needs to occur to close a transaction. Questions have always been the cornerstone of the sales process—but just because you want to ask questions doesn't mean your prospects and customers will respond favorably.

When I first started selling, I wanted to learn how to sell but even more importantly, I wanted to learn how to outsell the competition. Therefore, I read every sales book I could get my hands on. I also listened to audio cassette tapes and attended many different sales training programs in the hopes of mastering the strategic sale. When I got out into the territory, however, it became obvious that prospects weren't nearly as excited about answering my sales questions as I was about asking them. That's because every salesperson who called was asking the same old sales questions, and prospects didn't want to be bothered. I faced a similar problem getting prospects interested in listening to my sales presentation. Just because I had a great story to tell didn't mean prospects wanted to hear it. Once again, every salesperson who called claimed to have a great story.

Traditional sales methods were not helping to differentiate my product or my message. Prospects were less receptive than I had hoped, and the more sales calls I made, the more frustrated I became. To prospects, I was just another salesperson trying to get into their pockets. Even though I had not been selling for very long (at that point), it was clearly time for a new approach—something that would break down the traditional barriers of the sale to engage more prospects and significantly enhance my results.

Whether it was out of entrepreneurial instinct or desperation, I started to experiment with different techniques. Some worked quite well. Others failed miserably. When I found something that worked, I wanted to understand why it worked so I could repeat my success. Likewise, when something failed, I wanted to understand why it failed so I could avoid making the same mistake in the future. Over time, I compiled a battery of what-to-do's and what-not-to-do's that would forever alter the course of modern sales methods and training. Finally in 1996, I packaged this system into a strategic sales methodology called Question Based Selling.

Question Based Selling is a commonsense approach to sales based on the theory that what a salesperson asks...and how they ask, is more important than what they will ever say. This principle makes sense because in order to present solutions, you must first uncover a need. How do you find out what your prospects need? By asking questions. But not just any questions. To be effective in sales, you must ask questions that make prospects want to respond.

In QBS, we don't just tell you to go out and ask questions. That's not the way to be effective, especially not in a competitive environment. Instead, we show you how questions can be used to pique the prospect's interest and establish your credibility within the account. We show you how you can use questions to uncover greater needs and solicit more accurate information about where you stand in the sale. We also show you how to identify key players within the account, how to build internal champions that will support your product or service, and how to close more sales without having to face the traditional risks of rejection.

Question Based Selling will teach you how to engage more prospects in more productive sales conversation. We will show you how to move qualified opportunities forward in the sales process—toward a mutually beneficial exchange of value. Essentially, I reinvented the wheel so you don't have to.

While *Secrets of Question Based Selling* is ultimately about selling, your title need not be "salesperson" to benefit from this book. Consultants, architects, lawyers, accountants, recruiters, advertisers, public relations executives, and brokers all must sell to create and maintain clients. Small business owners and entrepreneurs must sell to stay in business. Even corporate managers have to sell their ideas to other managers, and to their subordinate teams. The truth is...everybody sells something.

Whether you're selling computer systems, life insurance, manufacturing equipment, advertising space, medical supplies, employee benefits, telecommunications, real estate, financial services, office furniture, consumer products, or professional services, many of the challenges are the same. You must break the ice with new prospects to find out what they need, and you must get them to want to hear about the solutions you offer. How do you get prospects and customers to take time out of their busy schedules? QBS will show you.

The QBS methodology is divided into three parts. Part 1 is a short course on QBS strategy. In the first five chapters, I explain the fundamental QBS strategies that differentiate QBS from other methods. Part 2 focuses on the most powerful tool in business—the strategic question. Here, we take an in-depth look at what to ask and how to ask it—showing how questions will enable you to accomplish your strategic objectives in the sale. In part 3, I show you how to implement each of the QBS strategies and techniques to help you more effectively navigate the sales process, contact new prospects, make better sales presentations, overcome objections, and close more sales...faster.

For me, QBS represents the culmination of a seventeen-year journey—one that has helped me realize that strategic questions are more than just staples of everyday conversation. Perhaps this marks the beginning of a new journey for you as well; not only as a motivated reader, but as a student of the question based sale. Congratulations on taking the first step. I wish you the best!

Thomas A. Freese
President, QBS Research, Inc.

Part One

A Short Course on QBS Strategy

O ne of the most difficult things about writing this
book was knowing where to begin. My intuition was
telling me to dive right into the heart of the sale, but I was
having trouble determining where the "heart" of the sale
actually was. It would have been easy to compile a list of
tips and techniques that would help in prospecting for new
business, making presentations, or closing sales. But
Question Based Selling is not just a compilation of tips and
techniques. It's a wholesale change in strategy.

To significantly increase your results, you must be willing to position yourself differently in the sale. This means
changing the way you uncover needs, understanding how
potential buyers are motivated, using references to create a
sense of momentum, and minimizing the risk of rejection
to increase your probability of success.

Part 1 of *Secrets of Question Based Selling* is a short
course on QBS strategy. The first five chapters are intended
to serve as building blocks for the rest of the QBS methodology, where you will learn how to break down traditional
barriers in the sale to engage more prospects in more productive sales conversation. Once you understand the fundamental strategies, parts 2 and 3 of the book will talk more
specifically about how to maximize your effectiveness in
every aspect of the sales process.

Chapter 1

INCREASING YOUR PROBABILITY OF SUCCESS

Selling has become increasingly more difficult. Prospects have less time...yet decision makers are receiving more sales calls than ever before. With a boom in the number of products being offered, "No" has become the standard response and the vast majority of sales calls end in rejection.

This creates an interesting dilemma for salespeople and sales managers. When the risk of rejection is high, sales productivity tends to be very low. QBS reverses this trend by showing salespeople that the best way to increase their probability of success is to decrease their risk of failure.

Selling is a creative act—one that requires salespeople to go out into their respective markets and create business opportunities that otherwise wouldn't exist. This means knocking on unfamiliar doors. It also means picking up the telephone and calling new prospect accounts. Of course, once you get in, the focus changes from that of engagement to further developing the opportunity. This includes uncovering prospect needs, building value around your solutions, and securing the prospect's commitment to move forward.

Sounds easy, doesn't it?

It isn't. In fact, for most salespeople it's becoming increasingly more difficult to secure a precious slice of the customer's time and attention, not to mention cracking into brand-new prospect opportunities.

Unless you sell commodity products at the lowest price, you're selling value—solutions that enable prospective buyers to save money, make money, or improve their existing condition. Just because your product or service solves a problem, however, doesn't mean prospects will automatically recognize an opportunity to enhance the status quo. That's why it's so important to engage new prospects in a productive conversation, to further explore their needs and the value you provide. Getting new prospects to want to engage is the challenge.

Much of my own background is in large account technology sales. This type of selling has its own unique set of challenges, starting with the fact that the corporate sales environment has changed significantly. While some prospect accounts have experienced explosive growth in their businesses, others have been forced to cut back. In either case, decision makers are being handed more responsibility without the benefit of additional resources.

In smaller sales, where salespeople are calling on small businesses or individual buyers, the situation isn't much different. Workloads continue to increase, competitors are noticeably hungrier, and the overall pace of business has quickened. This negatively impacts our ability to penetrate new accounts because potential customers cannot afford to spend time with each and every salesperson who comes calling.

In addition to having less time, prospects have also become much less accessible. Technological innovations such as email, voice mail, fax, cellular telephones, digital pagers, and the Internet have given prospects the freedom to execute their jobs away from their desks. While this is good in one sense, it also means your prospects are less likely to pick up the phone when you call.

Frankly, many prospects are reluctant to pick up the telephone anyway. With the rapid economic expansion that we have experienced in recent years, more vendors are offering more solutions than ever before. As a result, key decision makers are being inundated with a steady stream of salespeople who are all competing for the same thing—a chunk of the prospect's budget, but even more importantly, a slice of their time and attention.

Unfortunately, the sales profession in general has responded poorly to these business trends. As prospects and customers have had to become more judicious with their time, salespeople have started pushing even harder to get in. How do prospects respond to being pushed? Most push back in some way. When sellers call, some prospects get frustrated and hang up immediately. Other people program their phones to roll directly into a voice-mail system, or they use caller ID to hold salespeople at arms length. Invariably, the next salesperson who calls on the account will have to work even harder than the last—and they will also have to bear the brunt of any bad feelings that were created by previous callers.

When you combine all of these factors, it's no surprise that the average success rate when contacting new prospects has decreased significantly. Depending on which article you read, the average "hit rate" for engaging new prospects is between 2 and 5 percent. So, out of every one hundred sales calls, the average salesperson will uncover only a small handful of qualified opportunities.

This creates two problems for salespeople (and sales managers). First, given the low success rate when contacting new prospects, sellers are finding it difficult to fill the pipeline with revenue opportunities. As a result, otherwise diligent salespeople end up making call after call with little to show for their invested sales effort. Secondly, and even more importantly, when sellers know that they have a 95 to 98 percent probability of being rejected, it becomes very difficult for them to pick up the telephone and initiate contact.

Secret #1	Salespeople are being held at arms length, and rejection is making it more difficult for them to stay motivated.

Motivating salespeople is one thing. Getting them to stay motivated is another—and knowing that the vast majority of sales calls end in rejection is enough to demotivate even the most steadfast salespeople.

The Rules of Engagement Have Changed

Some sales organizations try to address this problem by telling their salespeople to make more calls. If you believe that sales is a numbers game, then increasing the number of calls you make should, in theory, increase the size of your forecast. Unfortunately, it doesn't work that way.

Say you want to penetrate a new prospect account, and through various contacts you find out that there are three key people who would need to sign off on a decision. You start calling and calling, leaving voice-mail messages with each person. When they don't return your calls, you continue calling, leaving daily messages for weeks on end. Now, let me ask you a question. Do you think your barrage of voice-mail messages would cause these prospects to view you as a competent professional, or do you think they would see you as more of a pest?

The other problem with the "make more calls" strategy is waste. Out of every one hundred sales calls, if only a small fraction turn into forecastable prospects, one has to wonder how many opportunities are being missed— prospects who have needs and budget, but haven't yet recognized an opportunity to improve their existing condition.

One sales book on my shelf tries to motivate sellers by changing the way salespeople view rejection. This particular author suggests that you should actually get excited every time you are rejected—because (in theory) every *no* moves you that much closer to a *yes*. With all due respect, I say, *"Hogwash!"* Show me a salesperson who gets excited about rejection, and I'll show you someone who is either chemically imbalanced, or who is much too comfortable with losing.

In addition to trying to fill the pipeline by making more sales calls, salespeople are also being directed to establish relationships with "gatekeepers," in the hopes that these relationships will eventually get them in to see the decision maker. In today's selling environment, this strategy is not as viable as it once was. Most of corporate America's gatekeepers have been replaced by automated telephone messaging equipment and as you might guess, it's virtually impossible to build a relationship with a voice-mail system. Consequently, salespeople end up leaving a professional sounding voice-mail message, in the hopes of provoking a return call.

The problem is that every seller who calls leaves a "professional sounding" message. Think about it. When a key decision maker retrieves his voice-mail messages, the majority of those messages are sales calls; and not surprisingly, many of them sound very much the same. To illustrate, here's a sample voice-mail message that a "typical" salesperson might leave.

> **Voice mail:** *"Hello Mr. Prospect, my name is Oliver Stevens, and I'm a senior sales representative with Continental Systems. We are the leading provider of productivity systems, and I wanted to take just a few minutes of your time to discuss how our family of products would positively impact your business. At your convenience, please call me back at (770) 555-6588."*

Sounds pretty good, doesn't it? It might even work—if it were the only voice-mail message on the prospect's machine. But chances are that it won't be. Key decision makers are constantly receiving cold calls just like this one from countless salespeople. In fact, it's not unusual for key players at lucrative prospect accounts to receive dozens of new sales calls on a weekly basis. The salesperson's name and the product they represent may be different, but the message they're attempting to communicate is essentially the same. As a result, lots of professional sounding messages are being left on voice-mail systems, but very few initial sales calls are ever returned.

Some salespeople get frustrated because prospects are so difficult to reach. They contend that it's not fair for prospects to ignore their sales calls. Ironically, I disagree. Even as a salesperson, I've always believed that just because an enthusiastic salesperson chooses to leave a voice-mail message doesn't mean the prospect is obligated to return the call. The truth is that most people don't have the time or the inclination to return every sales call that comes in, and frankly, they shouldn't have to. If a salesperson wishes to make contact, the burden is definitely on the seller. This raises an interesting question: What should salespeople do when their calls are not being returned? Should they leave a single voice-mail message and then wait indefinitely, or should they follow up with subsequent calls?

Persistence can still pay off, but only if salespeople understand that the rules of engagement have changed. In other words, sounding professional is no longer enough. Everyone sounds professional! And by definition, if you're just like everyone else, then you are average; in which case, you should expect average results. But average results don't pay the rent, and a success rate of only 2 to 5 percent makes it very difficult to populate a sales forecast and to generate enough revenue to succeed in sales.

While these may have been viable strategies in years past, competitive pressures along with market saturation have put a serious damper on what has traditionally been known as "smiling and dialing." Hence, there is a serious need to replace this churn and burn mentality with a new, and highly differentiated, sales approach.

Secret #2	In order to achieve above-average results, one must first be open to thinking about above-average concepts.

Question Based Selling offers a unique approach. While "old school" sales methods teach salespeople how to conform and sound like everyone else, QBS shows you how to be different, but not just for the sake of being different. Rather, we show you how to differentiate yourself for the sake of achieving above-average sales results. Now, everybody wins!

Selling Isn't about "Right" and "Wrong"

Training salespeople has always been a difficult task—one that ranks right up there with grooming attack dogs, or answering stockholder's questions at the annual meeting. Resistance is expected, and it's kill or be killed.

From the viewpoint of the salesperson, I completely understand how the training audience feels, as my own experience in corporate sales required me to sit through countless sales training programs—many of which were average at best. Let's be honest. Most of us don't want to be trained. Either we've heard it all before, or we're starting to realize that "old school" sales methods aren't necessarily the most productive approach. Nonetheless, salespeople are being asked to attend additional sales training programs, and they are expected to participate. But that doesn't mean they will buy into what's being taught.

Something else that makes sales training difficult to swallow is change. In order to increase your sales results, you have to be open to changing your behavior—after all, if you continue doing exactly the same things, you should expect exactly the same results. But like most people, salespeople are creatures of habit and they are naturally resistant to change.

Secret #3	A salesperson who continues doing exactly the same things should expect exactly the same results.

Before I assumed my current role as author, speaker, and trainer, I was just another salesperson in the audience. And like most of the other participants, I remember feeling a little uncomfortable, and sometimes even defensive, when the person leading the session started talking about change. *"What do you mean I should change?"* I would think to myself. *"Are you implying that my current approach to selling is wrong?"* Of course I was defensive. Who wants to be told they're doing it wrong?

But now that I'm on the other side of the podium, I see that lots of people are just as resistant to change as I was—some because they are already set in their ways, and others because they don't want to hear that their current approach to selling is wrong. Well, let me put you at ease. As a sales methodologist, I hold the same opinion now that I did when I was selling.

I believe there is no right way to sell. Conversely, it's pointless to tell someone else that their current approach to selling is wrong. Thousands of sales methods are being used at companies all over the world. Extrapolate this further, and you'll find that an infinite number of variations exist as individual salespeople apply standard methods within their own unique territories. Not surprisingly, some sales approaches are more effective than others. They yield better and more consistent results. But we have to be careful deeming any one approach to be the "right way," because technically, that would mean everything else is wrong. This is an inference that has unfortunately caused many sales trainers to fall on their swords.

Characterizing the sales process in terms of "right" and "wrong" overlooks the fact that everyone, and every sales situation, is unique. People you call on will have different needs, biases, and experiences. They will also respond differently in certain situations. Furthermore, what's right for one prospect, could be very wrong for another. People are just different; and for that reason, the next prospect you call on is likely to be very different from the last. Even when you're dealing with a specific individual, their situation will probably change over time, and what seems right today might be wrong tomorrow.

The truth is, terms like "right" and "wrong" are much too absolute to have any constructive value. After reading this book, I suspect you'll make some changes, but not because QBS is right and your current approach to selling is wrong. Rather, you'll make changes because you will discover new and more productive ways to approach the sales process, using techniques that will increase your probability of success and decrease your risk of failure.

A Methodology Based on Cause and Effect

Now that we've adequately disposed of the words "right" and "wrong," we still need to have some metrics for measuring progress in the sale. To accomplish this, we focus our attention in two areas: *probability* and *risk.*

In sales, success is achieved by managing a series of events and activities toward a specific goal—the sale. Obviously, it makes sense to incorporate those techniques and strategies that will move you closer to the desired goal, while disregarding other actions that produce undesirable results. But since every sale is unique, the sales process can never be a rigid formula that stays exactly the same in every situation. Instead, QBS has developed a framework that's based on cause and effect—a methodology that will help identify those things that will move you closer to making a sale and those things that will move you farther from it.

This framework allows us to begin categorizing the things we do in the sales process in terms of whether or not they increase our probability of success. When something we do causes prospects to respond favorably, this is good because it increases our probability of success and moves us closer to making a sale. On the other hand, if something we do causes an undesirable result, this is bad because it decreases our probability of success.

One of our goals in QBS is to simplify the sale. We accomplish this by identifying the events, activities, and strategies that will increase your probability of success, and incorporating them into the sales process. But rather than ignore the negatives, we also want to identify (and avoid) those things that will hinder our progress. Not every idea is a good one, and not every activity adds value.

The single most effective way to increase your probability of success in a sale is to decrease your risk of failure. It's one of the great secrets of consistent sales performance. Probability and risk share an inverse relationship in sales: when one goes up the other goes down. The greater your risk, the lower your probability of success. On the flip side, it's also true that lowering your risk of failure will increase your probability of success.

Secret #4	The most effective way to increase your *probability* of success is to decrease your *risk* of failure.

This is an important point, because it's no longer enough to pat salespeople on the back and send them out into a competitive marketplace. That's why our goal in QBS is maximizing your sales effectiveness by showing you how to increase your probability *and* decrease your risk.

The Greatest Challenge Salespeople Face

Most of the sales books I've read over the years talk about increasing probability, but very few talk about risk. Frankly, it's a discussion that doesn't fit in with all the hype, enthusiasm, and motivational hoopla that accompany so many sales training programs. I raise the issue because reducing your risk of failure is one of the ways that Question Based Selling is going to increase your success in sales.

Earlier, we said that selling is a creative act—one that requires sellers to create business opportunities that otherwise wouldn't exist. Of course, this is a risk/reward proposition. Every time you pick up the phone or knock on a door, a certain amount of risk is incurred. The prospect on the other end of the call could say no, which means your call would end in rejection. But you must call new prospects to increase the depth of your pipeline. It's a dilemma for many salespeople, because the risk of rejection is compounded with each additional sales call—and who wants to increase their own risk? This creates an interesting problem for sales managers too, as salespeople who feel a greater risk of failure are less excited about picking up the telephone and making calls.

Secret #5	The greater their risk, the more reluctant salespeople are to pick up the telephone and initiate contact.

Let's face it; rejection hurts. It's ominous and it's very personal, but it isn't new. As a kid, I remember how it used to feel to be the last one picked in gym class. I also remember agonizing for days before getting up the nerve to ask Tonya Buehler to the tenth-grade dinner dance. She was nice about it, but she still declined. I was crushed. Perhaps you've had similar experiences of rejection

So here we are, trying to build a career in professional sales, and guess what? It still hurts when somebody says, "*No thanks,*" or, "*I'm not interested.*" While your best prospects will let you down easy, other prospects might say no right to your face. Some will just take the easy way out and choose not to return your calls. Whatever the method, being rejected feels bad and makes it that much more difficult for salespeople to muster the courage to engage the next prospect.

The risk of rejection is the greatest challenge salespeople face. In sales, confidence is critical. But how self-assured can a salesperson be, given that the average success rate when trying to initiate a conversation with new prospects is less than 5 percent? Before you even dial the phone, the odds are stacked against you, which is enough to make anyone nervous.

Sales trainers are quick to point out that the risk of rejection is just part of the game; it's something every salesperson must learn to live with. "*Rejection comes with the territory,*" they say, "*so deal with it.*" In my view, this attitude misses the larger point, which is: just because the risk of rejection does exist, it doesn't mean that salespeople have to accept it.

Eliminate the Risk and Salespeople Will Run to the Phones

In addition to increasing your probability of success, Question Based Selling is also a risk-reduction strategy. I say this because every QBS technique and strategy that you will read about in this book is specifically designed to increase your probability of success and to decrease your risk of failure. In a sense, we enhance your sales effectiveness from both directions.

For sales managers, taking steps to proactively reduce a salesperson's risk can pay enormous dividends. To illustrate the point, here's a short parable that demonstrates what might happen if it were possible to completely remove all the risk from the sales process.

Only One Wish

Once upon a time, a QBS instructor was brought in to train a company's sales organization as part of their quarterly sales kick-off meeting. It was an energetic session in the ballroom of a major hotel, to an enthusiastic audience. Midway through the training, when it was time to talk about reducing the risk of failure, the QBS instructor walked over to a dusty old trunk that had been sitting off to one side of the stage. This was no ordinary trunk, however. It was a magic trunk. The QBS instructor slowly opened the trunk, reached in, and ever so gently removed a brass lamp.

This was no ordinary lamp, however. It was a magic lamp, and the instructor went on to explain that according to legend, inside this lamp lived an all-powerful genie. But the only way the genie would appear was if someone from the audience came up and rubbed the magic lamp. And as you might guess, this was not just an ordinary genie. He was a magic genie, one who was able to grant a single wish.

Before the QBS instructor even had a chance to ask for a volunteer, someone in the front row started waving their hand wildly. As luck would have it, this particular hand belonged to the vice president of sales, who bounded up to the stage volunteering to rub the magic lamp. Sure enough, out popped the magic genie to grant this sales executive a single wish. The vice president closed his eyes and calmly made his wish, which was instantly granted.

At first, everything seemed the same. Of course, the audience was on the edge of their seats, dying to know what the VP of sales had wished for. A million dollars? Beach-front real estate? What about peace on earth and goodwill toward men?

The genie explained, *"Your leader was very unselfish, for his wish was not for himself, it was for you—his salespeople."* The audience grew even more excited, wanting desperately to know what their VP had wished for. The genie continued: *"Because of your vice president's wish, every sales call you make (pointing to the audience) from now until the end of the month is guaranteed to produce a sale."*

Then, with a puff of smoke, the genie disappeared back into the lamp.

If we suppose for a moment that this story could really occur, how do you think these salespeople would respond? For the rest of the month, the genie has completely removed their risk of failure. No more, *"No thank yous."* Every sales call is 100 percent guaranteed to close! Do you think they would be excited? You bet they would be excited. People in this audience would likely share the same apprehensions about risk and rejection that we do. But since the magic genie has completely removed their risk, they can make sales calls without the usual trepidation that makes selling so difficult. Without the traditional risks of rejection, it's easier to pick up the telephone and knock on unfamiliar doors to initiate contact with new prospects.

| Secret #6 | Eliminate the risk...and salespeople will run to the phones. |

This story is a little corny perhaps, but it makes a very important point. If we can eliminate the traditional risks of rejection, salespeople will run to the phones. Not only will they make more calls, they will make them with greater confidence, and their productivity will soar. So will their sales performance. As we go deeper into the QBS methodology, you'll see that reducing your risk of rejection can do more than anything else to increase your sales productivity and your results.

The Ultimate Risk

Long before I landed a professional sales position, I got my first real taste of rejection when I started dating. As a younger man, I was never what you'd consider a hunk, but I didn't have one eye in the center of my forehead either. I was just an average guy with a below average self-image, especially when it came to asking that special someone for a date.

Some people call dating "the ultimate sale." That's a fair description, because just like sales, dating is a positioning ritual that either brings potential partners closer together or drives them farther apart. I call dating the ultimate risk—because when you get rejected, there's no place to hide. At least in sales, if a prospect chooses not to buy our product or service, we can easily deflect any feelings of rejection away from ourselves. I'm not saying it's right, but it's definitely common for salespeople who lose a sale to blame something other than themselves. Sometimes we blame the product. Other times we blame the parent company, the price, or the administrative staff. Some salespeople even blame the customer, because in their opinion, the customer made the wrong decision. I'm sure we've all done it.

With dating, however, there is no one else to blame. If the target of your affections says no, it's not the fault of the documentation, the support staff, or the price. With dating, you're the product—which is particularly scary when you realize that a "no" really means, *I'm not interested in YOU.* This type of personal rejection is very difficult to swallow. In addition to humbling even the most resilient egos, rejection discourages people from being persistent and asking for dates in the future.

For those people who are extremely self-assured, dating is a numbers game. I've known guys who were willing to walk up to complete strangers and ask them for a date. When they get rejected, they just move on and ask someone else. Most of us can't just ignore our feelings like that, however. Whether we're closing a sale or asking for a date, we're timid about popping the question because we don't want to be personally rejected.

The Best Sales Movie Ever Made

The risk of rejection is real, and the fear of failure can intimidate even the most well-intentioned salespeople. Unfortunately, this causes us to miss out on some otherwise lucrative opportunities because it's human nature to avoid risk, rather than jeopardize our confidence or endanger our self-esteem. Although it sounds self-defeating, it's a common reaction.

Whether it was dating or selling, the fear of rejection posed a real problem for me. In the dating arena, I used to shudder at the thought of having to walk all the way across the dance floor to ask someone to dance. If they said no, I would then have to walk all the way back, pretend I wasn't really interested, order a beer, talk to my friends, and use the restroom—all in a feeble attempt to deflect the feeling of having been rejected.

But while I was extremely averse to the risk that came with dating, I didn't want to spend the next fifty years as a monk either. Fortunately, out of adversity comes opportunity, and it was my own fear of rejection that led to the development of the technique that I am about to explain. The premise is simple. You can significantly reduce your risk of rejection by knowing where the other person stands before you actually pop the question. How do you find out where the other person stands? By sending a "single ping."

The idea came to me several years ago after watching a film that I now call the best sales movie ever made: *The Hunt for Red October*. For those who haven't seen it, *The Hunt for Red October* is an epic thriller starring Sean Connery and Alec Baldwin, based on a Tom Clancy novel by the same name. For those of you who have seen the film, you're probably wondering what a movie about Russian espionage and the defection of a nuclear submarine has to do with selling? You're about to see.

The Hunt for Red October

In a suspenseful moment midway through the film, the Soviet Union's flagship nuclear submarine (*Red October*), and its American counterpart (*USS Dallas*) suddenly find themselves less than one hundred yards apart, near the bottom of the North Atlantic ocean. Both submarine crews jump into action to arm their weapons, and they stand ready to fire upon the other vessel.

Alec Baldwin, a CIA officer on board the *Dallas*, acts on a hunch that the Russian captain wants to defect to the United States, and begs the American officers not to fire upon the *Red October*. After a few tense moments, the American captain reluctantly agrees to follow the young CIA officer's hunch. Instead of firing their weapons, the Americans attempt to communicate with the Russians.

Cautiously, the American captain sends a coded message asking the Russians if they wish to communicate. Sure enough, the Russians respond by sending a single sonar ping. In Navy terms, this is the equivalent of waving a white flag, only underwater. Once the American captain discovered that the Russians did intend to defect, they communicate further and the movie goes on to resolve itself—although I won't spoil the ending if you haven't seen the film.

What does a Hollywood movie scene about Soviet espionage have to do with sales? In this case, a lot. This scene shows us how we can reduce our risk of rejection by finding out where the other person stands, rather than just sticking our neck out and hoping that it doesn't get chopped off.

For salespeople, this solves a critical problem. Statistics show that the average sale requires five closing attempts before a prospect is ready to make an emotional commitment. In my experience, this is definitely true, as very few prospects hand over a check after the very first closing attempt. Instead, they need to get comfortable with the idea of owning the product or service before they are ready to make a purchase decision. But most salespeople, particularly those who are averse to risk, don't ever make it to the fifth attempt. Frankly, they stop asking—because of risk. As a result, many qualified sales opportunities are being left on the table. Perhaps this explains why, in most sales organizations, 20 percent of the salespeople generate 80 percent of the revenue.

> **Secret #7**   The average sale requires five closing attempts before prospects are ready to make an emotional commitment, but the average salesperson never makes it to the fifth attempt.

Now let's go back to our dating analogy. Suppose you wanted to ask someone out on a date. You could try the traditional approach, asking: *"Would you like to have dinner with me Friday night? I know a good restaurant."* It's direct and to the point, and she (or he) might say yes. But she could also say no. Even worse, she could give you a lame excuse; in which case you would tend to assume the worst, and it becomes very difficult to risk rejection and ask again.

Rather than forge ahead with the traditional high risk/high rejection strategy, I decided to try something different. By applying what I learned from watching *The Hunt for Red October*, I was able to significantly reduce my risk of rejection. You can reduce your risk too. It's simple. The next time you want to ask someone for a date, you can significantly reduce your risk of rejection by saying:

> **You:** *"This is fun talking with you. You know, (pause) we ought to do something sometime. (pause again)"*

You've successfully signaled your interest by sending a single ping. Granted, you haven't yet secured a date, but you haven't been rejected either.

This approach eliminates your risk for two reasons. First, because you haven't officially asked for anything, it's impossible to be rejected. Essentially, you are just making a suggestion. Second, and even more important, this approach is crafted in a way that almost guarantees a favorable response. Very few people, women or men, would respond by saying, *"No, let's not do anything, ever."*

Keep in mind that selling is a process, and it's usually not an effective strategy to push for the order in the initial moments of a sales call. The same is true when you're selling yourself. That's why we're not asking for a life-long commitment in this anecdote. Instead, we're simply trying to get one foot in the door so we will have an opportunity to build on our smaller successes.

Listen for the Return Ping

After you extend yourself by sending an opening ping, what happens next is extremely important. You'll want to pause and listen carefully for a return ping—to see if the other person wants to "do something sometime."

Because this approach is extremely nonthreatening, you make it easy for the other person to respond; and how they respond will likely reveal their level of interest. Let's play out a scenario. (We'll assume that the target of your affections in this example is named Alex.) Here's what might happen to complete the opening exchange:

> **You:** *"Alex, this is fun talking with you. You know, (pause) we ought to do something sometime. (pause again)"*
>
> **Alex:** *"That sounds good."*

Congratulations are in order as you successfully cleared the first hurdle! The target of your affections didn't say no, and you've sidestepped the traditional risks of rejection. But we're not finished yet, because we don't have a date. We also don't have enough information to know whether Alex is truly interested or just being nice. That's why it makes sense to continue the dialogue by asking the next logical question, which is:

You: *"Terrific! What kind of things do you like to do?"*

At a minimum, Alex will be flattered by your continuing interest. And once again, you have successfully sidestepped the risk of rejection, because you still haven't asked for anything. If the other person is interested in dating you, they will respond by telling you what they enjoy. For example, Alex might say:

Alex: *"I like dinner, movies, theater, golf, tennis, music, ..."*

> **Secret #8**   Once it's clear that a prospect is interested, securing their commitment to take the next step is easy.

This is a best-case scenario. Essentially, Alex's response is saying, *"Yes, I would like to get together, and here are some of the things I would like to do."* This makes your job easy. All you have to do is choose from the list and schedule an appointment (i.e., a date).

Persistence Does Pay Off

Now comes the tricky part. Not every single ping you send will yield a best-case scenario. Some people won't respond as eagerly with a list of activities that they would enjoy. Instead, they will be noncommittal and offer a vague response. Let's quickly replay the scenario and you'll see what I mean:

You: *"Alex, this is fun talking with you. You know, (pause) we ought to do something sometime. (pause again)"*

Alex: *"That sounds good."*

You: *"Terrific! What kind of things do you like to do?"*

Alex: *"Oh…just different things."*

Alex's response is noncommittal which means one of two things. Either this person is not interested in "getting together" with you and she is trying to dodge the question, or she doesn't understand Navy sonar language and she didn't catch the meaning of your initial ping.

But don't worry. Once your risk of rejection has been significantly reduced (because you still haven't asked for anything), it's much easier to hang in there. Again, you're simply furthering the dialogue by asking what they like to do. Remember, selling is a process. So, let's continue the scenario, only this time, let's take one more shot with Alex to see if there might be an interest:

> **You:** *"Alex, this is fun talking with you. You know, (pause) we ought to do something sometime. (pause again)"*
>
> **Alex:** *"That sounds good."*
>
> **You:** *"Terrific! What kind of things do you like to do?"*
>
> **Alex:** *"Oh...just different things."*
>
> **You:** *"What kinds of things?"*

In business and in dating, very few prospects will penalize you for showing interest. By following up on Alex's response, and asking, *"What kinds of things?"* you give Alex another chance to respond favorably, especially if she (or he) didn't understand your initial ping. If Alex is indeed interested, she will make a list, offering movies, dinner, golf, tennis, and just like before, you simply choose from the list and schedule an appointment.

What If They're Just Not Interested?

Like it or not, some people won't be interested in pursuing a relationship; in which case, you will probably get another ambiguous response like, *"I don't really go out that much."* This type of response means that you are probably not going to get a date—at least not now.

But it doesn't mean you've been rejected. The reason you sent a single ping was to eliminate your risk. You wanted to find out whether the other person was interested in "getting together" before you crossed the chasm of risk and asked for a date. If this approach uncovers an interest, you can choose from a list of options and schedule a date. But when it's obvious that the target of your affections is not interested, in my opinion, it's much better to approach them at another time, under different circumstances.

The old school of sales training contradicts this by suggesting that if you aren't going to accomplish the objective of securing an appointment, then you might as well go down in flames. This mentality actually encourages salespeople to keep pressuring prospects until they literally throw you out of their office. QBS disagrees with this for two reasons. First, while forceful tactics may pressure some people into saying yes, this type of aggression rarely fosters a lasting business relationship. Secondly, timing is critical in sales. Many of my biggest sales successes started with a no, but since circumstances do change, I always wanted to leave the door open to pursue the opportunity later—which isn't possible if your strategy is to either win now or go down in flames.

Opening the Floodgates of Opportunity

Whether it's cultivating new prospects or asking someone for a date, crossing the chasm of risk is difficult. But it doesn't have to be. You can use this and other QBS techniques to reduce your risk so approaching new prospects and asking for a commitment is no longer difficult. This will open the floodgates of opportunity and enable you to be more effective than ever before.

Secret #9	When you reach out to someone by saying, "*We ought to do something sometime*," the worst they can say is yes.

If we translate this single ping strategy into business terms, we find there are numerous ways to use questions within the QBS methodology to reduce or eliminate your risk. For example, when calling new prospects, I usually open the conversation by asking, "*Did I catch you at a bad time?*" In addition to being polite, it's a question that reduces your risk because very few people will blast you with a negative response. If the prospect says, "*No, this is not a bad time,*" then you have their permission to proceed. On the other hand, if they say, "*Yes, this is a bad time,*" then you know that plowing forward and interrupting them wouldn't have succeeded anyway. But rather than hanging up, I ask another positioning question, "*When should I call back?*" Again, very few civilized people will say, "*Don't ever call me back.*" Instead, they give me a time to call back. Now I have an appointment. We'll talk more specifically about penetrating new accounts in chapter 12, "Turn Your Cold Calls into Lukewarm Calls".

Here's another way to reduce your risk. To be an effective salesperson, you have to ask a lot of probing questions, right? But you first have to earn the right to ask. That's why one of the first questions I always ask is, "*Can I ask you a question?"* Virtually everyone will say, *"Sure."* It's a predictable response. Now I have secured the prospect's permission to proceed.

To cite another example of how to reduce your risk, suppose you are trying to close a sale that you've been working on for quite some time. You could take the direct approach by sticking your neck out and hoping that it doesn't get chopped off. But, as a risk-reduction strategy, I would much rather find out where the customer stands first by saying:

> **Salesperson:** *"Mr. Prospect, you've been considering our proposal for some time now. Does it makes sense for us to think about sitting down and wrapping up the details?"*

Notice that I'm not asking for a commitment to buy. I am simply asking if it "makes sense" to "think about sitting down." In most cases, the prospect's response will let you know exactly where they stand. If they don't agree that it makes sense to "think about sitting down," then the prospect is not ready to make a commitment—in which case, it's time to find out what the issues are and what else needs to occur to close the sale.

While these may seem like simple examples, this technique of reducing your risk will become increasingly significant as the QBS methodology unfolds. Note: I realize that we haven't addressed all of the issues that can affect your sales here in chapter 1. But that wasn't the point. The point was to change your mind-set—from thinking in terms of right and wrong, to focusing more on increasing your probability and decreasing your risk.

Summary

Success in selling is based on cause and effect. Everything you say and do in the sales process will either move you closer to a successful sale or farther from it. Likewise, everything we do throughout the rest of this book is designed to increase your probability of success and to decrease your risk of failure. This cause and effect relationship is fundamental to the successful implementation of Question Based Selling.

Increasing your probability of success and reducing your risk produces a dual benefit in terms of sales productivity. On one hand, your hit rate will increase when calling new prospect accounts. This means you will engage more prospects in more productive sales conversation. At the same time, your confidence will increase dramatically, enabling you to move existing opportunities through the sales process faster.

Chapter 2

MISMATCHING:
THE AVOIDABLE RISK

In high school physics, students learn that for every action, there is an equal and opposite reaction. That's exactly what happens in the strategic sale. The harder you push, the harder your prospects and customers push back. In Question Based Selling, this is a counterproductive response behavior we call mismatching.

In this chapter, you will learn what causes mismatching to occur, how it makes prospects more cautious and standoffish, and most importantly, how to minimize the effects of mismatching for greater sales results.

Have you ever had one of those conversations where the person you are talking with seems to clarify or contradict everything you say? You make a point, and they immediately take the opposite position. Or, you interject a comment, and they feel a need to share something better or more impressive. Needless to say, these are very frustrating behaviors that usually put a damper on any further discussion.

In everyday conversation, this occurs more often than you'd think. For example, make an innocent comment like, *"I hear it's supposed to be nice this weekend,"* and you might be surprised how often people will take the opposite position. In some cases, they will say, *"Really? I thought it was supposed to rain,"* or be *"too hot,"* or *"too windy,"* or *"too humid."* Perhaps they'll contend that the weekend is *"too far away,"* or *"too close,"* or maybe they'll just lament about the upcoming weekend because they have to *"clean the garage."* In each of these responses, the person is *mismatching* your original supposition that the weekend is supposed to be "nice."

Mismatching is a form of disagreement. It's an instinctive and emotional behavior that causes people to respond or push back in a contrarian manner, usually by taking the opposite viewpoint on what's being said.

The human body has certain natural reflexes. Blinking is a good example. If I were to flick my fist toward your eyes, you would blink. My action would cause an instinctive response. You wouldn't have time to evaluate the situation, and you would not make a conscious decision to contract your eyelid muscles. Reflexes would just take over, and you would instinctively blink.

While blinking is a physical reflex, mismatching is an emotional reflex, but it works much the same way. It's an emotional knee-jerk reaction that causes people to respond in a contrarian manner.

To see mismatching for yourself, try this simple experiment. Walk into a customer's office (or your manager's office) and cheerfully ask, *"Did I catch you at a good time?"* Watch carefully to see how they respond. More often than not, they will respond cautiously, saying something like, *"That depends on what you need."* Next, try the opposite. Walk into someone else's office and ask, *"Did I catch you at a bad time?"* Once again, observe their response. In many cases, they will instantly invite you in, saying, *"No, no. It's OK. What can I do for you?"*

People will mismatch just about anything. One afternoon while I was raking leaves in my side yard, I was lamenting to my neighbor that yard work is cruel and unusual punishment. He replied by saying, *"What do you mean? Working in the yard is relaxing and enjoyable."* Later on that same day, I thought it would be interesting to try the opposite—so I commented to my other neighbor that yard work is "relaxing and enjoyable." Sure enough, he took the opposite position, telling me why having to work in the yard was depressing. Was it pure coincidence that each neighbor took the opposing viewpoint? I don't think so.

> **Secret #10** Mismatching is the instinctive tendency of individuals to resist, push back, or respond in a contrarian manner.

Do people mismatch every time? Of course not. Mismatching is not a programmed response; it's a behavioral tendency. But mismatching does occur, especially for those of us in sales. Even when it's just an innocent comment, you might be surprised at how often prospects, customers, coworkers, and business partners will take the opposite position.

Agreement Brings People Together

In sales, buyers and sellers are coming together as partners in a mutual exchange of value. The key word here is *mutual*. When a sales transaction occurs, it should be good for the buyer and good for the seller.

This doesn't happen by accident, however. To have a mutual exchange of value, sellers must first get prospective buyers to agree that they have a need. Once a need is identified, then sellers must get prospects to agree that their product or service provides enough value to justify its cost. We show you how to uncover needs and present value later, but for now, let's focus on the psychology of the sales interaction.

Success in selling is largely a matter of bringing people together. We want prospective customers to feel comfortable, and we want them to openly share their needs, thoughts, feelings, and concerns. Essentially, we want to be invited to participate in a more in-depth conversation—because the more you know about the prospect's needs, the more opportunities you will have to provide valuable solutions.

Secret #11   Agreement is the emotional bond that brings people together to form mutually beneficial business relationships.

Contrast this with the feeling many prospects have when first meeting a new salesperson. Until they get a sense that the salesperson can truly add value, they usually are cautious and reluctant, unwilling to share their needs, thoughts, feelings, and concerns. The have not yet established a trust of the salesperson and, therefore, before you have a mutual relationship, prospects are more likely to push you away than invite you in.

Mismatching Is a Form of Resistance

For all the reasons agreement is your ally in the strategic sales process, disagreement is your enemy. Instead of bringing people together, disagreement drives them apart. In conversation, disagreement leads to an increased sense of resistance. When people disagree, they tend to distance themselves emotionally to avoid further confrontation or debate. They are also more cautious and reluctant to share ideas and opinions. Now let me ask, would you rather be openly invited into a more in-depth conversation or cautiously pushed away?

Mismatching is a form of resistance that communicates disagreement. As you saw earlier, someone who mismatches is essentially disagreeing with you. They're pushing back against something you said, or something you've done. Instead of agreeing that the coming weekend will be "nice," as in our example, mismatchers will disagree by saying it's going to be too hot, too windy, or too humid.

> **Secret #12** Mismatching communicates disagreement, which increases
> your risk and lowers your probability of success.

Because mismatching communicates disagreement, it has a destructive influence on sales conversations. Instead of fostering a sense of mutuality, mismatching causes discord, where people who mismatch are either trying to control the conversation or satisfy their own need to add value.

This is important because your ability to minimize the negative effects of mismatching can significantly reduce your risk, which in turn increases your probability of success. But to minimize the negative effects of mismatching, you must first understand what causes this behavioral tendency to occur.

Where Mismatching Originates

Because mismatching is a behavioral reflex, virtually everyone does it, albeit to varying degrees. In fact, when I explain mismatching to sales audiences, I can literally watch the expressions on people's faces change as they recognize their own behavior in some of the examples. Remember, mismatching is a very common and instinctive behavioral mechanism.

The question is, why do people mismatch? So far, we've talked about mismatching in terms of disagreement. This makes the act of mismatching sound like an intentionally malicious offense. Oddly enough, it's usually not. Mismatching is usually more of a defense mechanism than an intuitive response.

> **Secret #13** Mismatching is more of an instinctive defense mechanism
> than an intuitive response.

Mismatching is rarely driven by someone's desire to disagree; in fact, the opposite is true. It's usually driven by the need to feel valuable. Let's face it—most of us want to feel smart. We want to be respected and we want to feel that we are contributing something valuable in the conversation. Behavioral scientists would characterize this as our need to self-actualize.

People have an instinctive desire to feel valuable. We also have a need for social acceptance. But trying to add value in a conversation can unfortunately lead to mismatched responses. For example, if someone were to say, *"The ceilings in this house are very tall,"* and someone else responded by saying, *"I agree,"* how much value have they added to the conversation?

The answer is none. By simply agreeing, they are not offering any new ideas or additional information.

Therein lies the problem. People who want to feel valuable look for opportunities to interject new information into the conversation. They want to add something of value, something the other person may not have considered. In our very first example, the mismatcher interjected information in an attempt to share why the upcoming weekend might be something other than "nice."

Secret #14   A mismatched response satisfies the needs of the mismatcher more than it disagrees with the content of the discussion.

People are natural mismatchers—but not out of disrespect toward others. Rather, it's because we are naturally insecure. And that's the key point: while agreement is certainly an emotional bond that brings people together, it often fails to satisfy our internal and instinctive need to add value.

The Mismatching Instinct Comes in Four Flavors

I hope you're getting the picture that mismatching doesn't reflect poor behavior. In fact, some of the best-intentioned people are the most fervent mismatchers. But in the sales process, while we want prospects and customers to contribute to the conversation, we don't want their need to add value to foster a sense of disagreement. This would only make your sales conversations less productive.

The good news is, mismatching is an avoidable risk. By understanding why mismatching occurs and learning how to recognize a mismatch when it occurs, you can minimize its negative impact on your sales conversations.

In QBS, we have identified the four most common mismatch responses. Each of these behavioral tendencies is outlined below.

The Contradiction

Telling someone that they are wrong is one of the fastest ways to shut down a conversation. But that's essentially what happens whenever someone contradicts what another person says.

Contradiction is the most common mismatch—and it means just what it says. A contradiction is a reflexive response that directly rebuts a comment or statement. Our earlier anecdote about whether or not it was going to be nice weekend is a perfect example of a contradiction. Here's another example:

| Salesperson: | *"I've prepared an agenda for today's meeting. I would like to begin by talking about performance, cost effectiveness, and growth. Then we can talk about maintenance options."* |
| Prospect: | *"It's premature to worry about maintenance."* |

The prospect's knee-jerk reaction to the salesperson's prepared agenda is a classic mismatch. Rather than thoughtfully responding to what the salesperson has suggested, the prospect in this example immediately contradicts by saying the first thing that pops into his head. It's likely that maintenance issues will come up in the meeting, but for now, the prospect takes the contrarian position in an attempt to have some control over what's on the agenda.

In another example, if you were to say, *"The ceilings in this house are very tall,"* someone could easily contradict you by saying, *"Actually, the ceilings in this home are typical for houses in this part of the city."* Even when someone is trying to be helpful, a contradictory response still impedes the conversation's natural flow and discourages additional discussion.

The Unnecessary Clarification

My sales engineer joined me for a very important meeting with one of our most lucrative prospect accounts in the Southeast. The vice president of operations opened the meeting by sharing a problem that his company was having with unscheduled downtime.

| Prospect: | *"Our old system has consistently been out of service for approximately one hour per day to replicate files. This is unacceptable. We would like to find a way to reduce our system's downtime to no more than fifteen minutes. Can you help us?"* |

This was music to my ears. Reduced system downtime was one of the strengths of our solution, and this vice president had just built a perfect case for why he needed our product.

But then my engineer jumped into the conversation, in an attempt to add value.

| Engineer: | *"Actually, we reviewed your system logs and your downtime for replication is only 55 minutes per day."* |

Everyone looked bewildered. If the prospect's tolerance for downtime is fifteen minutes, what difference could it possibly make if the current system takes an hour or fifty-five minutes? Either way, the prospect still has the same problem—too much downtime. This is a good example of an unnecessary clarification, where the mismatch shuts down the conversation just as fast as a contradiction would.

Ironically, my engineer was just trying to participate. He was trying to add value by enhancing the accuracy of the discussion. Needless to say, pointing out a senior executive's inaccuracy is both counterproductive and unnecessary. We must remember that while we have an instinctive need to feel valuable, prospects and customers want to feel valuable too.

> **Secret #15**   Prospects and customers have an instinctive need to be perceived as valuable too.

Rather than listen to the essence of what's being communicated, chronic mismatchers have a need to clarify or restate everything that's being said. While a certain amount of detail is valuable, there's a point where clarifying unnecessarily becomes detrimental to your selling efforts.

One-Upsmanship

One-upsmanship is another type of mismatching. You see this with kids playing in the school yard, trying to outdo each other. One person makes a statement (or tells a story), and someone else jumps in trying to make an even bigger impact by saying, *"The same thing happened to me, only worse."*

One-upmanship is a mismatch because of what it communicates. Instead of acknowledging the value of another person's contribution, the mismatch actually reduces their significance by communicating, *"I'm better than you."*

Unfortunately, this behavior often finds its way from the school yard into many business situations. For example, prospects sometimes mismatch an overly-polished salesperson because the prospect wants to be perceived as equally charismatic. As a result, these prospects tend to say things like, *"If you think your proposal is aggressive, you should see the discount your competitor is offering!"*

Sellers can also one-up their prospects. After a prospective customer has finished describing their needs, countless salespeople have made the mistake of jumping in and saying something like, *"You think you have needs? You should see what another one of my customers is facing. They have so many problems with their systems that..."* Can you see why one-upping someone else creates a mismatched response?

In selling (and in life), a productive conversation shouldn't be a contest, and suggesting, *"I'm better than you,"* only increases your risk of failure.

The Dreaded "I Know"

Last, but not least, is the dreaded "I know" response. This type of mismatch occurs when the need to acquire additional information is superseded by one's own feelings of inadequacy or low self-esteem.

Have you ever noticed that some people aren't open to hearing your advice? College kids, for example, seem to know everything. Try offering some constructive advice to one and you'll see what I mean. It's amazing how worldly an eighteen- or nineteen-year-old can be. In most cases, however, this response is just a defensive reaction. Again, people want to feel valuable. Even my five-year-old daughter, after only three weeks of school, said, *"Dad, I don't need any more advice, because I'm in the kindergarten now."* While it takes most parents twenty years to raise a child, we finished in five. Wow!

It's not that people are averse to improving themselves. It's just that most people have a reflexive need to protect against feeling inadequate.

> **Secret #16**   Everyone wants to feel valuable, but most people have an even greater need to protect against feelings of inadequacy.

This knee-jerk "I know" response tends to close off a conversation and degrade the importance of another person at the same time—a double whammy. There are numerous variations of this mismatch, such as, *"I already knew that,"* or, *"So I've heard."* With this type of response, the mismatcher ends up sending the following message, *"I'm not stupid…so please keep to yourself next time."* As you might guess, this tends to shut down a conversation, which is problematic for sellers who are trying to engage new prospects. Here's a quick scenario to illustrate how the "I know" response can work against a seller.

Suppose a prospect shares what she believes to be an interesting point with her salesperson, Jennifer. Like most of us, contributing to the conversation makes prospects feel smart and valuable; and by listening intently, Jennifer has a wonderful opportunity to strengthen her relationship with this client.

All she has to do is listen and nod, but Jennifer has an intense desire to be perceived as knowledgeable. She's had to fight to get ahead in the business world, and she wants to be respected as an expert in her field. When presented with new ideas or information, Jennifer's reflexive tendency is to mismatch by telling prospects that she already knows.

Prospect: *"I've heard the county commission is considering a tax reduction for commercial property in North Fulton."*

Jennifer: *"I know. I heard that last week."*

The "I know" mismatch creates an interesting problem for Jennifer, and others like her. Because Jennifer's self-concept is largely based on being in the know, her need to mismatch is purely a defensive reaction. Essentially, she's more interested in protecting her own image (of being in the know), than in being attentive to the conversation and to her customer.

Jennifer isn't trying to create a problem. She's just trying to make sure that others see her as a credible professional. But this creates a problem when her need for credibility downgrades the importance of another person's input.

> **Secret #17**   Mismatching shows a lack of interest, which stifles conversation and chips away at the self-worth of other people.

Jennifer surely doesn't mean to degrade the importance of what her prospects are saying. To her, saying *"I know"* means the same as, *"I agree."* To the customer, however, "I know" usually sounds more like, *"I'm already aware of that piece of information, so shut up."* Jennifer's intent may have been pure, but her mismatched response sends a very different message—and there's a big difference between *"I agree"* and *"Shut up,"* don't you think?

What Mismatching Means for Salespeople

Prospects and customers have feelings too. They don't want to be contradicted, corrected, or one-upped, and they especially don't want salespeople to make them feel inadequate. Therefore, if you are mismatching your prospects or customers, you are literally undermining your own success.

> **Secret #18**   If you are a habitual mismatcher, then you are shooting yourself in the foot and you must STOP immediately!

Habitual mismatching is relatively easy to change. A manager, mentor, coach, or sales trainer should be able to work with you to identify the specific behavior and make the necessary adjustments. Correcting this behavior will significantly improve the quality and depth of your sales conversations.

Dealing with potential buyers who habitually mismatch is not so easy, however. You can't just tell them to stop. In fact, you will find that prospects and customers tend to mismatch salespeople automatically. Don't be offended. People are naturally cautious and skeptical of anyone who is trying to get into their pockets. I know how I feel when an overzealous salesperson walks up and asks, *"How can I help you today?"* Be honest. Aren't we all a little wary of being pushed into buying a product or service we don't really need? This caution breeds resistance—and the more cautious people are, the more likely they are to mismatch.

The old school of selling attempts to address this by coaching salespeople to be more aggressive. The strategy is: when prospects are cautious or reluctant, then you must push even harder to overcome their objections. But in today's selling environment, aggression usually backfires. We learned about this in high school physics. For every action, there's an equal and opposite reaction. In sales, that means the harder you push, the harder your prospects and customers will push back.

I use the following anecdote to illustrate the point.

The Hand-Push Analogy

The Hand-Push analogy is a simple exercise that we use in our QBS training programs to create a visual metaphor about resistance. It's one that sales audiences can easily relate to when it comes to dealing with a prospect's natural tendency to push back.

To demonstrate this exercise, I ask for a volunteer from the audience. Then we stand facing each other and I ask him (or her) to raise their right hand as if they were taking an oath of office.

This is a physical exercise, I explain, suggesting that they might want to brace themselves so they don't get knocked off balance. Carefully, I place the palm of my hand against theirs and start pushing—gradually at first. Then I increase the pressure until it's obvious to the rest of the audience that a significant amount of force is being exerted.

How do you think most volunteers respond? Without exception, they push back—harder and harder—in response to being pushed.

Secret #19   The harder you push, the harder your prospects and customers will push back.

The volunteer in this exercise reacts instinctively—pushing back in response to being pushed. It's a reflexive response, which proves an important point. Trying to push prospects, in an attempt to move them forward in the sales process, actually creates a problem for salespeople. That's because when prospects and customers feel "pushed," they usually respond by becoming even more standoffish, more cautious, and more resistant. As you might imagine, this is counterproductive to your selling efforts.

Telling Is Not Selling

The realization that prospects and customers are going to push back is a rude awakening, particularly for those sellers who go around telling prospects why their solution is superior. If we assume that most people have a natural tendency to mismatch, then telling customers why your product is great will often cause them to mismatch, telling you why it's not. It's a consistent pattern. Telling prospective buyers how superior your proposal is may cause them to point out areas where your offering is weak, or where your competition has an advantage. Moreover, if you tell prospects that you would like to wrap up the deal within a certain time frame, they're likely to start telling you why that's not going to happen.

Telling is not selling. This is an old saying in sales, but it's true. Most people love to buy, but very few want to be told, and even fewer want to be "sold." Buyers today don't want to be pushed, persuaded, or otherwise convinced. It's only natural; after all, who wants to feel that they're being manipulated into buying something they don't need?

Nonetheless, corporations spend millions of dollars each year telling their salespeople what to say. As a result, salespeople are being sent out into their respective territories to deliver some version of the following message.

Salesperson: *"Mr. Prospect, You should buy this product from me, because we offer you the best value, and you would benefit the most if I am the one who sells it to you."*

Very few salespeople would use these exact words, but this is precisely what customers hear when they're feeling pushed. I equate it to jamming one of those giant foam fingers you see at college football games into a customer's face saying, *"I'm going to sell you this product whether you like it or not."* Of course people mismatch. Wouldn't you push back too?

Perhaps you're starting to see the challenge. To succeed in sales, you must uncover needs and then educate prospects and customers on the value of your product or service. This is how you will help them recognize an opportunity to improve their existing condition. Using force to accomplish these objectives will only increase your risk and decrease your probability of success. There has to be a better way.

Five QBS Strategies That Reduce Your Risk

Just because mismatching is an instinctive response doesn't mean we have to passively stand by and let this behavior negatively affect our sales results. Similarly, just because a prospect mismatches doesn't mean we should write them off as not being a potential opportunity. Two of the largest sales in my career were made to chronic mismatchers.

But mismatching is not a typical objection; therefore, it cannot be handled like one. When people contradict, clarify unnecessarily, or respond defensively, they are usually trying to add value to the conversation in an attempt to satisfy their own needs.

Unfortunately, when a prospect mismatches something a salesperson says or does, many sellers jump into objection-handling mode—having been trained to squelch objections as they arise. They assume that if they can overcome the objection, it will go away. This formula doesn't work with a mismatched response, however, because you wouldn't want to squelch your prospect's need to add value, or their desire to contribute to the conversation.

When mismatches are treated as objections, salespeople end up finding themselves in the awkward position of trying to overcome a prospect's behavioral quirks—namely their intrinsic need to add value. Whoops!

> **Secret #20**   Mismatching is *not* an objection; therefore, it should *not* be handled like one.

The QBS strategies and techniques outlined in the rest of this book are intended to minimize the undesirable effects of mismatching on the sales process. For salespeople, this is a risk-reduction strategy. Instead of being pushed away, you will find yourself working with prospects and customers to create and nurture mutually beneficial business relationships.

Below are five key strategies you will learn that will minimize your risk of mismatching.

Ask More Questions and Make Fewer Statements

Minimizing the mismatching instinct starts with prevention. If we can identify and prevent those things that cause people to mismatch the things we say or do, then we can avoid a negative reaction.

In conversation, statements are easily mismatched. That's because most statements take a definitive position that can easily be disagreed with. For example, the statement, *"It's supposed to be nice this weekend,"* is easily mismatched when someone takes the opposite position, saying that it's going to be *"too hot," "too windy," "too rainy,"* or something else that disagrees with the original supposition.

The same thing is likely to happen if a salesperson tells a prospect, *"Your boss needs to be at the presentation next week."* Prospects can easily mismatch this statement by saying, *"There's no need for anyone else to be involved at this point."*

It's virtually impossible to make a statement that cannot be contradicted, clarified, one-upped, or interpreted defensively. In fact, the more definitive your statements are, the more susceptible they are to being mismatched. Cautious prospects are particularly wary of statements made by salespeople since they don't want to be pushed, persuaded, or otherwise convinced to buy a product or service they don't really need.

> **Secret #21**   If your current approach to sales is statement-based, then your comments will actually invite mismatched responses.

While statements are easily mismatched, questions are not. Questions help diffuse the emotional triggers that fuel the need to mismatch. That's because it's impossible to disagree with a question. If we go back to our now familiar example and change the statement to a question, we can avoid a mismatched response altogether by asking, *"Is it supposed to be nice this weekend?"* In reality, questions actually help to satisfy the other person's need to add value by inviting them to contribute to the conversation.

Asking questions, rather than making statements, also helps to minimize risk by giving sellers greater latitude in their conversations. I remember one instance where my company partnered with GE Capital on a multimillion dollar computer sale at the Georgia Lottery. David Reddaway of GE Capital and I took the senior vice president of the Georgia Lottery to an upscale seafood restaurant for dinner, where we had a nice mix of business and personal conversation. Because our guest was African American, I wanted to ask his opinion on a recent news story regarding racism in America. Most people would say that controversial topics like politics, religion, and sex should be avoided at all costs, particularly in a business setting. But in this case, I was truly interested in his opinion; so I asked.

I thought David was going to spit up his fish. His eyes got big, and I could feel his anxiety from across the table. He was shocked that I would bring up such a politically sensitive issue over dinner. In reality, it wasn't risky at all. Since I had taken no position on the subject myself (only asked a question), this prospect couldn't mismatch with an opposing viewpoint. Frankly, he was flattered that I was interested in his opinion. By the end of the evening, we had had a terrific meal and an insightful conversation; and we also closed the deal.

To minimize (or avoid) the risk of mismatching, it's important that sellers learn how to ask more questions and make fewer statements. This is one of the fundamental premises of Question Based Selling.

Credibility Reduces the Prospect's Need to Resist

If you agreed with our earlier conclusion that prospects are naturally cautious of salespeople, then you will probably also agree that the more credibility you establish with prospects and customers, the less standoffish they will be.

Establishing credibility should be one of your primary objectives in the sales process. In addition to communicating a greater sense of value, credibility also reduces your risk. Credibility reduces the prospect's need to mismatch because they start feeling comfortable with you, rather than cautious of you. It also opens the door to more productive conversation. People who believe that you are credible are more willing to openly share. Instead of pushing you away, prospects and customers will invite more in-depth conversation. Chapter 8 will show you how you can use QBS to develop strategic questions that can significantly enhance your credibility much earlier in the sale.

Curiosity Neutralizes the Mismatching Reflex

The opposite of resistance is intrigue. To intrigue someone is to arouse their interest, or make them curious, according to Webster. When someone is intrigued, they want to know more. In QBS, we raise the issue of curiosity, because we want prospects and customers to invite us into more in-depth discussions about their needs and the value of our product or service. This is how you can create more opportunities to provide solutions.

Making prospects and customers curious is the most effective way to engage them in a productive sales conversation. That's why curiosity is such a big part of the QBS methodology. People who are curious will want to hear more about your product or service, while those who are not curious won't. We cover this at length in chapter 7. For now, I just want to make the point that curiosity neutralizes the mismatching reflex. People cannot be curious and mismatch at the same time.

> **Secret #22**   It's impossible for someone who's curious to be inviting you in and pushing you away at the same time.

You can watch the dynamics of a conversation change when someone becomes curious. Curiosity causes them to physically lean into the conversation and give you their undivided attention. And when they ask a question to satisfy their curiosity, they are actually requesting your help—and it's impossible to ask for your help and push you away at the same time.

Reversing the Positive

Another way to reduce the negative impact of mismatching is to turn it around so that the responses you receive are actually in your favor. We'll discuss this at length in chapter 10 when QBS shows you how to neutralize the disposition of your questions—to solicit more open, honest, and accurate responses. But here's a preview of this technique to pique your curiosity.

Throughout the course of a day, I ask a lot of questions like: *"Did I catch you at a bad time?" "Am I interrupting?" "Is next week too soon for a presentation?" "Will the pricing in this proposal make your boss nervous?"*

Each of these questions has a negative tone, so when someone takes the opposite position they actually mismatch in my favor. This technique is called reversing the positive.

Reversing the positive is not a manipulation strategy, however. Sellers should not approach potential buyers saying, *"You don't want to buy any of this crap, do you?"* in the hopes that they will mismatch, saying, *"Yes I do...I do!"* But you can absolutely inject some humility into your questions by leveraging the negative so people will want to engage, rather than push you away.

Momentum Helps Reduce the Mismatching Instinct

Shortly after opening the southeast regional sales office for NetFrame Systems, I landed a meeting with the vice president of information systems at Georgia Pacific. NetFrame was a relatively small company at the time, and this was a huge opportunity for me, and for NetFrame.

The meeting was held in the executive suite on GP's mahogany row. People were seated around a huge conference table with giant leather chairs in a room with lots of windows and a fabulous view of downtown Atlanta.

At the time, NetFrame only had one other big-name account in the Southeast—Delta Air Lines. I was hoping to leverage our success at Delta so the people at Georgia Pacific would see how much better off they could be by purchasing our product. So, in the meeting, I told them how Delta had saved money by purchasing our solution as opposed to upgrading their existing equipment. I also showed them how Delta was able to reduce their system downtime and increase their productivity.

I went on and on talking about Delta until the vice president raised his finger and said, *"Hold on just a minute while I check something."* He wheeled his chair over to the window and began to look around. Everyone wondered what he was doing. When he finished scanning the area, he turned back to me and said, *"Just as I thought, we don't fly airplanes here at Georgia Pacific."*

That day, I learned a very important lesson about reference selling, and about mismatching. Individual references are easily mismatched. Remember when your parents used to say that you shouldn't jump off a cliff just because your friend Johnny did? It's the same with prospective buyers. Most won't make a buying decision just because the guy down the street decided to take the plunge. They need more evidence, which is why QBS approaches reference selling very differently. Instead of trying to motivate potential customers with individual references, QBS shows salespeople how to leverage the Herd Theory, which we will cover next in chapter 3.

The Herd Theory is a momentum play that also works as a mismatching reduction strategy. If everyone else already seems to be moving in a certain direction, prospects will feel much less of a need to resist or push back.

Summary

So far, we've discussed mismatching in terms of a verbal response. But it's important to note that mismatching also poses a silent risk. Some prospects will disagree, but they will remain silent—because they would rather disagree quietly than contend with the ego of a defensive salesperson.

Whether it's verbalized or silent, a mismatched response that takes the opposite position can affect your sales efforts negatively. But understanding this reflexive behavior gives you a strategic advantage over other sellers who are pushing to get into new accounts, pushing to move opportunities forward, and pushing to close deals by the end of the month, quarter, or year.

As we get deeper into the QBS methodology, you will see that forcefulness is not the best way to lead qualified prospects toward a mutual solution. Instead, QBS focuses on bringing people together, to increase your probability of success, and to reduce one of the most prevalent risks in the sale—the risk of mismatching.

Chapter 3

THE HERD THEORY

Traditional reference selling is highly overrated. Saying this may shock some people since virtually every sales training program created in the last thirty years talks about the importance of leveraging references to establish credibility and communicate value.

References are important, but so is differentiation; and it's no longer an effective strategy to use references just like everyone else. In QBS, we want to set ourselves apart from everyone else. This differentiation is achieved by leveraging the rest of the herd—which, ironically enough, includes "everyone else."

The use of references can help your selling efforts in two ways. First, a positive reference can increase your credibility by showing prospective buyers that the solution you are proposing has already been proven effective. Essentially, it's a way to show prospective buyers that the trail to success has already been blazed by someone else. By reducing the prospect's risk, you make it easier for them to move forward with a favorable purchase decision.

The second way references can be useful in the sales process is in stimulating buyer interest. When prospective buyers see that your product or service has already helped other customers solve a problem or improve their existing condition, chances are that they will want to know more about your solution. In this way, references can be used to pique a prospective buyer's interest.

| **Secret #23** | Potential buyers are instinctively trying to reduce their risk of making a bad decision. |

Prospects are at risk in the decision-making process. If they make a good decision, they can be a hero. If they make a bad decision, however, they will quickly become the goat. It follows, then, that buyers want to make the right decision. But even more importantly, they want to avoid making the wrong one.

Walk a mile in a prospect's shoes, and you'll find that most are scared to death of the unknown. They're having to wrestle with questions like, what if the product fails to perform as advertised? How can we be sure this solution will address our needs? Are we getting the best deal? Prospects would love to be able to peer into a crystal ball and see what the future holds before they make decisions, but crystal ball technology is only available in fairy tales. That's why buyers have to rely on the next best thing—references.

Problems with Traditional Reference Selling

The fact that other people or companies have already purchased, implemented, or deployed your solution is a proof statement that reduces the buyer's risk. It makes them feel more comfortable about your solution, and it increases their confidence about moving forward with a decision to purchase.

There are some problems with traditional reference selling, however, starting with the fact that positive references are a dime a dozen. Just about anyone can produce a list of happy customers. If five vendors are all vying for the same piece of business, chances are good that the prospect will receive five very similar lists of "happy" customer references. As a result, prospects tend to discount the value of these canned references—after all, why would a salesperson who wanted to win the business give out a bad reference?

In addition, individual references are easily mismatched (see chapter 2). Nothing irks a prospective buyer more than the suggestion that just because someone else made a decision to move forward, they should too. It's an aggressive position that makes prospects feel pushed, which is likely to cause them to respond by pushing back. Specific customer references are also mismatched because of differences that cause prospects to discount the validity of the reference. They think, *"Just because your solution worked in their environment, doesn't mean it's right for us."*

These problems put salespeople in an precarious position. Buyers still want to limit their risk before purchasing, but individual customer references aren't always enough to differentiate the uniqueness of your solution, especially if those references are being met with some resistance.

Why the Herd Theory Works

QBS changes the paradigm for reference selling. Rather than point to individual references to prove that a given solution is indeed viable, the

Herd Theory surrounds prospects with a sense of momentum—to establish credibility and convey a greater sense of value. This helps reduce the buyer's risk. It's a little like handing them a crystal ball.

If you could demonstrate that everyone else was already interested in, and excited about, your product, wouldn't that communicate a greater sense of value and lower the prospect's risk? That's precisely how the Herd Theory works. By showing prospects that "everyone else" is already moving in a certain direction, you can more easily motivate potential buyers to move in the same direction.

Here's a little metaphor that illustrates the Herd Theory in action.

A Quick Lesson on Cows

Have you ever noticed that a herd of cows all tend to move together in the same direction? Have you ever wondered why this phenomenon occurs? Let's take a closer look.

Imagine yourself driving down a country road, surrounded by rolling fields and farmland, as far as the eye can see. Suddenly, something catches your attention—it's a herd of cows up ahead, in a nearby field. Curiosity causes you to pull off the road to investigate further. And there you sit, in the middle of nowhere, watching the Herd Theory in action.

For unexplained reasons, you step out of your car, scramble over the fence, and catch up to the cows as the herd slowly makes its way across the field. Curious as to why they are all moving in the same direction, you maneuver yourself toward the center of the herd to ask a very simple question.

Fortunately for this metaphor, the cow in the center speaks fluent English. So you tap the beast on the shoulder, and ask: *"Pardon me, but…why are you walking in this particular direction?"*

When I tell this story in person, whether it's in Minneapolis or Madrid, I always ask the audience, *"How do you think the cow in the center of the herd will respond?"* So, let me ask you. How would you respond if you were surrounded by the rest of the herd?

I bet you answered with the same response I hear from salespeople all over the world. Invariably, they say, *"I'm moving in this direction because everybody else is."*

People too are strongly influenced by the direction of their surrounding herds. Just look at commercial advertising. All you have to do is switch on the TV, and you will see ads for all kinds of products that attempt to motivate the target audience by showing them how "everyone else" has benefited by moving in a certain direction. Think about it this way—other than using momentum, how else would large tobacco companies persuade young people to try cigarettes?

Leveraging "Everyone Else"

Buyers are influenced much more by the direction of their surrounding herd than by specific recommendations from individual references. Again, most prospects are reluctant to take the plunge just because someone else did. But they are definitely influenced when "everyone else" seems to be moving in a certain direction. Perhaps that's because there's safety in numbers and prospects would like to benefit from everyone else's successes. They would also like to learn from everyone else's mistakes. But one thing is for sure—nobody wants to reinvent the wheel.

> **Secret #24**   How the rest of the "herd" feels is more important than any one person's opinion or recommendation.

Surrounding prospects with the perception that "everyone else" is already moving in a certain direction is a very powerful QBS technique. We will show you how to leverage this strategy to penetrate more new accounts, build greater value in your sales presentations, and overcome objections. It also gives sellers a way to provide the emotional reassurance that prospects need to pull the trigger on a buying decision.

This approach is very different from traditional reference selling, however. With the traditional approach, sellers use references to suggest that *"since other customers are already using our solution, you should use it too."* This is a push strategy—one that attempts to encourage, nudge, and ultimately push prospects toward the desired result.

The Herd Theory is a pull strategy. Rather than pushing prospects by suggesting that they too should buy just because other customers have, The Herd Theory lets prospects know that everyone else is already moving in a certain direction, in order to ask, *"Would you like to know why?"* Essentially, we leverage the momentum of the surrounding herd to build credibility. The implication is if "everyone else" is already moving in a certain direction, then something about it must be good. As an example, how do you know whether or not a truck stop restaurant on the interstate has good food? By counting the number of trucks in the parking lot at meal time. More trucks, better food. (Make that a herd of trucks.)

But the Herd Theory also has a wonderful way of making prospects curious—so they'll want to know more. If your product or service appears to have momentum in the marketplace, then why wouldn't prospective customers want to know more about how it works?

How It Started: A True Story

Although the Herd Theory has evolved into a key component of the QBS methodology, this approach was conceived more out of desperation than design. Its origin dates back to 1990, when I had just accepted a position with KnowledgeWare, Inc., the leading provider of Computer-Aided Software Engineering (CASE) software.

At the time, KnowledgeWare was growing by leaps and bounds. They had just experienced a very successful initial public offering, and were in the process of rapidly expanding their customer base. As is often the case, they wanted to double the size of the sales force in order to penetrate more accounts. Consequently, I was brought in to sell in the Southeast.

This was an exciting opportunity; and, although my territory hadn't yet been assigned, I was chomping at the bit to get started. Product training was the first step, so I tried to learn as much as I could about CASE.

Two weeks into the job, the vice president of sales called me into his office and told me that there was a "slight" problem. Apparently, the company hired too many salespeople. After a recruiting frenzy, it was discovered that KnowledgeWare had staffed a total of seven salespeople in the Southeast region, but they only had six available territories. And because I was the last person hired, I was suddenly the odd man out. This was not what I expected to hear after only two weeks on the job.

"What does this mean for me?" I asked. The vice president didn't know, but he committed to find out and get back to me as soon as possible.

Numbly, I went back to my product training. Ten days later, I found myself back in the VP's office. Apparently, there was an opening in the Midwest. With five available territories in the central region, there were currently only four salespeople. *"How would you like to sell CASE tools in the Midwest?"* he asked. It didn't take a rocket scientist to figure out this was my only option, so I accepted.

The actual territory was still up in the air. During the previous sales year, the top performer in the Midwest was responsible for two states, Kansas and Missouri. To grow the business, KnowledgeWare's management had decided to cut his territory to make room for another sales rep (me). But since he had been the top producer in the region, he was allowed to divide the territory as he saw fit—and as you would expect from any hungry salesperson, he definitely took the better half.

"Tom, I've decided to keep Missouri," he announced. That made sense since he lived in St. Louis. *"But I'm also going to keep Kansas,"* he added, *"and you get Kansas City."*

Kansas City? *"That's not a territory,"* I remember thinking. *"Kansas City is just a dot on the map."* Having never been there, I couldn't help wondering how a cow town in the heart of the Midwest could ever be a desirable place to sell Computer-Aided Software Engineering tools. *"Should I go out and buy a western hat and some boots? Maybe I should learn to chew tobacco."* These and other wild thoughts ran through my head after being handed this "brass pig" for a territory. Not knowing what the future held, I was off to Kansas City.

The Standard Approach Wasn't Working

KnowledgeWare kicked off its new sales year on July 1. I had been on board just over a month. We received our annual quotas, and it was time to head out into the territory to start selling.

Armed with limited CASE tool knowledge, an extremely short list of prospects, and a telephone, I started calling prospects in Kansas City. Using the standard approach, my initial sales calls sounded something like this:

> **Seller:**   *"Mr. Prospect, my name is Tom Freese and I'm with KnowledgeWare, Inc., the leading provider of development software, based in Atlanta. We develop and sell Computer Aided Software Engineering tools, and I wanted to get together with you to discuss how our products can address your programming needs."*

Essentially, I was calling new prospects to see if they would be interested in investigating, evaluating, or hearing more about our product. Not surprisingly, I didn't get many hits. Most of the people I called were receiving a steady stream of sales calls that sounded very similar to mine. While prospects in Kansas City were always polite, I was having serious trouble getting my foot in the door. It wasn't the rejection that was bothering me, however. It was the fact that each *"No, thank you"* significantly reduced the size of my already petite territory.

My Desperation Move

Things were not going well. During my first thirty days in Kansas City, I worked hard to penetrate new prospect accounts, but with very limited success. I needed to try something different. So, in a desperate attempt to cultivate new business, I decided to host a KnowledgeWare product seminar.

KnowledgeWare's corporate marketing department featured a traveling "road show"—a group of presentation specialists who would blow into a city, provide an exciting "dog and pony" presentation, and then blow out. My strategy was: if I could fill the room with seminar participants, this event would give me an opportunity to generate interest, uncover needs, and motivate prospective customers to further investigate our solutions. I put a stake in the ground by scheduling a road show presentation in Kansas City for late August.

Fortunately, I was able to leverage KnowledgeWare's business partner relationship to secure the large auditorium at IBM's regional headquarters in downtown Kansas City. It was a terrific facility with all the trappings that would enable us to host a world-class event for up to one hundred people. This venue also gave us some much needed credibility and a built-in endorsement from the world's largest computer manufacturer—IBM.

All we needed was attendees, which was my responsibility. With less than a month remaining until the seminar, it was do or die. But if I was having trouble getting new prospects to meet with me, how in the world would I get them interested in attending a product seminar?

Mailing Invitations and Doing the Follow-Up

I decided to send out a mass mailing that would canvas every potential customer in the Kansas City area. But rather than send a blanket invitation to each company, I targeted individuals. I hoped this would give my invitations a personal touch. It would also give me a reason to follow up.

Shortly after the invitations were mailed, I started calling. Like an idiot, I used the same approach as before, hoping that prospects would be interested in coming to the seminar to hear about all the wonderful benefits our product offered. Unfortunately, most prospects just assumed that I was yet another salesperson begging them to attend another sales seminar.

As you might have already guessed, the first few prospects I contacted responded with the same level of disinterest as before. I quickly realized that responses like, *"It sounds good, but…,"* or, *"We'll think about it,"* were not accomplishing the objective. With limited success, I tried to confirm attendees; but once again, it was obviously time for something different. That evening, at a restaurant called The Golden Ox, on the lower west side of Kansas City, the Herd Theory was conceived. Little did I know how much impact this technique would have on my sales success.

The Rest of the Story

When the idea for the Herd Theory hit me, I was picking at my dinner, worrying that, with only two weeks before the seminar, very few attendees had been confirmed. My systems engineer and I were both nervous and not very hungry. In our favor was a solid company with a quality product, as KnowledgeWare had already become the industry leader in other parts of the country. We also knew that the road show event had been very well received in other cities, and we were convinced this format would produce a positive result if we could just get people to attend the presentation.

I started wondering, what if KnowledgeWare was the de facto standard for application development in Kansas City? What if everyone else was already using KnowledgeWare's products? Would that make someone who hadn't yet been exposed to KnowledgeWare's CASE tools interested in finding out more about the technology? In other words, if the rest of the herd was already moving in KnowledgeWare's direction, would other prospects in Kansas City want to know why? That was it! People would surely be interested in attending this event if they knew that "everyone else" was interested too.

The next day, I started calling prospects, but with a different purpose. I wanted to build a sense of anticipation and excitement around the event. So, rather than begging them to attend, I let prospects know that everyone else would be at this event, and my purpose in following up was to make sure they didn't get left out. The actual dialogue went something like this:

Follow-up Call *(Script)*

Seller: *"Hello Mr. Prospect, my name is Tom Freese, and I'm the regional manager for KnowledgeWare in Kansas City. I wanted to contact you about the CASE application development seminar we are hosting at IBM's Regional Headquarters on August 26. Do you remember seeing the invitation we sent you?*

Frankly, we are expecting a record turnout—over one hundred people, including development managers from US Sprint, Hallmark Cards, Pepsi Co., Yellow Freight, Kansas Power & Light, the Federal Reserve Bank, Northwest Mutual Life, American Family Life, St. Luke's Hospital, Anheuser-Busch, MasterCard, American Express, Worldspan, and Trans World Airlines, just to name a few.

I wanted to follow up because we haven't yet received an RSVP from your company, and I wanted to make sure you didn't get left out."

Granted, this is a highly positioned approach, but it's also 100 percent accurate. I wanted prospects to know that IBM was endorsing this event. I also wanted to let them know that "everyone else" was going to be there. I accomplished this by rattling off an impressive list of marquis company names that we were "expecting" to attend. Most importantly, I wanted to make sure that they *didn't get left out.*

"Left out of what?"

Leveraging the rest of the herd has a customer service flavor, more than the traditional sales role. Rather than begging prospects to attend, I was simply calling to make sure that they didn't miss out on a very important opportunity. That's the beauty of this technique; if you say to someone, *"I just wanted to make sure you didn't get left out,"* the next four words they will say are, *"Left out of what?"* When prospects become curious about what it is that they might miss, they almost always ask for more information.

> **Secret #25** When you're trying to make sure someone doesn't get "left out," their next four words will be, *"Left out of what?"*

Nobody wants to miss out on a potential opportunity, particularly if "everyone else" already seems to be moving in a certain direction. Keep in mind that while most prospects are naturally cautious, they are also naturally curious—and their desire not to be left out will likely generate a request for additional information. How did I respond when prospects asked for more information? That was easy. Their request was my invitation to pique their interest further by getting them excited about the upcoming event.

Securing Their Commitment to Attend

After piquing the prospect's interest, there's no time like the present to close. In this case, that meant getting them to agree to attend our presentation in Kansas City. Once we let them know we were expecting a record turnout, it was easy to ask for a commitment by saying, *"Do you have your calendar handy?"* Everyone has their calendar handy. Now the only question was, were they available on the date of the seminar? If so, I simply asked if they would like me to reserve them a seat. Mission accomplished!

If the prospect was not available to attend the presentation on August 26, but was interested in finding out why "everyone else" was interested in KnowledgeWare's CASE tools, I suggested one of the following alternatives:

Would You Like to Send Someone Else? Perhaps there was someone else on their staff or in their organization who could attend the presentation in their absence. This would certainly help get our foot in the door.

Could We Schedule a Make-up Event? For those people who had conflicts, I would probe to see if there was any interest in scheduling a second event.

What about an On-Site Presentation? Some people don't like public seminars. For them, I might suggest that we come on-site for a more detailed discussion about KnowledgeWare and how our CASE tool products could enhance their specific development environment.

I even used the Herd Theory to let prospects know what other companies who had scheduling conflicts were doing. I also made it a point to expand each opportunity by asking prospects if there was anyone else in their company who would benefit from attending this event. I offered to contact these referrals, but I always asked the prospect to forward a note letting them know we had talked. If you ask nicely, most people are happy to accommodate this request. Then the person who they referred you to won't mistake your call as just another salesperson who's cold-calling into the account.

Results Speak for Themselves

By the time August 26 arrived, we had already confirmed attendees from most of Kansas City's largest corporations. Development managers, programmers, and software engineers from US Sprint, Hallmark Cards, Pepsi Co., Yellow Freight, Kansas Power & Light, the Federal Reserve Bank, Northwest Mutual Life, American Express, Master Card, and Anheuser-Busch were all coming, largely because "everyone else" was going to be there.

Sure enough, when they arrived, everyone else was there. We had a record turnout of 119 attendees! IBM's auditorium was packed, and our event in Kansas City set an attendance record for KnowledgeWare road show seminars that went uncontested for the rest of the sales year.

Many prospects thanked me for calling and making sure they didn't get "left out." The momentum we had communicated became a self-fulfilling prophecy—people were excited about the presentation because everyone else seemed excited. Even the IBMers who attended were astonished, as they too would benefit from this event. It was a win/win for everyone involved.

When it came time to kick off the actual presentation, I took the stage and introduced the program. I thanked everyone in the audience for their time and reviewed the objectives of the event. Then, before the seminar began, I took one more opportunity to leverage the herd by saying,

"Before we actually get started today, I would like to turn your attention to the back of the room." Everyone turned around in their chairs. There stood thirty-seven IBM sales reps, lined up against the back wall. I continued, *"I would like to thank IBM for their support of this event; and to give you (the audience) an idea of just how exciting KnowledgeWare's product is, when was the last time you saw this many blue suits, white shirts, and red ties in one place?"* Everyone clapped!

The truth is, in the days prior to the seminar I invested the time to call every IBM sales rep in the Kansas City office (over fifty people) to make sure they knew we were hosting one of the year's largest seminar events. I also made sure that they knew "everyone else" was going to be there. Not surprisingly, the local IBMers didn't want to be left out either.

Secret #26	Most prospects are very interested in, and highly influenced by, what "everyone else" is doing.

After this seminar, there was no longer a shortage of opportunity in Kansas City. We knew all along that we were selling a valuable solution, and we also knew that people would buy if we could just get them to evaluate our product. By the end of the year, my brass pig of a territory finished No. 1 in sales, and KnowledgeWare became the de facto standard for CASE software in Kansas City. We also closed more new-name accounts than any other commercial sales territory in the country—all because we leveraged the momentum of the surrounding herd.

Momentum Comes in All Shapes and Sizes

When people think of references, they think of "happy" customers. This makes sense since salespeople would want customers who are satisfied with their products and services to positively influence other potential buyers. Happy customers are not the only source of momentum in your strategic sales, however.

The Herd Theory can be just as effective with non-customer references. That's essentially what we used in Kansas City. We let prospects know that "everyone else" was interested in hearing more about our CASE tool solutions. Even before we had customers, we were able to leverage other prospects to create a sense of momentum that helped us establish credibility and generate interest. As a result, everyone wanted to know why the rest of the herd was moving in KnowledgeWare's direction.

> **Secret #27**   If the rest of the herd seems to be moving in a certain direction, other prospects and customers will want to know why.

Non-customer references give sellers an excellent opportunity to be creative. Herd momentum comes in all shapes and sizes and you can customize the surrounding herd to meet the needs of your specific sales situation. For example, if you are talking to a bank, you might leverage your success at other financial institutions like Citibank, First Union, Transamerica, Chase Manhattan, Bank of America, Bank of Boston, American Express, and VISA. If you call on regional hospitals, you might tell them about your success at St. Jude's Children's Hospital in Memphis, Mt. Sinai in Miami, Emory University Hospital in Atlanta, Sloan-Kettering in New York, and Humana Hospitals in Nashville.

You can build momentum using the media too. *"Ms. Prospect, would you like to know why the Wall Street Journal, Forbes Magazine, Newsweek, USA Today, and Entrepreneur Magazine have all featured articles about the success of our newly announced product?"* If your product is relevant to their business, they will surely want to hear more.

You can also leverage your partners, particularly if your company has strategic industry relationships or if your product is sold through reseller channels or distribution. Letting prospects know that you are currently partnered with companies like IBM, Microsoft, Andersen Consulting, Ernst & Young, Deloitte & Touche, Coopers & Lybrand, Forrester Research, and the Gartner Group can be very powerful for establishing credibility and piquing the prospect's interest.

If you represent a brand-new company or you sell a product that has just been released, you may not yet have the luxury of existing customers. The Herd Theory can still work by drawing a parallel between yourself and other success stories that create a sense of momentum. (Call it guilt by association.) As an example, it wasn't long ago that Microsoft was just a fledgling start-up company. Now, they are one of the most successful businesses ever. Perhaps you can build a parallel by letting prospects know that your company will do for the Internet or cable TV business what Microsoft has done for PC software. If you sell pharmaceuticals, perhaps you can create momentum by letting prospects know that your product is expected to be as popular as Tylenol. The key is linking yourself with a success story that prospects can easily relate to.

You Can Even Leverage Your Competition

Most salespeople would agree that using a prospect's direct competitor as a reference can be a little dicey. For example, it would be hard to say to Chase Manhattan Bank, *"You should buy our product because Citicorp is one of our best customers."* You are more likely to get an immediate mismatched response like, *"We don't want to be like Citicorp."*

If you change the underlying message, however, you can absolutely leverage the momentum of competitive companies. For example, if you're selling a product whose marquis customers include telecommunication giants like AT&T, MCI, Sprint, and US West, and you are trying to penetrate other new accounts in the same industry, you can very effectively leverage the Herd Theory. You can accomplish this by rattling off an impressive list of telecommunications companies that are already moving in your direction, then ask, *"Would you like to know why all these companies are already using our product?"* Who wouldn't want to know why other companies are moving in a certain direction—especially when they are competitors?

Popcorn Credibility

We've all heard the unmistakable sound of popcorn popping. It's that rapid-fire, popping sound that tells us that the popcorn is bursting with activity. You know, Pop, pa, pa, Pop, Pop...Pop, pa, pa, Pop, Pop!

After a few minutes, when most of the kernels have popped, the popping sound slows down in a way that's also unmistakable. It's how you can tell that the popcorn is finished—when the popping sound slows to an intermittent, Pop ....Pop….....…...Pop….Pop….....….......Pop sound.

Applying the Herd Theory is more than just naming a list of references. You must also be able to name those references with a certain amount of credibility—popcorn credibility. It should sound like popcorn popping, as you demonstrate a higher level of competence and credibility by confidently rattling off an impressive list of customers, prospects, media references, or partners.

In the context of a sales call, it might sound like this:

Salesperson: *"Mr. Prospect, you mentioned that you wanted to increase revenue and decrease expenses. That's exactly why companies like Delta Air Lines, Citibank, Lockheed Martin, Compaq, Goldman Sacs, Lanier Worldwide, Motorola, and Transamerica have all chosen our product. Would you like to know what they're doing to accomplish the same objective?*

Lots of salespeople can name two or three customers, but then their popcorn stops popping. From there, it's a struggle to name more—in which case, they actually lose ground because they can't demonstrate credibility.

> **Secret #28**   When surrounding prospects with herd momentum, you gain credibility as long as your "popcorn" keeps popping.

Now that you understand the concept, here's an exercise you can use to increase your own popcorn credibility when dealing with prospects and customers in the strategic sales process.

Exercise: Increase Your Popcorn Credibility

In our live QBS training programs, we show audiences how to increase their popcorn credibility using a simple exercise. I usually start by asking everyone in the audience to get a partner. For our purposes here, you can practice this exercise by yourself.

Once everyone has a partner, I ask each participant to make a pre-exercise commitment. On a piece of note paper, write down how many herd references you think you can name in rapid succession. This will give you a baseline for assessing your results. *Hint*: Top salespeople can usually rattle off between 25 and 30 herd references.

For the actual exercise, I ask partners to stand facing each other. While one partner holds up their hands and counts on their fingers, the other person rattles off as many herd references as they can name—with popcorn credibility. It's best to begin with customer references. This enables participants to focus on the technique. Later, I encourage you to try this same exercise using prospect references, partner references, and media references.

When everyone is ready, I give the signal, and participants begin naming references until their popcorn stops popping. Long pauses indicate that you are no longer gaining credibility so the counting stops. The number of herd references that were counted is how many you can name with popcorn credibility. Now, compare your score to the number of reference names you wrote down prior to the exercise.

How does your pre-exercise commitment compare to your actual results? The typical salesperson who participates in this exercise can name between eight and fifteen reference names in rapid succession. That's good for the first time through. Do not despair if your results were lower than expected. I've seen experienced salespeople stumble after naming only three or four references. The key is increasing your skills so you can quickly create a robust list of herd references to establish greater credibility in the sales process.

Practice Makes Perfect

The best way to increase your popcorn credibility is to improve your recall. Sellers who can confidently rattle off an impressive list of herd references can surround their prospects with a powerful sense of momentum. To do so, you must be able to easily recall herd references out of memory. This is not a function of IQ, however, it's a function of practice.

Sellers can easily increase their popcorn credibility if they are willing to practice ten minutes a day for a full week. For this relatively small investment, you will be shocked at how large the benefit is. For best results, take out a piece of paper and physically create several different herd lists, categorizing reference names by industry, size, or how long they have been customers. By taking the time to write them down, these references will be more accessible in your memory for easy recall later.

Then each day, practice naming the references you've listed. Practice naming them by category and make it a point to learn a few specific data points about each member of your herd. As you get more sophisticated, practice rattling off your reference names by geographic location or in alphabetical order. The more specific you can be, the more credibility you will convey. In just a few days, your confidence will soar, and you will be well equipped to leverage a sense of momentum that will make your prospects and customers feel more comfortable, and motivate them to move forward in the sales process.

Do You Have a Pencil?

Sooner or later, most prospects will ask for references. They will want to contact a handful of other customers in an attempt to uncover any potential "gotchas" before making their final decision.

The problem is, while most sellers are quick to respond with a canned list of satisfied customer references, prospects usually get a similarly generic response from every vendor—a list of five or six account names, laid out on nice paper, with glowing remarks about each. Vendors hope this gesture will make prospects feel more comfortable, but it often doesn't.

If you really want to differentiate yourself, here's something you can try. The next time a prospect asks you for references, say, *"Sure. Do you have a pencil?"* (Note: Don't ask for a pen. It sounds too rhetorical. Instead, ask if they have a pencil and you're more likely to get a favorable response.)

Once they're ready to write, you start naming references from memory. Include the name of the company and the primary contact in the account. For maximum impact, I like to rattle off their telephone number (and extension) as well. Be sure to give your prospects a chance to write all the information down. You might even give them a quick synopsis about the issues these references faced, and how their issues were resolved by implementing the proposed solution.

You can literally watch a prospect's face light up as you name five, ten, even fifteen references off the top of your head. This is the ultimate implementation of popcorn credibility and the Herd Theory. It is also a terrific way to demonstrate that you know your business better than any other salesperson they have ever encountered. You want them to come away thinking that some of your competitors don't even know their families as well as you know your customers. Your credibility will skyrocket; and chances are, they won't even call your references. Why bother? Your demonstration of competence will make prospects feel more comfortable than a hundred canned references ever could.

> **Secret #29**   A salesperson's ability to demonstrate account-specific knowledge translates into greater credibility.

Memorizing account-specific detail isn't difficult. Most salespeople talk to their best references so often that they know a great deal about these accounts already. But if you have trouble remembering details, make a cheat-sheet. Put a list of pertinent facts in your daily planner, so you can glance at it while prospects are writing down the references you name. Salespeople get just as many points for being prepared as they do for having a good memory.

Applying the Herd Theory throughout the Sales Process

The Herd Theory is a powerful technique for establishing credibility and generating interest at the beginning of the sales process. Prospects will surely be curious when "everyone else" seems to be moving in a certain direction—and if they're curious, they will want more information. The Herd Theory is also useful later in the sales process to provide the emotional reassurance prospects need to pull the trigger on a purchase.

Buyers are nervous, particularly when they're faced with an important decision. That's why herd references are so valuable. The same momentum that you used to pique the prospect's interest can also be used to overcome objections and show customers why your product provides the best solution.

Feel, Felt, Found: A Distant Cousin

When an objection is raised, many salespeople gravitate to a technique that's commonly called Feel, Felt, Found. This is how I was originally taught to handle objections and reassure prospects that they were indeed making the right decision.

Here's how Feel, Felt, Found works. When a prospect raises an objection, the salesperson acknowledges the concern by saying, *"I understand how you feel."* The salesperson is then supposed to cite at least one example of how other customers have *"felt"* the same way, but here's what they *"found"* that helped resolve their concern. The actual dialogue might sound like this.

Prospect: *"I'm concerned that your price seems too high."*

Salesperson: *"I understand how you feel. Other customers have felt the same way. Take Nationsbank, for example, who had similar concerns about price until they found that the value of our product far outweighed its cost."*

The intentions of this Feel, Felt, Found strategy are admirable, but the problems are two-fold. First, this approach tends to invite mismatching. As we said before, pointing to individual success stories makes it easy for prospects say, *"But we're not Nationsbank."* The other problem with Feel, Felt, Found is that you can only use it once per sale. Otherwise, using this technique over and over to address multiple objections makes you sound like a broken record.

Secret #30   Surrounding prospects with a credible herd reduces your risk because you become the messenger, not the message.

The Herd Theory accomplishes the same objective as Feel, Felt, Found, but without the risks. Most objections aren't unique and many of the prospects you engage will have similar questions and concerns. But rather than trying to use individual successes to make people feel comfortable, the Herd Theory uses momentum to make objections easier to overcome.

In fact, you can use the same herd that you rattled off earlier in the sale to give your prospects a clearer sense of direction. To accomplish this, let them know that companies like US Sprint, Hallmark Cards, Pepsi Co.,

Kansas Power & Light, the Federal Reserve Bank, Yellow Freight, Northwest Mutual Life, and Anheuser-Busch have all had similar concerns. Then ask, *"Would you like to know what they did to ensure their success?"*

Of course they will say yes. Now you're providing a valuable service. Rather than trying to talk prospects into buying, you're letting them know that many of your existing customers had similar questions before they finalized their decisions. This gives you an opportunity to share what these customers (i.e., the rest of the herd) did to ensure their success. This positions you as the messenger and not the message, which significantly reduces the likelihood of a mismatch.

Summary

By creating a sense of momentum in the sale, you will have a strategic advantage. Since the beginning of time, it has always been easier for people to follow the crowd than to strike out on their own. That's why leveraging the Herd Theory is such a powerful strategy in QBS. If you can reassure prospects that they are indeed moving in the right direction, you will increase your probability of making a sale, and you will also reduce the buyer's risk. It's the perfect win/win scenario.

Chapter 4

GOLD MEDALS & GERMAN SHEPHERDS

To succeed in sales, sellers have to motivate potential buyers to want to take action. But we (as sellers) also have to recognize that people are motivated in different ways. While some people are motivated to run fast toward gold medals, many others will run even faster from German Shepherds.

In QBS, we show you how to motivate both kinds of buyers. By adjusting the way you position your value, you can double the number of benefits your product or service offers, and increase your probability of success in making the sale.

"I go fishing up in Maine every summer," Dale Carnegie wrote in the mid 1930s. "Personally, I am very fond of strawberries and cream, but I find that for some strange reason, fish prefer worms. So when I go fishing, I don't think about what I want. I think about what they want. I don't bait the hook with strawberries and cream. I dangle a worm or a grasshopper in front of the fish and say, 'Wouldn't you like to have that?'"

This story prompts me to ask, why not use the same common sense when fishing for customers?

Secret #31	If you want to motivate people, then it's more important to think about what they want, rather than what you want.

Most salespeople love to talk about the solutions they offer. They get excited about the value of their product or service and want to share this good news with qualified prospects. While some are more strategic in their delivery, others get excited and start spewing benefits like a volcano. In either case, their objectives are the same—sellers are trying to establish enough value in their solutions to justify a favorable purchase decision.

But as Mr. Carnegie points out in his timeless and meaningful message, just because something's important to us (as salespeople) doesn't mean it's important to the customer. Sales presentations are breeding grounds for this type of disconnect. For example, have you ever had the experience where some portion of the audience is absolutely riveted to your presentation, while other people in the same audience are just sitting there with a glazed look, as if they are completely missing the point? In the real world of selling, this happens because people have different buying motivations.

Always Positive Isn't the Most Productive

Salespeople have tried numerous ways to address the fact that prospects are motivated differently. One of the most prevalent sales tricks is to try and motivate prospects with "happy gas." For decades, sellers have been told that attitude is everything, and the more enthusiastic you are, the more excited your prospects will become. You know the drill—flash a big smile and bubble over with energy in an attempt to get prospects excited about your product. Gag me! This fluffy cloud approach to selling is just a facade that causes many salespeople to miss out on some otherwise lucrative opportunities.

Salespeople who are not filled with happy gas still tend to emphasize the positive, pointing out all the wonderful benefits their product or service offers, in an attempt to get prospects and customers excited. But as you are about to find out, always positive isn't always the most productive approach. True professionals are not "always positive." Instead, they radiate competence, capability, and expertise by being serious and self-assured. This is very different from the eager salesperson who communicates value by having a permanent smile plastered on his or her face.

> **Secret #32**   Competence, credibility, expertise, and value will outsell overeagerness every time.

I'm not saying that you shouldn't be proud of your product or excited about a new opportunity. I'm merely suggesting that being super-positive is not the best way to motivate *all* prospects. And as you'll see throughout QBS, being super-positive is not even the best way to motivate *most* prospects.

Problems with Behavioral Selling

Salespeople have also tried to address the fact that people are motivated differently by adjusting their own behavior. The last fifty years of behavioral research has generated numerous selling models that attempt to categorize prospective buyers into subgroups of people who have common personality characteristics and behavioral tendencies. Some of these subgroups include: Drivers, Amiables, Analyticals, Expressives, Sensors, Thinkers, Intuitives, Judgers, and Feelers…just to name a few.

With a behavioral approach to selling, the thought is: if you can identify the type of person you are dealing with, and better understand how they are motivated, then you will be able to more effectively position the value of your product or service. I agree with this premise. The problem is, most behavioral selling models are very difficult to implement in the real world. I say this because after trying twice to implement this approach, I found that:

- When first engaging new prospects, it's impossible to know, in the early stages of a conversation, whether you are dealing with a Driver, Amiable, Expressive, or Analytical. This puts you at a significant disadvantage, because prospects are going to form their impressions of you long before you will know how to position yourself.

- *You can't judge a book by its cover.* Have you ever met someone who at first seemed like a "crusty old bird," but then once you got to know them, you found out that they were just an "old softy?" Other people are sweet until you aren't looking, and then, wham! They stab you in the back. Needless to say, misjudging someone can be detrimental to your sales efforts.

- Very few salespeople (and I emphasize the word few) have the acting talent required to instantly transform their own personality to match their prospect's behavior without bumbling around or sounding fake.

- Lastly, when you are dealing with multiple people in a strategic sale, who all have different personality profiles, whose personality style should you match? I would hate to address the needs of the Driver, and then find out later that I failed to meet the needs of the Amiables, Expressives, or Feelers.

These problems lead me to conclude that behavioral selling models make for interesting reading; but trying to categorize people according to their personality type and then match your behavior to theirs is an ineffective way to manage the sale. The truth is, many salespeople end up outsmarting themselves by first misjudging their prospect and then mishandling the situation.

My experience has been that most salespeople perform at their best when they are just being themselves. They appear more comfortable and sound more confident, which allows them to focus on delivering value rather than try to be something they're not.

Secret #33	Keep it simple. You will be more effective just being yourself, rather than trying to be something you're not.

This brings us right back to square one, where we concluded that people are motivated differently. While I have always agreed with the premise that knowing how people are motivated allows sellers to more effectively position their value, I knew that there had to be a better way to manage these differences.

Solving the Problem

People who are motivated differently can get excited about the same product for different reasons. This became apparent in 1992 when I started selling Superservers for NetFrame Systems. What's a Superserver? Simply put, it's a computer system that's powerful enough to handle large corporate networks.

NetFrame put all its new field salespeople through a one-week orientation at corporate headquarters in the Silicon Valley. There we learned how to qualify new opportunities and how to position NetFrame's family of products. Upon completing the training, we were sent back to our respective territories *to create business opportunities that otherwise wouldn't exist.*

At first, I toed the company line—telling prospects how exciting our new technology was. I told them how NetFrame's unique system architecture would improve their performance, productivity, and reliability. I also explained how our systems were easy to manage and how they saved money.

As it turned out, some prospects did get excited about all the wonderful benefits NetFrame offered. But as time went by, I noticed that some prospects just weren't getting it. No matter how many "wonderful benefits" I threw out, they still weren't registering value, and I wasn't getting any closer to making a sale.

Finally, ignorance gave in to curiosity, and I started asking customers what they wanted. Guess what I discovered? While some prospects were very interested in all the positive benefits NetFrame offered, others were more interested in avoiding potential problems—things like maintenance headaches, support issues, or overloading the network with excess traffic. I found out the prospects had very different reasons for buying our product; and to motivate more prospects, it was clear that I needed to change the way I was positioning value.

The Metaphor That Stuck

In 1996, the Summer Olympic Games were held in my home city of Atlanta. As I watched athletes from all over the world perform in their respective events, I remember wondering what motivated them to compete at the highest levels. On the surface, it seemed logical to assume that these world class athletes were driven by all the positive rewards that would go to the champion—fame, admiration, and of course, the gold medal. After training for most of their lives, who wouldn't want to experience "the thrill of victory"?

But as I watched the games unfold, it became obvious that while some athletes were motivated by *positive rewards*, many others were trying to avoid "the agony of defeat." Rather than think about all the accolades that would come from success, some athletes were motivated to run even faster, and jump even higher, because they were trying to avoid an undesirable outcome.

Carl Lewis, arguably the greatest track and field athlete of all time, and nine-time Olympic gold medalist, was an excellent example of this. After his last event in Atlanta, when he won the gold medal on his final attempt in the long jump, the sportscaster asked, *"Mr. Lewis, what were you thinking about just before you jumped?"* As it turned out, Carl Lewis wasn't thinking about medals, money, or any of the accolades that would come from a victory. Instead, he said his primary motivation was that his family was in the stadium and he didn't want to disappoint them by losing his final Olympic event.

Isn't that the way many customers feel? Rather than hoping to benefit from all the "wonderful things" your product or service offers, they're trying to avoid potential problems, uncertainty, or even failure. QBS realizes that people are motivated differently—and while some are motivated by positive reward, many other people are motivated even more by negative aversion.

> **Secret #34** While some people run fast toward *gold medals*, many others run even faster from *German Shepherds*.

The fear of failure is a powerful influence. Imagine what would happen if a pack of German Shepherd dogs were actually chasing the Olympic athletes down the track toward the finish line. That would certainly motivate me to run faster; how about you? So what motivates your customers: *gold medals* or *German Shepherds*? In reality, some prospects you meet will be driven by positive benefits (*gold medals*), while others will be motivated by their need to avoid potential problems and feelings of uncertainty (*German Shepherds*).

The fact that people are motivated differently shouldn't surprise you. We see evidence of this every day. For example, why do people exercise? Isn't it true that some people exercise because physical activity is invigorating and it makes them feel energized all day (*gold medals*), while other people exercise because they're trying to lose weight or they want to reduce their risk of heart failure (*German Shepherds*)?

Why do people take vacations? Again, some people want to spend time with their families and see the world, while other people take vacations because if they don't, they'll go nuts. Can you see the difference?

I applied this principle to selling Superservers at NetFrame and quickly discovered that while some prospects were interested in positive benefits like better performance, productivity increases, and state-of-the-art technology, other prospects were more interested in protecting themselves against negative issues like downtime, maintenance problems, and corrupted data. Once I realized that my product could be positioned to address *gold medals* and *German Shepherds* (both), my sales took off; and it was truly amazing to see prospects who used to just sit there with that glazed look, suddenly come alive.

The question is, what type of prospects do you want to sell to, those who are motivated by positive rewards or those who are motivated more by negative aversion? If you're like me, you'll want to sell to both.

Double Your Benefits to Double Your Value

If you want to sell to people who are motivated by both *gold medals* and *German Shepherds*, then it's important to position benefits in ways that both will understand. How do you do this? I'll show you.

Positioning benefits is how sellers establish value. Ultimately, we want to establish enough value to justify the cost of our solution. Extrapolate this further, and we can logically conclude that the more benefits you bring to the table, the more value you can present to prospects and customers—which will ultimately increase your probability of success for making a sale.

So let's make a list of benefits. Whenever I deliver a QBS program to a live audience, I ask each participant to make a list of the compelling benefits their product or service offers. Then I go to the flip chart, and together we aggregate these benefits into a larger list that summarizes their company's value proposition. What we end up with is a flip chart filled with benefits—much like the following diagram. To follow along, I encourage you to make a list of the specific benefits that you and your product offer your customer.

The tendency is to position benefits positively, as *gold medals*. That seems to make sense, given that the dictionary defines a benefit as *something that promotes or enhances one's well-being*. Consequently, sellers all over the world run around telling prospects how terrific their product is because it provides wonderful benefits like reliability, cost effectiveness, lower overhead, ease of use, and the list goes on. These benefits are wonderful, but only for those people who are motivated by *gold medals*. Other prospects, who are motivated more by *German Shepherds*, fail to register these positive benefits; in which case, sellers only connect with a portion of their intended audience.

* *More Reliable*
* *Cost Effective*
* *Less Overhead*
* *Easier to Use*
* *Easy to Manage*
* *Upgradable*
* *Proven Solution*
* *Performance*

We definitely want to motivate prospects who get excited about positive rewards. But we also want to reach those people who are trying to avoid potential problems, uncertainty, or even failure. You can accomplish this by positioning the benefits you offer both ways—as a *gold medal* and a *German Shepherd*.

Take one of the benefits from our diagram (cost effectiveness, for example). In addition to emphasizing the positive aspects of your product's cost effectiveness in terms of *gold medals*, it's just as important to let prospects know that your solution will also protect them against potential *German Shepherds* like hidden expenses, high maintenance costs, or a low return on investment.

The same logic applies to other benefits like reliability and performance. To increase the value of your offering, you'll want to position these benefits both ways too. Let me illustrate.

Seller: *"Ms. Prospect, our reliability features will increase your productivity (gold medal) and reduce all those pesky interruptions that would otherwise handcuff your business (German Shepherd)."*

– or–

"Performance is also an advantage—for two reasons. Because our systems use advanced technology, you can access more information than ever before (gold medal) without any risk of overloading the system with excess network traffic (German Shepherd)."

Are you getting the picture? You can take any benefit from any company, for any product being offered, and position it both ways—as a *gold medal* and also as a *German Shepherd*.

Positioning benefits both as *gold medals* and *German Shepherds* accomplishes two very strategic objectives in the QBS sale. First, it's a risk reduction strategy. Instead of having some portion of your audience glaze over because they're simply not getting it, you will connect with more prospects by positioning value in a way that motivates them. Also, positioning benefits both ways means you no longer have to guess whether you are dealing with a Driver, Amiable, Expressive, or any other personality type. You'll know in advance that prospects are motivated either by positive rewards or by negative aversion. This allows you to score points with those prospects who are motivated by *gold medals*, and with those prospects who are motivated by *German Shepherds*.

> **Secret #35**   By positioning both *gold medals* and *German Shepherds*, you will get more bang out of each benefit.

The flipchart diagram on the previous page listed eight specific benefits. The problem is that many of your competitors will claim that they too provide the same list of benefits. But you'll have the advantage if they focus only on the positives (as most sellers do), because they will address only eight value points. A QBS salesperson, on the other hand, who positions each of these benefits in terms of *gold medals* and *German Shepherds*, will expand their value proposition to include sixteen value points, rather than just eight.

Here's the best part. Very few people are motivated only by *gold medals*, or only by *German Shepherds*. While some might lean one way or the other, the vast majority of prospects and customers are motivated by a combination of the two. Now do the math. Your ability to present twice as many benefits gives you an opportunity to present twice as much value; it also gives your prospects and customers twice as many reasons to move forward with a favorable purchase decision. This technique will ultimately help you justify your solutions and close more sales. As an added bonus, positioning *gold medals* and *German Shepherds* (both) will differentiate you from any competitors who are still being taught to focus only on the positive.

QBS Didn't Invent Human Behavior

The realization that prospects are motivated by positive reward and by negative aversion will forever change the face of professional sales. Those sellers who are willing to adapt and change the way they position benefits will reap significant rewards, while those who focus only on the positive will find themselves fighting against a severe competitive disadvantage.

Question Based Selling shouldn't receive all the credit, however. We didn't invent human behavior. Potential buyers have been responding to *gold medal* and *German Shepherd* motivations for a long time. Just look at the advertising industry. Marketing executives figured out long ago that in order to generate greater returns on their advertising investments, they needed to target multiple segments of the consumer population. Do you remember the TV commercials for Fram Oil Filters—where the greasy mechanic looks directly into the camera and says, "*You can pay me now* (to change the filter), *or pay me later* (to replace the entire engine)?" Fram recognized that while some people buy oil filters to make their engines run more smoothly (*gold medal*), many other people buy oil filters to avoid potential engine damage (*German Shepherd*).

Don't be alarmed! Targeting multiple market segments has become a common advertising practice for everyday products. Here's another example. Why do people buy Johnson's baby shampoo? Some people buy it because it's gentle on the hair (*gold medal*), while many other people buy Johnson's baby shampoo because it won't sting their baby's eyes (*German Shepherd*). Remember the slogan? "No more tears."

I can keep going. Why do people buy Miller Lite beer? Some people buy it because it "tastes great" (*gold medal*). Other people buy Miller Lite beer because it's "less filling" (*German Shepherd*).

The following chart highlights a number of everyday products and how they are being positioned to appeal to both kinds of buyers.

Product	Gold Medals	German Shepherds
Volvo Automobiles	Efficient and stylish	Safe to protect family
Tandem Computers	Maximum performance	Eliminates downtime
Microsoft	Technology leadership	Fewer integration issues
Johnson's Baby Shampoo	Gentle on the hair	No more tears
Miller Lite Beer	Tastes great	Less filling
Fram Oil Filters	Smoother running engine	Prevents costly repairs
Life Insurance	Retirement savings	Financial protection
Diet Food Products	High in taste	Low in fat
Organic Detergents	Natural cleaning agents	Protect the environment
Weight Loss Programs	Look and feel better	Lose those ugly pounds

Positioning Gold Medals and German Shepherds

Don't mistake this for negative selling. Positioning *German Shepherd* benefits is not intended to threaten, intimidate, or scare prospective customers. We are simply acknowledging that prospects are motivated differently, which gives you an opportunity to position your benefits in a way that will more effectively meet their business and emotional needs.

Corporate Marketers Take Note

In every company I have sold for, the corporate marketing group played an integral role in the success of the sales organization. But I have noticed that the vast majority of product literature and corporate marketing programs are full of *gold medal* benefits, but they hardly mention *German Shepherds*. Like salespeople, corporate marketers have also been taught to put their best foot forward when positioning benefits, in an effort to communicate all the wonderful aspects that their product or service offers.

Ironically, the way marketing departments position *gold medal* benefits is often in direct conflict with the sales organization. Sales managers want salespeople to go out into their respective territories looking for *German Shepherds*—problems or issues that are causing pain. But this causes an emotional disconnect whenever a salesperson uncovers a prospect who is motivated by *German Shepherds*, and then turns around and starts positioning their company's value in terms of *gold medals*. That's essentially what happens every time you deliver a canned corporate pitch or hand someone a product brochure.

This problem can be solved if salespeople probe for both *gold medals* and *German Shepherds*, and corporate marketers make it a point to position solutions in a way that speaks to both motivations.

Champions Also Need to Position Both Ways

What if you're selling to someone who is motivated exclusively by one or the other? For example, suppose you've been working with a major account for the last several months, and your champion (Matthew) is motivated by positive reward. Matthew is an energetic optimist who likes state-of-the-art technology and high performance solutions, and he is definitely motivated by *gold medals*. Knowing this about Matthew, should you position your solution (to Matthew) in terms of *gold medals*, *German Shepherds*, or both?

Traditional thinking would suggest that you should communicate with Matthew in terms that are most likely to motivate him. In that case, you would focus on *gold medals*. In QBS, we'd say just the opposite. Even if Matthew is absolutely driven by *gold medals*, that doesn't mean the rest of the committee or the person who ultimately signs the check will be motivated the same way. Most strategic decisions involve more than one person, and someone other than your champion may have very different buying motivations. Therefore, it makes sense to talk about both *gold medals* and *German Shepherds* so your internal champion can buy into the total value of your product and then position it both ways to other people in the organization.

Even Managers Can Apply This Principle

Does your company have sales awards? A performance trip? Bonuses for reaching or overachieving sales quota? Most companies do. By offering incentives for good performance, management can encourage the sales organization to perform at the highest levels. But incentives like these only tap into some portion of how salespeople are actually motivated.

Lots of salespeople are motivated by positive rewards—no question about it. But salespeople are also motivated by negative aversion. While many sellers are motivated to go the extra mile to receive a trip or an attractive bonus, others work just as hard because they have an intense desire not to fail. That's how it was for me. I appreciated all the bonuses, accolades, and awards that came with success, but I was also motivated by the fear of having an empty sales forecast, facing a disgruntled sales manager, or missing the annual performance trip.

Being motivated by *German Shepherds* is not some demented form of paranoia or pessimism; nor does it equate to having a negative attitude. Rather, the fear of failure is a very powerful and constructive motivational influence that, when channeled properly, can improve both your performance and your results.

> **Secret #36**   Some of the world's most successful people get to the top because of their intense desire *not* to be on the bottom.

There's a lesson here for husbands, wives, parents, teachers, even sales managers. Accolades and rewards can motivate people to perform in desirable ways. But so can the need to avoid problems, uncertainty, or even failure. The message is this: if you want ordinary people to perform in extraordinary ways, then it's important to motivate them with *gold medals* and *German Shepherds* both.

Summary

Knowing that prospects and customers are motivated by *gold medals* and *German Shepherds* causes salespeople to approach the sales process differently. Being able to connect with a larger audience puts a bounce in their step and bolsters their confidence. That's because Question Based Selling does what Dale Carnegie suggested so many years ago—we teach salespeople to focus on what the customer wants, rather than what *we* want.

In order to have an opportunity to position value, however, sellers must first uncover a need. That's what we talk about next in chapter 5. We show you how to uncover prospect needs that will fuel the sales process.

FUELING THE SALES PROCESS

Buyers are motivated by what they need. If someone needs to protect against financial loss, for example, they buy insurance. If someone needs to keep pace with industry trends, they upgrade their technology. Virtually every purchase is an attempt to solve a problem, and thereby satisfy a need.

By helping prospective buyers identify potential needs, sellers can expand their opportunity to provide solutions—and more opportunities means increased sales. In this chapter, we'll examine how you can help prospects recognize greater needs, and how those needs will fuel a successful sales process.

Ring...ring... ring... Begrudgingly, I closed the newspaper, climbed out of my comfortable chair, and lunged for the telephone. Sure enough, it was another one of those pesky sales calls. You know, where the phone rings just after you've crashed into the La-Z-Boy, following a long day at the office.

On the other end of the call was a salesperson named Brent, who was selling septic tank improvement products. *"Septic tank improvement products?"* I remember thinking, *"That's a new one on me."* But as a consummate student of the sale, I indulged him—at least for a few moments.

Brent was an energetic young salesman who successfully secured a few minutes of my time, and then dove headfirst into his sales pitch. He explained that he represented a company that distributes chemical enzyme systems. (What's a chemical enzyme system, you might ask? Apparently, it's a chemical process that enables septic tanks to function more efficiently.) Brent rattled off a list of product features and their corresponding benefits. Then he added, *"Our products are EPA approved and environmentally safe."*

After his opening barrage, I asked, *"How much do your septic tank improvement products cost?"*

"Our products are extremely cost effective—less than three dollars per month," Brent responded confidently. He then tried to close the sale by offering a five-year supply of his product for the special low price of $179.

"There's only one problem," I replied, *"I subscribe to the theory that if it ain't broke, don't fix it. And as far as I know, my septic system is working just fine, which makes your product too expensive at any price. But thank you anyway."* (click). Then, before settling back into my chair, I forwarded my calls to prevent any further unwelcome interruptions.

Brent didn't sell me his product, but it wasn't because he lacked a good solution or because his sales pitch was ineffective. Frankly, he could have been the world's greatest salesperson offering the best septic tank improvement product and the answer would have been the same—*No thanks*. The reason is simple. I wasn't a qualified prospect because I didn't perceive a need.

> **Secret #37**   Without needs, there are no solutions; and without solutions, it's virtually impossible to establish value.

Brent was convinced that homeowners would save money by using his product. But it doesn't really matter what the salesperson believes. The buyer is the one who actually makes the decision, and since my septic tank seemed fine, there was no reason to spend $179. Brent failed to uncover a need that would fuel the sales process; therefore, he missed an opportunity to either solve a problem or improve my existing condition.

This scenario makes an interesting case study because salespeople all over the world try some variation of this approach—offering solutions without first identifying a need. But buyers don't have needs just because you offer solutions. It's the other way around. You can only offer solutions if the buyer has needs. Guess whose job it is to uncover needs? The salesperson's.

Where Do Needs Originate?

Sellers cannot provide value until the prospect first recognizes the existence of a need. Needs are what initially motivates them to investigate potential solutions and needs are ultimately what motivates them to buy. Of course, the more needs you uncover, the more likely it is that prospective buyers will find value in the solutions being proposed.

Too often, sellers are taught that the best way to find qualified opportunities is to go out looking for pain. That's essentially what my friend Brent was doing. He was calling to see if I was currently experiencing a septic tank problem. The assumption is, if prospects are currently experiencing a problem, then they must have needs. On the surface, looking for pain makes sense because pain causes prospects to seek relief. It also motivates them to want to prevent problems from occurring in the future.

Searching for problems is not a bad strategy. Pain can be a very powerful motivator indeed. In fact, frustration and discontentment have been the catalysts for some of the most lucrative opportunities of my sales career. But we must realize that pain is not the only cause of prospect needs.

Needs are also created by desire. Otherwise, why would anyone spend $80,000 to buy a new Mercedes Benz? It's not because they're feeling some sort of pain. More likely it's because they desire the luxury and elegance that only Mercedes Benz can offer. These desires *are* needs, but they are hardly problems in the traditional sense. If the customer's objective was simply to solve a problem, they could have purchased a Honda for less money and still had adequate transportation.

Needs Come From Both

The same is true with artwork, fine jewelry, pleasure boats, furniture, oriental rugs, sporting goods, video equipment, musical instruments, and vacation property. People purchase these products to satisfy a need—a need that comes from desire, rather than pain.

In QBS, we define a need as a discrepancy between *what is* and *what could be*. In layman's terms, needs are formed when people who are dissatisfied with the status quo (*what is*) recognize that they would be better off if their situation was improved (by *what could be*). Prospects who are currently experiencing pain will seek relief, while those who wish to satisfy a desire will buy things to improve their existing condition—and the larger the discrepancy, the more your prospects will need a solution.

Secret #38   To alleviate *pain*, prospects will seek relief. To satisfy a *desire*, prospects will attempt to improve their existing condition.

A discrepancy can manifest itself as either a lack of something required (to alleviate pain), or a lack of something preferred (to satisfy a desire). To illustrate, suppose your laptop computer crashes for the third consecutive day. If you depend on a PC to run your business, then you suddenly have a serious problem—a pain caused by a lack of something required. Having lost my own computer system before, I know that this situation can quickly manifest itself into a need by creating a discrepancy between *what is* (an unreliable laptop) and *what could be* (a system that works).

A discrepancy can also be created by desire—a need to improve the status quo. If an MCI salesperson showed a corporate CFO how to reduce his company's telecommunications costs by changing carriers, and the CFO became excited about saving money, then a discrepancy would be created between *what is* (his current long distance expenses), and *what could be* (significant reductions in cost). As a result, the CFO's contentment with his previous carrier would be replaced by a desire to improve the status quo.

In Question Based Selling, this is important because we must recognize that needs come from both pain and desire. If your goal is to uncover needs and provide solutions, you can significantly expand your opportunity (to sell) by offering relief to those prospects who are currently experiencing pain, and a vision of value for those who wish to improve their existing condition.

Perception Isn't Everything

Going back to the story of the septic tank salesman, I want to point out an interesting irony about needs. Just because Brent didn't successfully uncover a need doesn't mean a problem (or an opportunity) didn't exist.

I didn't think we had septic tank problems, so I did not perceive a need for the product Brent was offering. But after a few days, Brent's call prompted me to wonder if our septic system was indeed functioning properly. For all I knew, it could have been seeping raw sewage into the ground. What did I know about septic tank maintenance?

As I thought more about it, I remembered seeing septic tank service trucks around the neighborhood. These service trucks would indicate that our neighbors were either currently experiencing problems with their septic systems, or they were trying to prevent problems from occurring. I made a few calls and discovered that septic tanks do need regular maintenance, so I scheduled an appointment with a local company, AAA Septic Services, to come out and give us a "complimentary" evaluation.

The service rep asked, *"When was your system last serviced?"* My honesty revealed my ignorance, which he used as an opportunity to educate me further. He explained that like anything else, septic systems need to be serviced on a regular basis to function properly; otherwise, the homeowner could face any number of undesirable and costly consequences.

As I learned more about septic tanks, it was obvious that we did have a need. It was a classic case of what you don't know *can* hurt you. Gladly, I authorized a work order for AAA to service our system. In addition, I agreed to purchase the very same maintenance product Brent had offered less than a week earlier to help avoid potential problems in the future.

When My Perspective Changed, So Did My Needs

When Brent called, I didn't think I needed septic system maintenance. But within seven days of his call I was signing a purchase requisition for the very same septic tank improvement product. The question is, what was it that changed?

Oddly enough, my actual needs didn't change between Brent's call and AAA's recommendation. The status of my septic system was virtually the same as it had been a week earlier. What changed was my perspective. New information created a discrepancy between the current status of my septic system, and the recommendation I was getting. When I found out that septic systems do need regular maintenance, and that there are serious consequences if regular maintenance is not properly performed, I quickly recognized the existence of a need.

As you can see from this anecdote, the actual need had been there all along. Brent simply missed an opportunity to make a sale because he didn't understand the difference between active needs and latent needs.

Active Needs

People who are currently experiencing problems, frustration, pain, or an intense desire, have immediate needs. In QBS, we call these *active needs*. If you were driving on a desolate stretch of interstate highway, for example, and your low fuel warning light started to flash, you would have an immediate need; in this case, for gasoline. Since you would be on the verge of running out of fuel, you would have an active need to resolve the problem.

Similarly, if you were in a computer superstore and saw that the price of the laser printer that you've been eyeing for the last several months had suddenly been reduced for a "today only" clearance sale, you might have an immediate need to take advantage of the opportunity. This is an example of an active need that comes from desire.

Active needs occur whenever a person is no longer satisfied with the status quo. Whether their dissatisfaction is caused by pain or desire, prospects with active needs are easy to approach because they are open to change. In many cases, they're already out there actively looking for a solution.

> **Secret #39** *Active needs* occur when prospects recognize that they are no longer satisfied with the status quo.

Not surprisingly, people with active needs make wonderful prospects. In addition to having already recognized their needs, they appreciate a salesperson who is willing to work with them to find a solution. Consequently, the sales cycle tends to be much shorter, and decisions are made more quickly. In some ways, it's like feeding a hungry baby. All you have to do is dangle a few benefits out in front of someone with an active need, and they get excited.

It would be nice if every prospect had active needs. But that's not reality. While it's enticing to think that people out there are desperately seeking our solutions, the reality is prospects with active needs represent only a small portion of your overall market opportunity.

Latent Needs

The larger and more significant portion of the market is comprised of prospects who do have needs for your product or service, but haven't yet recognized those needs. In QBS, we say that these prospects have *latent needs*.

Latent needs are needs that do exist but haven't yet surfaced as problems or desires. Prospects with latent needs fail to recognize that they are no longer satisfied with the status quo. As an example, suppose you and I were standing beside your car when suddenly we noticed that one of your tires was worn down to the cords. Instantly, you would have a need for new tires. The question is, did you have a need for new tires yesterday? Sure you did. The tread on your tire didn't wear itself down overnight. But until you recognized the problem, your need for new tires was latent. This is essentially what happened when Brent called me. I absolutely had a need for septic tank improvement products, but my need was a latent need.

Salespeople encounter prospects with latent needs all the time—especially prospects who say things like: *"I don't need life insurance because I'm not planning to die any time soon."* Or, *"We don't have time to evaluate new technology, because we're too busy putting out fires."* Here's my personal favorite: *"We can't afford sales training right now, because our sales have been down."*

Hello! The best time to buy life insurance is when you're not planning to die. Similarly, new technology might help eliminate some system problems; and it makes all kinds of sense to invest in sales training if your sales numbers are weak, or your competition is getting tougher.

> **Secret #40**   *Latent needs* exist when prospects fail to recognize that they are no longer satisfied with the status quo.

The primary reason latent needs exist is ignorance. When prospects are not aware of a problem (or an opportunity to improve their existing condition), they have no reason to change the status quo. Another source of latent needs is a false sense of security. Going back to a previous analogy, if your car was just serviced and everything checked out fine, then it would be easy to assume that there's no need for additional maintenance.

The Lion's Share of Opportunity

The easiest way to create opportunities that otherwise wouldn't exist is to go out into the marketplace looking for prospects with active needs. But as we've said, active needs represent only a small fraction of the overall market opportunity, while latent needs make up the lion's share. For every prospect who is currently feeling pain, or who recognizes an opportunity to improve their existing condition, there are many more who could also benefit from your product or service. In fact, this relationship is highly skewed where prospects with active needs are more the exception than the rule. You can see this better if we extrapolate some numbers.

Everyone needs insurance, right? One might think so, but studies have shown that while 60 percent of middle-class Americans are under-insured, less than 2 percent are "in the market" to buy additional coverage. What does this mean for insurance salespeople? It means that sixty out of every one hundred prospects needs more insurance, but only two out of those people would be eager to have a discussion about buying additional coverage. These two people would have active needs.

Total Market Opportunity

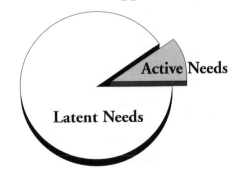

Active Needs

Latent Needs

If you do the math, you will also find that prospecting for active needs is unproductive. Using the previous example, an insurance salesperson who prospects for people with active needs would have to make fifty calls (on average) just to find one new opportunity. That's an extremely low return on investment. If that same salesperson went after the larger market segment, by targeting the other 60 percent who have latent needs, the number of opportunities that could be harvested from the same pool of prospects would increase dramatically. In other words, out of every fifty prospects, thirty would have a latent need for additional insurance and a potential interest in the products being offered.

Most top sales performers will attest that the overwhelming majority of their sales success comes from their ability to transform a prospect's latent needs into active needs. This transformation is also how you escalate the prospect's sense of urgency to move forward with a favorable decision.

Increasing the Prospect's Sense of Urgency

Dangling potential solutions out in front of a prospect with latent needs is a low percentage play. No matter how good your solutions are, prospects with latent needs are not going to buy. That's because they're complacent. They're already satisfied with the status quo, and the opportunity for improvement isn't enough to initiate or justify a change.

The opposite of complacency is urgency. Urgency motivates people to take action when problems are painful enough, or opportunities are enticing enough, to justify making a change. How can you increase a prospect's sense of urgency? Easy. All you have to do is transform their latent needs into active needs. And the greater the prospect's needs, the more incentive they have to alleviate the pain or satisfy the desire.

Secret #41	*"How badly you're bleeding usually dictates how fast you drive to the hospital."* The greater the prospect's sense of urgency, the more likely they are to act on your solutions.

The following diagram illustrates the relationship between latent needs and active needs. Actually, it's a logical progression. As the prospect's perspective changes (like mine did in the septic tank story), latent needs are transformed into active needs, and the prospect's sense of urgency for finding a solution will increase automatically. So will your probability of completing a successful sale.

Escalating Needs Increases Probability

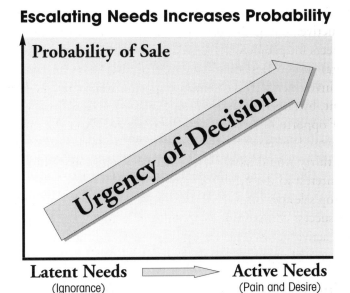

Turning a prospect's complacency into an active desire is the real game in professional selling. This is what allows sellers to go after the broader market opportunity—those prospects who do have needs but haven't yet recognized the opportunity to improve their existing condition. It's also what separates top sales performers from the rest of the masses.

While it's natural for prospects to find comfort in the status quo, sellers have to realize that prospective buyers can't take advantage of opportunities they don't know about. This boils the sales function down into a process of mutual discovery, where sellers work together with prospective buyers to uncover problems and opportunities that otherwise wouldn't have been identified. Have you ever heard a prospect say, *"I wish I had known about your product sooner?"* Just like you and me, they can only act on the information they have at the time.

Secret #42   Uninformed prospects are much less likely to make a favorable buying decision.

The easiest way to increase a prospect's sense of urgency is to change their perspective. You can accomplish this either by offering new information or by asking questions that will help them discover opportunities to improve their existing condition. The following anecdote illustrates the point.

Changing the Prospect's Perspective

Pat Daley sells home security systems in Sacramento, California. Like many salespeople, Pat makes sales call after sales call, trying to uncover potential opportunities by asking people if they are currently "in the market" for a new home security system. His prospecting efforts have been diligent, but sales have been slow. Most of the people he talks to either have a security system already, or they feel secure enough without one.

Robert Dickens also sells home security systems in Sacramento. Even though he's calling on the same pool of prospects as Pat, Robert's business is booming. His pipeline is overflowing with new opportunities and his company is swamped with new orders. Business couldn't be better. In fact, his organization is straining to keep up with a rising demand for home security.

What's the difference between Robert's approach and Pat's, given that they are selling similar products within the same geographic area?

The difference is their target market. Pat is prospecting for people who already have an active need for a security system. Robert, on the other hand, works closely with his prospects to develop their need for home security. Robert has figured out that his greatest opportunity to make sales lies in his ability to create demand, by helping potential buyers recognize latent needs. In his view, who wouldn't be interested in protecting their home and family?

To foster a demand for home security, Robert focuses on raising the prospect's awareness, which is the first step toward changing their perspective. His typical sales call sounds like this:

Robert: *"Hello Mr. Prospect, my name is Robert Dickens, and I'm with SafeGuard Security Systems of Sacramento. Sir, are you aware that within a five mile radius of your home, the number of break-ins, thefts, and violent crimes has nearly doubled in the last year?"*

Prospect: *"Really? I wasn't aware of that."*

Robert: *"Yes. It's unfortunate, but true. In fact, six incidents of criminal activity have been reported in your area within the last ninety days. That's why I'm calling. To protect people like yourself, SafeGuard Security has implemented a community-wide plan to eliminate these security breeches. Would you like to know how this plan works?"*

Prospect: *"Yes, I would."*

Robert: *"Through the end of next month, our company is offering residents in East Sacramento a complimentary security evaluation—and there's no obligation to buy anything. For those people who are* *interested in protecting their homes and families, we will dispatch one of our certified security experts to inspect your property and identify any security risks. That way, you can minimize any temptations that might otherwise invite criminal activity."*

After getting the prospect's attention by raising their awareness, Robert schedules an appointment for himself or one of his company's security experts to come out and provide a complimentary evaluation.

What does a complimentary security evaluation consist of? Essentially, it's forty-five minutes of uninterrupted sales time. It's also an opportunity for Robert to transform the prospect's latent needs into an active desire by identifying potential security problems.

As property owners learn more about how intruders target houses with insufficient lighting, inadequate door locks, or overgrown shrubbery, they begin to feel less secure. With each deficiency that Robert or one of his security experts points out, homeowners begin to visualize how burglars, rapists, or murderers could easily gain access into their home. Consequently, their sense of urgency for buying a security system increases significantly. According to Robert, once a homeowner takes the time to consider the risks, they invariably jump to the next question, which is, *"How much does a security system cost, and how soon can you have it installed?"* Bingo!

Secret #43   Urgency sells! It increases the prospect's desire to satisfy their needs, and it also increases your probability of success.

Robert is successful because he works together with his prospects to identify potential problems. That's not the case with Pat. Pat isn't trying to escalate the prospect's sense of urgency. Instead, he just goes after the small percentage of homeowners who already recognize their need for home security, but haven't yet purchased a home security system.

Robert is not only providing a valuable solution; he is rendering a valuable service. By giving his prospects an eye-opening dose of reality, he helps them to realize that they may not be as safe as they thought. This realization creates a discrepancy between "what is" (potential risks), and "what could be" (peace-of-mind protection). Keep in mind that Robert hasn't created the problem (crime), nor has he created the prospect's need for home security. He simply brings the issues to the forefront, so prospects can make informed decisions about enhancing their status quo.

Summary

Although the previous example deals with home security systems, the same philosophy applies whether you're selling insurance, technology, software, consulting, real estate, pharmaceuticals, financial services, industrial supplies, or heavy equipment. Transforming latent needs into active needs will escalate the prospect's sense of urgency for finding a solution; which in turn, increases your probability of making a successful sale.

Identifying needs is fundamental to any successful formula in selling. No matter how exciting your solution may be, prospects who don't recognize their own needs won't recognize the value of your product or service. How can salespeople help prospective buyers recognize needs? That's what part 2 of the QBS methodology addresses. Come with us now and we'll show you how to leverage the most powerful tool in sales.

Part Two

Leveraging the Most Powerful Tool in Sales

Everybody says you have to ask questions. Sales managers, sales trainers, and sales consultants all advocate the importance of questions in the sales process. First, you must ask for the initial appointment; then you must ask questions to uncover needs; and when you reach the end of the sale, you must ask for the order.

Questions are important. Even the Bible says, *"Ask and ye shall receive."* In addition to helping sellers gather information, questions can also be used to establish your credibility, uncover prospect needs, and develop mutually beneficial business relationships. Used properly, strategic questions are the single most powerful tool in your sales arsenal. But too many questions can make prospects feel uncomfortable, and asking the wrong questions at the wrong time can kill a conversation in its tracks.

In part 2 of *Secrets of Question Based Selling*, we're not going to tell you to ask questions—you already know that. Instead, we're going to examine the strategy of *what* to ask, and *how* to ask it. As a result, you will discover that every question you deliver has three strategic attributes—a *Scope*, a *Focus*, and a *Disposition;* and how you manage these three attributes will ultimately determine how productively your prospects and customers respond.

Before you start blasting prospects with questions, however, you must first earn the right to ask. In other words, prospective buyers must want to engage. What makes a prospect "want to" engage? That's what you're about to find out.

Chapter 6

CONVERSATIONAL LAYERING

Prospects won't buy from every salesperson who comes calling. They can't even afford to spend time with everyone who calls. This makes it tough on salespeople who are trying to break into new accounts. To uncover needs and present solutions, salespeople must first earn the right to engage.

Relationships are the key to selling effectively. You've heard it many times before: people buy from people. But this raises an important question. If relationships are the key to selling effectively, what's the key to building an effective relationship? In QBS, the answer is Conversational Layering.

Some people enjoy mountain biking. Other people like tennis, fishing, or horseback riding. Me, I like golf. Several months ago, I had an interesting experience during a golf outing one Saturday morning. Since I was a single, I was paired with three other players to complete a foursome. I shared a golf cart with a lively fellow named Bud.

Bud and I were strangers to each other, so we chitchatted for a few holes before broaching the subject of business. *"Bud, what do you do for a living?"* I asked. Bud said that he worked for a small software company in Atlanta. Then he went on to tell me a little about his business. I would have guessed that Bud was in his early fifties.

"What do you do?" he reciprocated.

I said, *"After seventeen years in sales and management, I developed a strategic sales methodology called Question Based Selling. Now I travel all over the world teaching salespeople and sales organizations how to be more effective."*

For some reason, what I said struck a nerve with my new friend Bud. His face lit up and he turned to me in the golf cart and said, *"I'll have you know that you're sitting next to the greatest salesperson on the East Coast!"* While this seemed like a bold statement, I could tell he wasn't kidding. Now I was curious.

"Really?" I replied. I wasn't trying to challenge his assertion, and I wasn't being judgmental. I was, however, very interested in knowing what made him the "greatest salesperson on the East Coast." So I said, *"I'm not trying to challenge you, but I have to ask…What makes you the greatest?"*

"Relationships," Bud said confidently. *"Relationships are the key! Tom, you have to understand,"* he added, *"that people buy from people, and customers have to feel comfortable enough to share their true feelings and concerns."* On that, I agreed. Relationships are important. But I still wanted to know what made him the greatest salesperson, so I persisted.

"Bud," I said. *"The reason I'm asking is because next week I'll be speaking to several hundred salespeople, and I'd like to tell them that I played golf with the greatest salesperson on the East Coast. I'd also like to tell them that you said relationships are the key to selling effectively. Then I'd like to share some of your secrets. So my question is, What are the four or five things that give you an advantage in developing business relationships?"*

A blank expression suddenly came over Bud's face. After making such a bold declaration, he pondered my question about having relationships for a moment and then said, *"I guess you just have them."*

His response was par for the course (no pun intended). I mean, it's incredible how many books and sales trainers espouse the importance of relationships in the sales process, but then don't tell you how to be more effective in creating and maintaining them. I found this very frustrating as a salesperson. So, when I hear people like Bud say, *"I guess you just have them (relationships),"* I can see why so many salespeople focus on having relationships without ever thinking about what causes those relationships to occur. Fortunately, this is about to change with the introduction of QBS's Conversational Layering Model.

Introducing the Conversational Layering Model

Relationships are important in the strategic sale because people *do* buy from people. But that doesn't mean salespeople should just head out into their respective territories to have relationships with prospective customers. Instead, we must ask ourselves: if relationships are the key to selling effectively, then what's the key to building effective relationships?

The answer is Conversational Layering. Whether you're trying to crack into a brand-new prospect account or expand an existing opportunity, the sale ultimately breaks down into a series of events and activities that are intended to engage qualified prospects in productive sales conversation, and then move them forward in the sales process toward a mutual exchange of value. The key word here is process.

We said earlier in chapter 1 that the QBS methodology is based on cause and effect. In that vein, sellers must first "earn the right" to have a relationship. As sellers, we can't just pick up the telephone and start pummeling prospects with questions about their needs. Likewise, we can't just start telling them about our solutions. Instead, we must first earn the right to engage prospects in a conversation about their needs and the value we provide.

By applying this same logic to the entire sales process, we created a layered model that defines each of the prerequisite steps that must occur on the way to a successful sale (see diagram below).

Conversational Layering

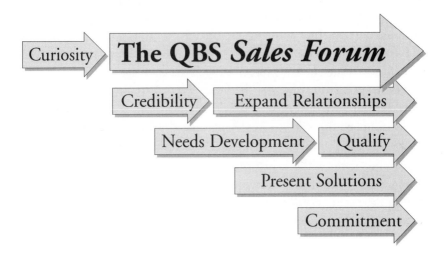

This is the Conversational Layering Model. In this model, relationships are a key component of the sales process, but as you can see from the diagram, relationships are not the catalyst of the sales process. Imagine how you would feel if a salesperson called and said, *"Hi, this is Kerry Thomas of ABC Company, and I would like to have a relationship with you."* Most people wouldn't respond very favorably to this approach. That's because the salesperson hasn't yet *earned the right* to engage you in a business relationship.

Jumping Ahead Increases Your Risk

I always thought that a career in the military would have been great if it were somehow possible to enlist as a colonel. Think about it—instant rank, a company car, a plush office, and lots of medals. Unfortunately, it doesn't work that way. To achieve the rank of colonel, one must first earn the right, which means climbing a ladder that starts at the very bottom—in boot camp.

Similarly, it would have been great to be a concert pianist, especially if it was possible to jump ahead to the professional ranks without having to study or practice. As an instant success, I'd play beautiful music before packed audiences in Carnegie Hall. But I took piano lessons for a couple weeks, and quickly discovered that piano players don't just jump ahead to Carnegie Hall.

The same argument could be made about selling. We could take the position that salespeople can't jump ahead in the sales process—but in reality, they can. Most sellers don't have anyone looking over their shoulder, so there's nothing to stop them from jumping ahead. As a result, many sellers do exactly that. They try to jump ahead (to uncover needs and present solutions) without first securing the prospect's interest or their attention.

I say, if you're going to jump ahead in the sales process, then why not jump all the way to the end? Here's an idea. Pick up the telephone to call one of your most lucrative prospects and say, *"Hi, Mr. Prospect, I've got Thursday afternoon open on my schedule, so why don't I bring by a stack of purchase orders and sign you guys up? That way, we can save you the hassle of having to work through a diligent evaluation."* Of course, this is silly—because you can't ask for a commitment without first presenting a solution.

Jumping ahead in the sales process is a high-risk proposition, one that significantly reduces your probability of success. But that's exactly what salespeople are doing when they ask for a commitment without first accomplishing each of the prerequisite steps in the Conversational Layering Model. The same thing happens when you try to jump ahead into a relationship without first earning the right to engage.

> **Secret #44**   Jumping ahead in the sales process increases your risk of failure and reduces your probability of success.

The belief that relationships are the key to selling effectively causes many sellers to jump ahead and focus all of their energy on building relationships, hoping to create new prospect opportunities to sell. The problem is, jumping ahead in the sales process is not a very effective means of creating relationships. So we're back to the same question, If relationships are the key to selling effectively, then what's the key to building an effective relationship? The answer to this question will change your perspective about sales. It will change the way you think about your prospects and customers, and it will also change the way they think about you.

Crossing the Sales Chasm

The very first sales training class I ever attended was one of the well-known Xerox sales courses. I remember one of the premises of this course was: if you want prospects and customers to openly share their thoughts, feelings, and concerns, you have to ask *open-ended* questions. As a young buck who didn't know much about professional sales, getting people to open up by asking open-ended questions sounded reasonable, so that's what I tried. Great in theory, perhaps, but it was a different story when I approached real prospects with my newfound questioning strategy.

It's one of the great ironies of selling. Salespeople are taught to "open" their conversations with open-ended questions, but prospects and customers are usually reluctant to open up and share their thoughts, feelings, and concerns with someone they don't know, especially a salesperson. Think about how you would respond if a cold call interrupted your dinner, and the salesperson said, *"Hello, Mr. Prospect, my name is Joe Skinner, and I'm with Mutual Equity Brokers. What are your financial goals and objectives for the next five years?"* While some people might actually answer this question, most won't. Instead, they're more likely to think, *"You don't have the right to ask me that,"* and hang up.

> **Secret #45** Unless a relationship already exists, most prospects are reluctant to openly share, especially with a salesperson.

I often ask audiences (in live QBS programs) to raise their hands if they sometimes receive sales calls like the one I just described. Sure enough, most everyone's hand goes up. *"Now, I want you to keep your hand raised if you afford the salesperson more than fifteen seconds."* Everyone puts their hand down. Even salespeople don't like to be on the receiving end of a cold call—and most don't even stay on the phone long enough to find out what's being offered.

It's safe to assume that prospects in your target market probably feel the same way. Like us, they have better things to do with their time than enter-

tain sales calls, and they don't want to have a relationship with every ped-
dler who comes calling. As a result, prospects tend to be cautious, standoffish, and hesitant, especially when it comes to answering a bunch of open-
ended sales questions.

This presents an interesting problem for the strategic salesperson. In order
to have an opportunity to provide value, the strategic salesperson must first
uncover a need. We talked about this in chapter 5. But just because we want to
probe for needs, it doesn't mean prospects are ready to openly share their
thoughts, feelings, or concerns. This creates a *chasm* between their needs and
your value—until something happens that causes prospects to want to engage.

The Sales Chasm

What
Makes
Prospects
Want to
Engage?

Most prospects are reluctant to openly share with someone they don't
already know (and trust). Even qualified prospects who have a sense of
urgency and an active need are cautious of salespeople who jump ahead and
start asking questions that are too aggressive or too personal. Consequently,
sellers are caught in a catch-22—where prospects are reluctant to participate
in a meaningful conversation without an existing relationship, but sellers
can't initiate a relationship until the prospect is willing to participate in a
meaningful conversation.

It's a Paradigm Shift

One of the most significant differentiators between Question Based Selling
and other sales methods is our belief that salespeople shouldn't be trying to *get*
prospects to make a buying decision. We shouldn't be trying to *get* prospects to
answer questions, and we shouldn't even try to *get* them to listen to our pitch.
Instead, QBS focuses on getting prospects to *want* to buy, to *want* to answer
questions, and to *want* to listen. It's more than semantics. It's a paradigm shift.

What makes prospects and customers want to engage? If you refer back to the previous diagram, you'll notice that the Conversational Layering Model is a series of prerequisite steps that must be completed to move an opportunity forward in the sales process. For example, in order to ask for a commitment, sellers must first present solutions. Presenting a solution is the prerequisite for securing a commitment. That makes sense—after all, why would anyone move forward with a purchase without a thorough understanding of the proposed solution?

But just as you can't ask for the order without presenting a solution, you can't just show up and start presenting your solutions either. You must first accomplish certain prerequisite steps. Working backwards in the Conversational Layering Model, you will see that sellers can only present solutions if they have uncovered a need and qualified the opportunity. Again, prospective buyers would only *want* to attend a sales presentation if the solution being offered was able to address a specific need.

> **Secret #46**   To secure a commitment, you must first present a solution; but to present solutions, you must first uncover a need.

By continuing to work backwards in the Conversational Layering Model, we can very quickly identify each of the prerequisite steps that must be accomplished in order to move an opportunity forward.

Needs development is one of the most important components of the sales process. It's a prerequisite for presenting a solution. But as we already mentioned, you can't just blast your prospects with a bunch of sales questions in an attempt to uncover needs. You must first earn the right to ask, which means building a mutually beneficial business relationship.

The Key to Building Effective Relationships

Relationships are definitely important in the QBS sales process, but I still can't agree with my golfing partner's philosophy that salespeople should just "have" them. For sellers to successfully establish relationships, prospects must want to engage further. What makes them *want* to? Once again, working backwards in the Conversational Layering Model, it's clear that the key to building effective relationships in the strategic sale is credibility. Credibility is the prerequisite for every relationship.

Can you see the difference? Rather than jumping ahead and trying to force a relationship, QBS focuses on getting prospects to want to engage by leveraging credibility. We believe that without credibility, you can't possibly have a truly productive relationship. Why would you or anyone else enter into a relationship with someone whom you didn't consider credible? Fortunately, the converse is also true. The more credibility you can establish as a competent professional, the more your prospects and customers will *want* to engage.

> **Secret #47**   Credibility is the basis for every relationship; and the more you have, the more your prospects will *want* to engage.

Unfortunately, salespeople have a bad habit of trying to communicate credibility by claiming their own greatness. This isn't a very effective strategy because competitors are out there telling prospects that they're great too. In chapter 8, QBS will show you how to establish credibility by asking questions, but not the typical open-ended questions that I admonished earlier. Rather, you will learn how to significantly enhance your own credibility by asking a series of diagnostic questions.

It's not time yet, however, to ask diagnostic questions because we must first earn the right to ask. While credibility is the prerequisite for relationships, it's still not the beginning of the sales process. In other words, sellers can't just pick up the phone and rattle off a bunch of diagnostic questions. Instead, they must first secure a *forum* for selling.

The QBS Sales Forum

In order to have an opportunity to earn credibility, build relationships, uncover needs, present solutions, and ultimately secure a commitment to buy, we must have an environment that's conducive to selling. That means we must have two things: the prospect's time and their attention.

In QBS, we call this combination of time and attention a *sales forum*. This is where the sales process actually begins. To successfully engage new prospects (or existing customers) in a productive conversation, we must have a slice of their time and attention. While this may seem like a fundamental concept, I make the point because we sometimes forget that we are not the only ones calling on lucrative prospect accounts. Just ask your customers how many sales calls they have to fend off on a daily, weekly, or monthly basis.

Prospects also have to manage the hustle and bustle of their daily routine—which oftentimes isn't so routine. In fact, it's amazing how many people are vying for the decision maker's time and attention. If the boss calls an important meeting, or if a project needs to be completed by the end of the week, prospects suddenly have less time, and it becomes that much more difficult for a salesperson to get their attention.

As if that's not enough, sellers also have to compete with all the non-business things that can occupy the prospect's mind. If the kids are home sick, the car is in the shop, or the prospect has a community service meeting later that night, these scenarios tend to eat away at the prospect's availability, and their time and attention.

Now ask yourself this question, Given that prospective customers have more responsibility than ever before, and they are being pressed to accomplish greater results in less time, why should they give *you* a precious slice of their time and attention? This is the challenge that every salesperson faces.

> **Secret #48**   Sellers have to compete with everyone (and everything) for a slice of the prospect's time and attention.

Some salespeople try to secure their prospect's time and attention by being persistent. They leave a continuous barrage of professional-sounding voice-mail messages in the hopes that prospects will eventually call them back. The problem is that if you're not the only salesperson calling on the account, then your "professional-sounding" messages are likely to sound just like everyone else's—in which case, you'll fall victim to a phenomenon we call *Charlie Brown's Teacher Syndrome.*

Charlie Brown's Teacher Syndrome

Do you remember Charlie Brown—the ever popular Peanuts character most of us grew up with? Although it has been a while since the original comic strip cartoon was created, it's amazing how many people still remember Linus, Lucy, Schroeder, Snoopy, and the gang. But do you remember Charlie Brown's teacher? Trust me when I say that most of your prospects do.

When I present Question Based Selling to live seminar audiences, I like to ask the following question: *"How many people in the audience use the telephone to make sales calls?"* Virtually everyone raises their hand. *"I want you to raise your hand again if you find yourself leaving lots of voice mails when making these calls?"* Once again, everyone raises their hand. Then, I ask the tough question. *"How many prospects actually return your call after you leave a message?"* For most salespeople, the answer is *"not very many."*

Do you know why your prospects aren't calling you back? I could guess, but if you would like to know for sure, then I suggest you try a little experiment. It's one of the exercises we do in the live QBS sales training program, and it's designed to show salespeople why their prospects aren't calling them back. Even though reading a book is different than attending a live QBS presentation, I encourage you to work through this exercise with us here.

To start, it's important to capture the type of messages you are leaving on your prospect's voice mail. To accomplish this, let's create a role-playing scenario. Picture yourself dialing the phone and calling a new prospect (who in this case, is me). After a few rings, the call rolls into voice mail where you hear a standard greeting that says: *"Hello, you have reached the voice mail of Tom Freese. I'm not able to take your call at this time, but if you leave your name and number, I'll call you back* (beep)." What would you say? Whatever it is, write it down.

At this point in the exercise (in the live program) we've captured a room full of professional-sounding voice-mail messages. We use these messages to play out the scenario from the prospect's point of view. But, as you're about to discover, the messages we leave on a prospect's voice mail are often very different from what the prospect actually hears when he plays them back.

To show the audience what I mean, I briefly disappear backstage and then reemerge playing the role of the prospect they just called. For effect, I lumber up to a mock desk, and say (to myself), *"I can't believe I've been in meetings since 7:00 A.M. this morning. Now, it's after 1:00 P.M. I'm hungry—but the cafeteria is closed and I've got a staff meeting in a half-hour. On top of that, the monthly report is due tomorrow, I have to meet with the company auditors, the kids are home sick, the car is in the shop, and the boss is in a bad mood. Oh well, I guess I'll check my voice mail."*

Next, I pretend to dial the phone and do my best impression of the electronic voice that tells how many messages are waiting in the queue:

Voice-Mail Recording: *"Extension 324…you have sixteen new messages."*

Now, if I'm an important person at a key prospect account, how many of these voice mail messages might have been left by salespeople? Probably a bunch. And to put it in perspective, yesterday I would have received a bunch of sales calls, and I can probably look forward to the same tomorrow. While many prospects would like to ignore their voice mail, they can't—because an important customer or the boss may have called and left a message.

To simulate this prospect listening to his voice mail messages, I call on various audience members to read the messages they left on my hypothetical voice-mail system earlier in the exercise. With me still playing the role of the prospect, the rest of the simulation goes something like this:

—BEEP— (I choose someone in the audience to read their message.)

Seller: *"Hello, Mr. Prospect, my name is Justin Wilson, and I'm with XYZ Manufacturing, a company that prides itself on providing the highest quality products in the industry. I'm calling because I want to see if there is an opportunity to get together to discuss your manufacturing requirements and the capabilities of our product. At your convenience, would you please call me back at (209) 377-9900."*

—BEEP— (I choose someone else to read their message.)

Seller: *"Hi, Mr. Prospect. This is Gail Truman of ABC Company. I was hoping to get a few minutes of your time to see if there's a potential fit between your company's needs and the solutions we provide. When you get a chance, would you please call me back? My office number is (315) 653-8782."*

BEEP. Someone else reads their voice-mail message. BEEP. Another message. BEEP. I keep going until we accomplish the objective of the exercise; which is to discover that it doesn't take long before all these professional-sounding voice mails start to sound the same. With the exception of the caller's name and the company they represent, these messages are virtually interchangeable.

This is a tough lesson. But while sellers are often proud of the messages they leave, prospects are quick to tune out whenever the next salesperson's message sounds just like the last one. In QBS, we have a name for this. We call it *Charlie Brown's Teacher Syndrome.* Do you remember how Charlie Brown's teacher sounded? We never see the teacher in the actual cartoon, but we do hear a muffled voice that sounds like a muted trumpet. No real words, just noises—something like: *"wah…wah…wah …wah…wah."*

If your voice-mail message sounds just like everyone else's, then your prospect is more likely to hear a recorded message that sounds a lot like Charlie Brown's teacher. By the time the prospect gets to the fifth or sixth voice-mail message (out of seventeen), they are more likely to hear:

—BEEP—

Seller: *"Hello Mr. Prospect, my name is Justin Wilson, and I'm with XYZ Manufacturing, a company that prides itself on…wah…wah.*

> *I'd like to…wah…wah…wah…so we could have the opportunity to discuss…wah…wah…wah."*

Voice-mail messages from Charlie Brown's teacher are quickly deleted. Even if you take the time to craft what you think is a spectacular message, what you say may be very different than what the prospect actually hears. To them, you are just one of many callers; so when your prospects hear "*wah…wah…wah,*" it's easy for them to immediately gravitate to the position, *"No thanks, we already have enough…wah…wah…wah."* As a result, the salesperson fails to secure the prospect's time and attention.

Securing the prospect's time and attention is fundamental to your success in selling. In essence, if you want to have a chance to take a swing at the ball, you must first give yourself an opportunity to stand up to the plate.

Overcoming Prospect Reluctance

Charlie Brown's Teacher Syndrome isn't restricted to voice mail. This phenomenon can also occur when prospects pick up the phone or when you meet them face-to-face. Within seconds, prospective buyers start forming their first impressions, and if your approach sounds just like everyone elses' (i.e., *wah…wah…wah*), they will quickly tune out.

Sellers have tried to overcome this phenomenon in a number of different ways. Some even try sneaking up on their prospects. Commando selling, I call it. That's where the salesperson devises a strategy that will hopefully get them in and out before the prospect knows what happened. I'm not a big fan of commando tactics, but surprisingly, there are plenty of books out there on the subject.

In Question Based Selling, we want prospects and customers to want to engage. Rather than tricking them, we want them to want to give us their time and attention so we can have a mutually beneficial discussion about their needs and the value of our products. What makes a prospective buyer want to give a salesperson their time and attention? The answer is in the upper left hand corner of the Conversational Layering Model—curiosity.

The Spark That Makes Prospects "Want to" Engage

Have you ever noticed that top performing salespeople are consistently penetrating new accounts while average performers have to struggle for every appointment? It's not because top performers are better conversationalists. It's also not because they're better closers. It's because they know how to secure a prospect's time and attention—by piquing their curiosity.

If you take another look at the Conversational Layering Model (see diagram on page 83), you will see that curiosity is the key that unlocks the rest of the sales process. Curiosity creates the spark of interest that makes prospects want to know more about the solutions you offer.

It's a simple formula. Curious prospects will choose to engage. But if a prospect is not curious about you or the solutions you offer, you won't succeed in getting their time or their attention.

Secret #49   Curiosity is the key that unlocks the rest of the sales process.

Rather than try to force a relationship with prospects who are naturally cautious of salespeople, QBS initiates the sales process by piquing the prospect's curiosity to secure their time and attention. It's what gives you an opportunity to establish credibility, build relationships, uncover needs, present solutions, and ultimately secure the prospect's commitment to buy.

This model is almost too straightforward to be considered strategic. But consider this. When a prospect is curious, and they also believe that you are indeed credible, engaging them in a mutually beneficial business relationship is easy. It's one of the great secrets of Question Based Selling.

Summary

There's an old saying that you can't teach an old dog new tricks. If we translate this into sales terms, it means some salespeople would rather press on using a familiar approach than try something different. Change *is* difficult, and I'm not offended when people resist a new approach. Not everyone can be a top performer. But for those of you who strive to achieve the next level of success in sales, Question Based Selling offers a proven and repeatable sales model that will enable you to engage more prospects in more productive sales conversation.

That said, some salespeople cringe at the thought of appending additional steps onto the front end of the sales process. They figure it's tough enough to build relationships without having to think about making people curious and establishing credibility too. To them, having to *earn the right* to engage seems like extra work. Let me assure you, it's not.

Extra work is all those sales calls that end in rejection. Extra work is also all the voice-mail messages that fail to generate a return call. QBS's Conversational Layering Model is designed to save you all this "extra work."

Even better, it serves as another risk reduction strategy. If you can make prospects curious, they will automatically want to know more. And the best part is, a curious prospect will not only call you back, they'll call you back first.

> **Secret #50**   Salespeople who understand how to make prospects curious will never have to worry about being successful.

What can you do to make prospects and customers curious? That's the subject of chapter 7. Our objective here in chapter 6 was more strategic. We wanted to point out the difference between jumping ahead to force a relationship, and instead, think about what makes prospects want to engage. Hopefully, we've made you curious enough to read on.

WHAT MAKES
PEOPLE CURIOUS?

Successfully engaging new prospects in productive sales conversation starts with your ability to make them curious. Again, it's a simple formula. Prospects who are curious will choose to engage, while those prospects who are not curious won't.

Curiosity is the first step in the Conversational Layering Model. It's also the spark that makes people want to find out more about the products and services you offer. In this chapter, you will learn how to leverage curiosity as a strategic tool to secure a greater share of your prospect's time and attention.

The newly hired salesperson, trying to rationalize his lack of production during the first month on the job, explains to his boss, *"Sir, I can lead the 'horses' to water, but I can't always make 'em drink."*

"Make 'em drink?" the sales manager sputters. *"Making customers drink is not your job. Your job is to make them thirsty!"*

The sales manager in this anecdote makes an interesting point. It's not a salesperson's job to make people buy. The salesperson's function is to uncover new opportunities and then pique the prospect's interest, so they will want to know more about the products and services being offered.

> **Secret #51**   The more curious your prospects become, the more opportunities you will have to add value and provide solutions.

In Question Based Selling, we want prospects to be curious. We want them to ask questions, and we want them to be "thirsty" for more information about the value we provide. But this requires a change in strategy. Rather than launch into a litany of features and benefits in an attempt to pique your prospect's interest, QBS recommends piquing the prospect's interest first, in order to create new opportunities to uncover needs and present solutions.

If you want to engage new prospects in productive sales conversation, you essentially have two choices. You can be aggressive and try to force your way in, or you can make prospects curious enough to "want" more information about the value you provide—so *they* will invite you in. Not surprisingly, most of us would rather be invited in than have to force our way in.

The Conversational Layering Model (from chapter 6) shows us that curiosity is the key that unlocks the rest of the sales process. If a prospective buyer is curious about who you are or what you can do for them, you will get their time and attention. If they are not curious, however, you won't even get to first base. This is actually good news because it simplifies the sales process. It also puts you in control of your own destiny. In other words, if you can make prospects curious, then you will have an opportunity to establish credibility, build relationships, uncover needs, present solutions, and secure a commitment to move forward with a sale.

Now, the question is, what makes people curious?

The Easiest Way to Make Someone Curious

There are lots of ways to make people curious. You can make people curious by saying something that piques their interest. You can also make them curious by leaving provocative voice-mail messages or by sending intriguing emails. We will analyze each of these as the chapter unfolds, but for starters, let's begin by talking about the easiest way to pique someone's curiosity.

Making people curious doesn't have to be difficult. In fact, the easiest way to pique someone's curiosity is to simply say, *"Guess what?"* Virtually everyone you say this to will immediately stop what they're doing and say, *"What?"* That was easy. Now you have their time and their attention.

You can produce a similar result by saying, *"Can I ask you a question?"* That's another easy yes. Test it out for yourself. Simply walk up to the next person you see and say, *"Can I ask you a question?"* This question usually stops people in their tracks because they automatically start wondering what you are about to ask.

Both of these questions are designed to create what we call a *mini-forum*. We said earlier that you must first have a prospect's time and attention in order to position the value of your product or service. In the Conversational Layering Model, we characterized this as having a *forum* for selling. But sometimes (especially in sales) you have to walk before you can run.

At the very beginning of the sales process, we haven't yet earned the right to ask for several hours of the prospect's time. It's more likely that we are just trying to get through the first few minutes of the call. By asking for smaller commitments, you make it easier for prospects to engage—at least initially. Then, what you do to pique the prospect's interest further will determine whether the sales process moves forward or stops.

> **Secret #52** Making prospects curious only takes a minute, but it gives you an opportunity to establish relationships that can last a lifetime.

The reason this is important is because the larger sale is a compilation of smaller successes; and if you can establish a mini-forum, you can easily create opportunities to expand your conversations. For example, I don't start probing for needs without first saying, *"Can I ask you a question?"* Likewise, I rarely give feedback without asking, *"Would you like to hear some feedback?"* We use this technique throughout QBS to secure the prospect's time and attention, which is much more effective than trying to bully your way in.

I would like to add that making people curious is not a manipulation strategy. Quite the contrary. Asking questions to make sure it's OK to proceed is not only good manners, it demonstrates that you are sensitive to the prospect's situation and you are also very respectful of his or her needs.

Voice Mail: Friend or Foe?

For many sellers, voice mail is the enemy. It's the gatekeeper that stands in the way of a salesperson talking directly with the prospect they are trying to reach. As we said in chapter 1, thousands of voice-mail messages are being left every day, but only a small fraction of these calls are ever returned.

Prospects, on the other hand, think voice mail is terrific. Automated messaging systems have given them the flexibility to be out of the office and away from their desks, yet they can still receive important messages. Voice mail also enables key decision makers to screen incoming calls, so they can focus on their business, rather than be interrupted by constant solicitations.

Some sales trainers teach salespeople to hang up when they get a prospect's voice mail, and not leave a message. Instead, they would rather you keep calling and calling until the person you're trying to reach actually picks up the phone. The busier the prospect, or the more averse they are to receiving sales calls, the less productive this strategy is, however.

Other sales trainers suggest that you should leave increasingly forceful voice-mail messages so prospects will feel a sense of obligation to call you back. The problem is, these messages often fall victim to *Charlie Brown's Teacher Syndrome* (chapter 6) because salespeople end up leaving the same old worn-out messages over and over.

In QBS, we want to differentiate ourselves from the typical sales caller, but not just for the sake of being different. We want to differentiate ourselves for the sake of being more effective. This means leveraging curiosity to engage more prospects in productive sales conversation.

> **Secret #53**   Rather than positioning value to pique the prospect's interest, QBS piques the prospect's interest in order to position value.

Once I learned how to make people curious, voice mail became a terrific asset and a good friend. In fact, one of the secrets of my success in selling was that 95 percent of the voice-mail messages I leave would generate a return call. Let me say that again: 95 percent of the prospects I called, called me back. Why did they call back? They returned my calls because when I left a message, I didn't think about features, benefits, solutions, needs, or relationships. The only thing I thought about was what will make this person curious enough to *want* to call me back.

Making people curious does require some thought and creativity. There are no magical scripts that will guarantee your success on each and every call. But there are many ways that you can leverage curiosity (when leaving voice-mail messages) to engage prospects in more productive sales conversation. Here are a few ideas to get you started.

A Question That Only You Can Answer

Salespeople aren't always calling new prospects. Sometimes we're calling existing customers, business partners, or other contacts in our industry. Calling someone familiar is much easier than making cold calls, but you still have to compete with everything else that's vying for that person's time and attention. So rather than leave the same old "professional-sounding" message, you might say:

Salesperson: *"Hi Susan, this is (your name). I'm calling because I have a question…that only you can answer. If you would, please call me back. I'll be in my office this afternoon until 4:00 P.M."*

Will Susan return the call? If your voice-mail message makes her curious, she will. This technique is particularly effective because it's personal without being offensive, and it conveys a certain sense of urgency. After all, any question that "only you" can answer must be important. It's also very easy to implement. Before you dial the phone, just think of a question that only your prospect can answer. Examples include: *"Susan, how do you feel about _____?"* or *"What is your opinion on _____?"* These are questions that only Susan can answer (by definition) because you are soliciting her feelings and opinions. By the way, most people love to give their opinions, and they'll probably be flattered that you asked.

Something Made Me Think of You

If you'd rather try another approach, you can make existing contacts curious, so they will respond to your call, by leaving a voice-mail message that says, *"Hi Richard, I decided to pick up the telephone and call because something happened today that made me think of you. When you get a minute, call me back. I'll be in the office until 5:00 P.M. My telephone number is (770) 394-0727."*

If you were Richard, would you return the call? Most people would, especially if they receive the message before 5:00 P.M. They would want to know what happened that made you think of them. For best results when they do call you back, be ready with a story or anecdote that will lead the conversation into your business reason for calling.

Secret #54 The more curious prospects become, the sooner they'll call you back.

What's a County Tax Record?

Dave Brown is a commercial real estate agent in Atlanta. After hearing about Question Based Selling through a mutual friend, Dave offered to buy me a steak dinner if I would give him a few pointers. Because I'm usually a sucker for a good steak, I accepted his invitation.

Over dinner, Dave went to great lengths to explain that selling commercial real estate is different from other types of sales. *"How is it different?"* I asked. Then he started to describe an all too familiar scenario, where he was making call after call, and leaving message after message, but very few prospects were calling him back. So far, selling commercial real estate didn't sound much different than selling anything else.

He went on to explain that the game in commercial real estate is matching landowners who want to sell their property with builders who need land to develop. The problem is, most property owners who *do* want to sell have already enlisted another agency, while those who don't (want to sell) would rather not be bothered. Keep in mind that Dave is just one of many commercial real estate agents in the Atlanta market lobbing cold calls into landowners who, for all practical purposes, are usually not very excited to hear from yet another salesperson. Consequently, it's difficult to find new opportunities.

After dinner we drove to Dave's office, where I asked him to show me how he makes sales calls. He plopped down behind a large wooden desk and pulled out a list of prospects. Then he dialed the telephone, waited for the answering machine to beep, and left the following message.

Salesperson: *"Mr. Prospect, my name is Dave Brown, and I'm with ABC Realty, the leading commercial real estate brokerage firm in Atlanta. Our firm specializes in getting landowners the highest value for their property. I would like to have an opportunity to talk with you about the possibility of listing your property. Please call me at (404) 972-4545."*

I asked Dave if he remembered the Charlie Brown cartoons. He did, and we both chuckled when he realized his opening blurb sounded like Charlie Brown's teacher. Everyone who is trying to sell commercial real estate in Atlanta is essentially calling the same pool of prospects, and they are leaving some version of the same professional-sounding message. Of course, by the time a prospect hears Dave's message, it sounds more like: *"Hi, this is Dave Brown with...wah...wah...wah. We specialize in...wah...wah...wah, and I wanted to...wah...wah...wah.*

The root of Dave's problem was easy to identify. Since the voice mails he was leaving sounded just like everyone else's, prospects weren't giving his message any more attention than the other real estate calls they were receiving on a regular basis. Dave recognized the problem: if he couldn't even get up to the plate, he would never have an opportunity to take a swing at the ball. Dave knew it was time for something different. He just didn't know what.

I pulled out a diagram of the Conversational Layering Model and explained the role curiosity plays in the QBS sales process. I explained that curious prospects will choose to engage while those who are not curious won't. Now Dave was curious. All we had to do now was figure out what would make his prospective landowners curious.

Having never sold real estate, I didn't profess to have all the answers. But if we nosed around his office, I thought we could come up with some ideas.

"What kind of books are these over here on your shelves?" I asked.

"Those are real estate law books," Dave said.

"What about over there inside your glass cabinet?" I probed.

"Those are multiple listing guides." he answered.

Dead ends on both counts. *"What about this?"* I asked, as I pointed to a large computer printout on Dave's credenza. It was a stack of county tax records. What's a county tax record? Apparently, in the state of Georgia, real estate agents can print a county tax record for any parcel of property—complete with a description of the property, tax information, and the original purchase price. *"Now, that's interesting,"* I said. *"Can you print one of these for the next person on your prospect list?"*

While I drafted a calling script, Dave headed into the adjoining office to print out a copy of Mr. Jones' county tax record. When he returned, I asked him to sit down in his usual place and handed him the script that I had just created. *"If you get Mr. Jones' voice mail, this is the message I want you to leave."* In addition, I said, *"When you make the call, I want you to be holding Mr. Jones' tax record in your hand."* I didn't care if he held it behind his back or over his head, so long as it was in his hand. Then, Dave dialed the telephone, listened for Mr. Jones' voice mail, and then left the following message:

Salesperson: *"Hi, Mr. Jones, my name is Dave Brown, and I'm with ABC Realty. I'm holding a copy of your county tax record in my hand...and I have a question. If you would, please call me back at (404) 972-4545. I will be in my office tomorrow morning until 11:45 A.M."*

Do you think Mr. Jones will return the call? You betcha he will! Wouldn't you? What's more important is why he'll call back. Dave's message was designed to do one thing—to make property owners curious. As we have said, curious prospects *will* choose to engage. It's important to note that while this particular messaging technique is highly positioned, it's also 100 percent accurate. When Dave makes these calls, he *is* holding a copy of the prospect's county tax record in his hand, and he *does* have a question.

I like to use this anecdote because it encourages salespeople to start thinking outside the box. At a minimum, this technique is very different from leaving the same old "professional-sounding" message.

The next question is, what do you say when Mr. Jones calls you back? Were you wondering this too? It's simple as telling the truth: you tell him exactly why you called. Let's play out the callback scenario and you'll see what I mean.

Mr. Jones:	*"This is Ed Jones returning your call. You left a message on my machine—something about my county tax record?"*
Salesperson:	*"Yes, Mr. Jones, let me pull your file."*

Mr. Jones, as I said on the message, my name is Dave Brown, and I'm with ABC Realty in Atlanta. We are currently working with three developers who are looking for one hundred–acre tracts of land for various projects. I have no idea if you would ever be interested in listing or selling your property, but I noticed on your county tax record that you currently own 242 acres; so I thought I would pick up the telephone and see if it makes sense for us to have a conversation." (pause)

Not everyone who calls Dave back will be ready to sell their property. Some may never be ready. But if you want to have an opportunity to take a swing at the ball, you must first get yourself up to the plate. This means getting real "live" prospects on the telephone, and engaging them in a productive conversation about their needs and the value you provide.

You might be shocked to know that most prospects who return Dave's call actually thank him for calling. That's because rather than trying to force his way in, Dave is providing a valuable service. Owning land is an important investment, and most investors are interested in knowing about potential opportunities when they arise. Even if they aren't ready to sell their property at this time, this approach still initiates a conversation where Dave can build a relationship that may yield potential opportunities in the future.

When was the last time *you* were thanked for making a prospect call?

Creating an Associative Reference

When targeting new prospects, it's always a good idea to look for possible inroads into the account. Perhaps you have a previous contact or an existing relationship in some other part of the business that you can leverage to get to the decision maker. Having an "in" is definitely to your advantage. When there are no inroads into a new account, however, most of us tend to gravitate to some version of the same old cold-calling script.

QBS takes a different approach. Salespeople can't always count on an existing relationship or a reference to pave their way into a new account, but they can always create and leverage an associative reference.

What's an associative reference? An associative reference is a contact you manufacture within your targeted prospect accounts that gives you a reason to get with key decision makers and initiate a productive dialogue.

Essentially, an associative reference creates a sense of familiarity that makes decision makers curious enough to want to engage further.

Here's an example. Suppose you wanted to penetrate a division of Ford Motor Company, but you currently have no inroads into the account. Sure, you could just pick up the telephone and start lobbing cold calls into Greg Simms, the general manager of the division and ranking decision maker. But I wouldn't—because Greg Simms probably gets deluged with sales calls from all kinds of vendors who want a share of his time and attention.

Most strategic salespeople have been taught to target the end user, rather than go through the purchasing department. That makes sense because the end user typically has the need and the budget, while purchasing just facilitates the transaction. Nonetheless, it may be a good idea to start with purchasing (or some other department), because they often make great associative references.

Hence, I might lob a call into the purchasing department. After a few rings, a gruff sounding person usually answers the phone, her name is usually Doris, and she's usually in a bad mood. Perhaps you've had the occasion to talk with her. Here's how that conversation "usually" goes:

Purchasing: (ring...ring) *"Purchasing, this is Doris!"*

Salesperson: *"Hi Doris, my name is Tom Freese, and I'm with XYZ Corporation. I've got a little problem that I was hoping you could help me with. Did I catch you at a bad time?"*

Purchasing: *"No, no...this is fine. What can I do for you?"*

Doris may provide a wealth of information—in which case, I would ask for information about decision makers and find out what she knows about upcoming projects. I would also ask about the purchasing process for the products I represent. Generally, I would try to have as productive a conversation as Doris would allow. Then, once I got off the phone with Doris, I would call Greg Simms and leave the following voice-mail message:

Salesperson: *"Hi Greg, this is Tom Freese with XYZ Corporation. I just got off the phone with Doris in purchasing...and I have a question. If you would, please call me back at (770) 565-5342. I'll be in my office today until 4:00 P.M."*

Do you think Greg Simms will call me back? If he's curious about what's up with Doris in purchasing, he will. Once again, this approach is highly positioned, but it's also 100 percent accurate. I *did* just get off the telephone with Doris, and I *do* have a question. So, what should I say when Greg

Simms wants to know why I was talking with Doris in purchasing? Again, I would simply tell him why I called.

> **Salesperson:** *"Mr. Simms, thank you for returning my call. As I said on my message, I'm with XYZ Corporation, the leading provider of widgets in North America. Recently, I heard that your company was getting ready to fund a large project in the Northeast. I wasn't sure who to contact, so I called Doris in purchasing to see if it would make sense to have a conversation about your needs and the products we offer. Then I called you. Are you the person I should talk with about this?"*

Doris in purchasing is an associative reference. She's not the end user, and she typically doesn't make the actual decision. She might not even be able to help identify the right person. But whenever you leave a message saying you "just got off the phone with Doris in purchasing," the recipient of your message will call back because they'll be curious about what's up with the person you referenced. Furthermore, it's much easier to engage someone when it appears that you have already made it past the gatekeeper.

Associative references don't have to come from the purchasing department. This technique can be implemented just as effectively by contacting the decision maker's counterpart within the same company. Talking to Greg Simms, for example, creates an opportunity for me to call John Hutchison, the General Manager of another division. Using the same approach, I would leave a voice-mail message saying, *"Hi John, this is Tom Freese and I'm with XYZ Corporation. I just got off the phone with Greg Simms over at the Birmingham plant, and I have a question that I was hoping you could answer. If you would, please call me back at (770) 565-5342."*

Leveraging curiosity provides a wonderful opportunity for salespeople to be creative, but it's absolutely critical that you don't cross the line. Sellers don't have to breach their integrity to make people curious; and if you are creative and consistent, you won't have to.

> **Secret #55** A highly positioned, curiosity-inducing strategy can only be effective if it is also 100 percent accurate.

I've just cited a few examples of how salespeople can use voice mail to make prospects curious enough to return their sales calls. But there are thousands of ways to make prospects curious. Whether you sell to doctors, accountants, lawyers, corporations, or individuals, if they are curious about whom you are or what you can do, they will choose to engage. If they are *not* curious, then you will *not* have an opportunity to sell. It's that simple.

Sending Intriguing Email Messages

Do you take email for granted? Many salespeople do. They fall into the trap of thinking that email is an enabling technology that gives them easy access to prospects and customers. In their minds, all they have to do is send an email message and they will automatically get through to a busy prospect. The problem is, email provides easy access for everyone, including your competitors. As a result, prospects and customers are now being deluged with electronic mail messages, and it's no longer unusual for decision makers and key influencers to receive fifty, eighty, and even a hundred email messages per day. Prospects then have to sift through all the fluff to get to the really important information.

When I send an email message, I don't consider it "fluff." To me, it's important information. I want the recipient to read the message I've created, and I want them to read it sooner than later. That's why I focus on making my recipients curious, in order to secure their time and attention.

When you send email messages to prospects, customers, or coworkers, they usually check email by downloading their messages onto a personal computer. These messages are then displayed in a list that shows the date and time of the message, who the message is from, and its subject. The date and sender fields are automatically assigned, but the "subject" field provides a wonderful opportunity for you to pique the prospect's curiosity and get them to prioritize your message.

When a prospect reads their email, you can assume that they are going to prioritize messages by sender and by subject. Messages that appear to be urgent are undoubtedly going to be opened and read first. But so are the messages that make these prospects curious.

Salespeople have a bad habit of using the subject field to tell recipients what the message is about. There's some irony in this practice. If you tell the recipient what your message is about (in the subject field), then why do they need to read it? Their curiosity would have been satisfied.

In Question Based Selling, we view the subject field as having only one purpose—to make people curious. So our objective is simple. We want prospects, customers, and coworkers to notice the subject field, become curious, and then open the email to see what it says. As an example, here's a subject heading that I have used many times in my email messages to pique the recipient's curiosity:

To:	mrprospect@largecorporation.com
From:	tfreese@QBSresearch.com
Date:	May 23, 2000
Subject:	What would happen if...?

Most people who receive an email that says, *"What would happen if...?"* will instantly double click on the subject to find out what the message is about. As an added bonus, if your message heading makes them really curious, it's likely that yours will be one of the first messages they read.

Again, be creative. There is an infinite supply of subject phrases that you can use to make your email messages more provocative. Here are some other phrases that will accomplish the same objective.

Subject Phrases: *Guess what?*
Have you ever thought about...?
On second thought...
Don't look now, but...
What did your boss mean when he said ...?

Each of these subject phrases is intentionally vague. That's by design. The subject field's only purpose is to pique the recipient's curiosity so they will *want* to open the message and read it. And just like voice mail, the more curious they become, the more they will want to read your email.

> **Secret #56** With email, the subject field should be used to make people curious so they will open and read your messages.

Leveraging curiosity is not a manipulation strategy. In QBS, we are not trying to get prospects to buy something they don't need, and we aren't trying to *force* people to listen to our pitch. We're simply trying to initiate a conversation to see if it makes sense to engage further. What makes prospects and customers *want* to engage further? That's what we will examine next.

Five QBS Strategies That Make Prospects Curious

Curiosity is a very powerful human emotion. It's also the catalyst for the rest of the sales process. But we still haven't answered the question: what makes people curious? Actually, there are five things—curiosity inducers, I call them—that you can use to make prospects *want* to engage. These include provocative questions, partial information, glimpses of value, newness, and momentum.

Provocative Questions...and Statements

Provocative questions (and provocative statements) tend to make people curious. They make people wonder why you asked (or said) what you did. Earlier, we made the point that the easiest way to grab someone's time and attention is to say, *"Guess what?"* This is an example of a provocative question, one that causes most people to wonder, *"What?"* The same thing happens when you say, *"Can I ask you a question?"* Whomever you ask will surely say yes, but they will also automatically start to wonder what you are about to ask. It's human nature.

I used a provocative question to name this chapter: What makes people curious? I used this question because I want readers to wonder what the chapter is about—and if they do, they will probably start reading. On the cover of the book, I used the same technique to create the subtitle, only with a provocative statement that reads: *"How the most powerful tool in business can double your sales results."* Again, I want the reader to become curious enough to open the book to find out how the most powerful tool in business can double their sales results. Even the preface has a curiosity-inducing title: *"The best sales experience...I hope you'll never have."* It is designed to pique the reader's curiosity so they will notice the story that kicks off the book. Does it work? You tell me.

In addition to piquing the prospect's interest early in the sale, there are numerous opportunities to use provocative questions and statements later on in the sales process to lead potential buyers toward a favorable decision. You will see this technique used throughout Question Based Selling.

Partial Information

Some sellers spend lots of time trying to satisfy their prospect's curiosity, but little time creating it. They just assume that their value lies in the information they provide, so they go around spewing features and benefits about the value of their company and products.

But, if you believe that making prospects curious is the key that unlocks the rest of the sales process, then satisfying a prospect's curiosity would eliminate their incentive to engage further. Think about this: if the prospects you call on already have all the information they need, then they don't have any reason to meet with you. Likewise, if prospects aren't curious after your initial meeting, then there's no reason to schedule a presentation. They would already have all the information they need. And if prospects get everything they need in your presentation, then there's no reason to follow up afterward.

> **Secret #57**   Average sellers try to satisfy their prospect's curiosity. Top
> performers try to make prospects even more curious.

If you want prospects and customers to *want* more information, then rather than trying to tell them everything up front, you have to leave some meat on the bone. That means sharing enough information to pique their curiosity and communicate value, but not so much that you remove their incentive to participate in the next step of the sales process.

As an example of using partial information to make a prospect curious, suppose a salesperson approaches a prospect and says:

Seller: *"Ms. Prospect, my engineer ran a series of tests on your system over the last several days and he thinks you are about to have a serious problem."*

Prospect: *"What kind of problem?"*

Wouldn't you be curious if someone told you that you are about to have a serious problem? Of course you would; in which case, you'd want to know more. Once you have your prospect's attention, you can appropriately guide the sales process by asking additional questions.

Seller: *"In researching your network configuration, we found that one of your file servers may be corrupting data. The good news is, we think we have a solution. Can you get the committee together so we can discuss the problem and present possible alternatives?"*

Partial information can also be a very effective strategy later in the sales process. Curiosity is what motivates prospects to attend presentations, and curiosity is also what gets decision makers to sit down at the negotiating table—to work out the details of a purchase. If you want to wrap up a deal, for example, you might try saying:

Seller: *"Mr. Prospect, several weeks ago we submitted a proposal for your upcoming project. If our management was willing to offer you a special deal, would you be ready to sit down and work through the details of a purchase?"*

The prospect may say, *"No, I'm not ready."* But then again, they might say yes. Frankly, most prospects will say yes because they will be very curious about what you meant by the phrase "special deal." Keep in mind that you're not asking them for a commitment here. You are simply asking if they would like to sit down to discuss something that may be beneficial for both parties.

Some sellers push back against this concept of partial information. They worry that withholding information might breach their integrity or seem unprofessional. If you have similar concerns, then I want to ask you a question. How long does your very first interaction with a typical prospect usually last? Five, ten, maybe fifteen minutes? Prospects *are* busy people, and it's virtually impossible for a salesperson to articulate the full value of their offering within such a limited window of time. You just can't cover all the features, benefits, cost comparisons, configuration details, upgrade options, support options, and warranty information in a single meeting or sales call. Consequently, salespeople end up dealing in the world of partial information, whether they like it or not. So, do you want to give prospects information that satisfies their curiosity, or would you rather provide information that makes them *want* more?

One note of caution about using partial information as a strategy to pique your prospect's curiosity: prospects will interpret messages that are too vague as either devious or unimportant. That's why we've suggested that you should leverage partial information, as opposed to no information.

Glimpses of Value

Another way to pique a prospect's curiosity is to use glimpses of value. This is a powerful strategy because dangling valuable benefits in front of potential buyers entices them to want more information. If they ask for more information, you've accomplished the primary objective. You've made the prospect curious enough to invite you in to further discuss the match between their needs and your solutions. This technique actually combines provocative questioning with partial information to give prospects a "glimpse" of the "value" they could receive. Here are just a few examples.

Seller: *"If our product could increase your productivity by 40 percent, would you be interested in seeing a demonstration?"*

"With one small change, you could dramatically improve your return on investment. Would you like me to show you how?"

"Other customers have saved lots of money by synchronizing their maintenance contracts. Would you like to know how much?"

Talk about glimpses of value! Who wouldn't want to know how to save money, increase productivity, or improve their return on investment? Asked any of these questions, most prospects would instinctively respond by wanting more information. Now you have a curious prospect who is willing to give you their time and attention.

You can also use this technique to identify problems and indicate to prospects that you can provide a solution. That's how I sell QBS sales training. Whenever I am on conference calls with various vice presidents of sales, I know that most of them like to cut through the chaff and get directly to the substance. That's why I make it a point to bring up some of their most difficult challenges right away. The conversation usually goes something like the following:

Seller:	*"One of the biggest challenges in sales today is penetrating new accounts. Salespeople are out there making lots of calls and they're leaving lots of voice-mail messages, but very few prospects ever call them back. Does this happen to your salespeople?"*
VP of sales:	*"Yes, and it's getting even tougher to get in."*
Seller:	*"Question Based Selling solves this problem."*
VP of sales:	*"How do you do that?"*
Seller:	*"I'll get into that in a moment...but can I ask you another question?"*
VP of sales:	*"Yes."*
Seller:	*"Do some of your newly hired salespeople ramp up very quickly while others seem to take months and months, and sometimes never get over the hump?"*
VP of sales:	*"Unfortunately, that's true."*
Seller:	*"QBS can solve that, too."*

> **Secret #58**   By letting prospects know that you *can* solve their problems, they will become curious and want to know more.

In chapter 9, we will use glimpses of value to create *solution questions*. Solution questions are hypothetical closing questions that essentially ask, *"If I could show you how to improve your existing condition, would you be interested in taking the next step?"* This is a wonderful closing technique that will help move your sales opportunities forward.

Newness and Exclusivity

New things are exciting and people *always* want to be "in the know." More importantly, people don't want to be left out. Perhaps that explains why prospects and customers have an insatiable appetite for information about new products and upcoming announcements. This gives us another opportunity to make prospects curious by saying:

Seller: *"Mr. Prospect, we are about to announce two products that will change the way people do business on the Internet. The question is, does it make sense for us to bring you up to speed on the impact these announcements will have on your business?"*

If your new announcements are relevant to the prospect's business, of course it makes sense for them to be "up to speed." You could make this offer even more exclusive by letting prospects know your company is limiting the number of prospects who can sign a non-disclosure agreement. How will they know if your product is valuable to their business? By engaging in an in-depth discussion about their needs and your solutions.

Leveraging Momentum

Last but not least, momentum is another curiosity-inducer that you can use to capture a prospect's time and attention. We talked about momentum in chapter 3 when we introduced the Herd Theory. If you remember, one of the strategic benefits salespeople gain from leveraging the momentum of the herd is credibility. The other is curiosity. If "everyone else" seems to be moving in a certain direction, prospects *will* become curious and more often than not, they will want more information.

One of my favorite applications of the Herd Theory (for making prospects curious) occurs when prospects cut you short in the first few seconds of a sales call to ask, *"What's this about?"* Rather than be caught off guard by this and fumble to describe your value to a prospect who doesn't really care, you might try saying:

Salesperson: *"Frankly, Mr. Prospect, we solve a very important problem that most of the companies in your industry have."*

Prospect: *"What problem is that?"*

This one sentence is usually enough to make the prospect curious—and of course, curious prospects will choose to engage. When the prospect hears that you "solve a problem most companies have," they will want to know what the problem is and how you solve it. Bingo!

Summary

We started this book off by saying, *"Selling is a creative act."* It's clear that individual salespeople have to differentiate themselves from everyone else who is also competing for the prospect's time and attention. One of the most effective ways to set yourself apart is by leveraging curiosity. If you can make prospects curious, you will penetrate more new accounts, uncover more needs, communicate more value, overcome more objectives, and your sales results will increase dramatically.

The proper curiosity strategy will vary depending on whether you're leaving a voice-mail message, sending an email, or talking directly with the prospect. It will also depend on whether you have an existing relationship or are trying to penetrate new accounts from scratch. On one hand, you don't want to be too aggressive. On the other hand, you want to be bold enough to successfully engage potential buyers in a conversation that will lead to an opportunity. We will explore many of these subtleties later in chapter 12, when QBS shows you how to "Turn Your Cold Calls into Lukewarm Calls."

For now, realize that making someone curious is not the end of the sales process. Rather, it's just the beginning—as curiosity will help you secure the prospect's time and attention to establish your credibility, build relationships, uncover needs, present solutions, and move the opportunity forward toward a favorable purchase decision.

Chapter 8

ESTABLISHING
CREDIBILITY IN THE SALE

Credibility is critical to your success in sales. The old saying is true: people do buy from people. It's also true that we inherit all the negative biases that prospects have about salespeople; and until it's proven otherwise, most prospects will just assume that you have no credibility.

In this chapter, QBS shows you how to establish credibility very early in the sale by narrowing the scope of your questions. Then, as you gain the prospect's confidence, we show you how to broaden the scope of your questions to engage them in a mutually beneficial sales conversation.

Credibility is *not* a tangible item. You can't touch it or feel it, and you certainly can't pull it out of your briefcase and hand it to a prospective customer. Instead, credibility is an impression that people form about you. It's a sense of trustworthiness, believability, and perceived competence that lets other people know you are able to provide valuable solutions, you deal honestly, and you can be trusted to help them make good decisions.

> **Secret #59**   Sellers begin to have credibility when prospects form a favorable impression about their competence and value.

When you are perceived as credible, opportunities to provide valuable solutions will be abundant. Doors will open, and qualified prospects will gladly invite you in to learn how your product or service can address their needs. If you are not perceived as credible, however, gatekeepers will hold you at arm's length, conversations with prospective customers will be kept to a minimum, and opportunities to position your product offering will be scarce. That's why credibility is such an integral part of the QBS sales process.

Back in chapter 6, we introduced you to the concept of Conversational Layering. There, we explained that to achieve the desired result, sellers must first accomplish each of the prerequisite steps in the sales process. We already talked about the first prerequisite in chapter 7— piquing your prospect's curiosity to get their time and attention. As you can see from the diagram, once prospects *want* to engage, and you have successfully secured a forum for selling, the next objective in the sales process is establishing credibility.

Conversational Layering

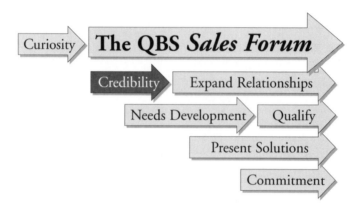

The Conversational Layering Model positions credibility as a prerequisite for building and expanding mutual relationships. In order for any salesperson to have an opportunity to uncover needs, present solutions, and ask for a commitment, prospects must first perceive you as a credible resource. We can take this idea one step further by suggesting that the greater your credibility, the more comfortable prospects and customers will feel, which increases your probability of success and decreases your risk. What can you (as a salesperson) do to establish as much credibility as possible early in the sales process? The answer to this question might surprise you.

Sellers Start with Near-Zero Credibility

When salespeople call on new accounts, prospects begin to form their impressions in a matter of seconds. So, what's a typical first impression? Do you think prospects say to themselves, *"Hooray, an eager salesperson is calling!*

Now I get to talk with someone who wants to show me how they can solve all my problems." Of course they don't. It's more likely that prospects are trying to figure out the best way to get off the phone. First impressions of salespeople are typically not good, and prospects usually aren't eager to entertain new sales calls for that very reason.

Some people think this sounds negative, but I'm merely being realistic. To illustrate the point, let's try a simple experiment. In your mind's eye, I want you to take a few moments and create a mental list of all of the things you've done in the last thirty days. Include everything from business meetings to answering email, power lunches to eating dinner with your family, and paying bills to watching TV. Once you have compiled a comprehensive mental list, I want you to prioritize it—putting those things that are most important at the top of your list, and those things of lesser importance nearer to the bottom.

Now, where on your list does taking cold calls from salespeople appear? Be honest. For most of us, receiving cold calls from salespeople is at the very bottom—ranking just slightly higher than going to the dentist for a root canal or being audited by the IRS.

Even salespeople don't like receiving sales calls. Isn't that ironic? We make our living trying to penetrate new accounts, yet we are just as cautious and just as reluctant as our own prospects when another salesperson comes calling. Before we even know what they're selling, we turn them away, assuming that they offer little or no value. That's because all salespeople enter the sales process with *near-zero credibility*. Like it or not, we inherit all the negative baggage and prejudices from other sellers who have previously called on an account—and until you prove otherwise, prospects will automatically assume that you have little or no credibility. Consequently, they will assume that you provide little or no value.

Secret #60   Salespeople enter the sales process with near-zero credibility.

When salespeople are perceived to have near-zero credibility, prospects are reluctant to engage—which makes it difficult to uncover needs, and even more difficult to provide value. In the American justice system, people are presumed innocent until proven guilty. Salespeople, on the other hand, are presumed valueless until they establish credibility. Don't be offended. Prospects and customers have become increasingly skeptical because of their previous experiences with pushy salespeople who were less than honest, or who reneged on promises that were made.

Salespeople these days face an interesting challenge—one that could be compared to the dilemma graduates face when trying to land their first job out of college. Companies want to hire people with experience, but in order to gain experience, college graduates first need to get hired. It's a catch-22. The same is true in sales. Prospects are reluctant to engage unless you are a credible resource, but the only way to establish credibility is to engage the prospect in a productive conversation. Because of this paradox, salespeople who don't get a chance to demonstrate that they are indeed credible miss out on many lucrative sales opportunities. Frankly, without credibility, sellers won't even get a chance to take a swing at the ball.

It's clear that credibility is a prerequisite for building mutual relationships, and salespeople do need to be perceived as credible in order to succeed. So, let's take a look at how you can establish credibility in the sale.

Three Ways to Establish Credibility

One of the best ways to establish credibility in a sale is to leverage existing relationships. Perhaps you have a friend or an acquaintance within a targeted prospect account who would give you a personal endorsement. Or, maybe you already have a business relationship in some other part of the company, and can leverage your contacts there. In either case, personal references are excellent for building credibility with new prospects.

If you already have a relationship you can leverage, then I'd encourage you to use it. A credible reference is often worth its weight in commission checks. But where most salespeople struggle is establishing credibility in accounts where no relationship currently exists. That's the real challenge as salespeople try to create new business opportunities that otherwise wouldn't exist.

Salespeople who don't have an existing relationship to leverage often try to claim their own credibility. Although this is not a very effective strategy, many sellers are quick to jump into their spiel about how great their company or product is. In an attempt to get prospects to form a positive impression, they blast them with claims of greatness that end up sounding like this:

Seller: *"Hi, Mr. Prospect, my name is Johnny Rocket, and I'm the District Sales Manager for JKL Company, the world's leading provider of intelligent systems. Our track record for success is unmatched in the industry and we pride ourselves on how much we care about our customers. In addition to being the top performing office in the state, we also have the best staff, and I have been the top salesperson for the last five years. Why, I have even accomplished..."*

Claiming your own greatness is a strategy that usually backfires. More often than not, trying to claim credibility causes cautious prospects to mismatch, withdrawing even further. I know I usually tune out whenever an eager salesperson starts telling me how great they are. How about you?

QBS recognizes that sellers don't always have an existing relationship to leverage. We also assume that most sellers want to avoid the problems that come with claiming their own greatness. That's why we teach salespeople how to establish credibility by asking questions. But not just any questions. We show you how to establish credibility and build relationships by managing the *scope* of your questions.

Managing the Scope of Your Questions

Scope is the first of three attributes we use to characterize strategic questions in QBS. The other two are *focus* and *disposition*. Every question you ask has a scope, a focus, and a disposition, and how you manage these three strategic attributes will ultimately determine the productivity of your questions, and the quality of the responses you receive.

Scope refers to a question's broadness or narrowness. Are you familiar with the traditional labeling of questions as open-ended or closed-ended? Open-ended questions are broader in scope. They are designed to expand a conversation by getting people to open up and share their thoughts, feelings, and concerns. Examples of open-ended sales questions include:

Salesperson: *"What are your goals and objectives for the next five years?"*

"What are the three biggest issues you currently face?"

"How would you rate the effectiveness of your current vendor?"

The scope of these questions is extremely broad, which gives prospects an opportunity to take the conversation in many different directions. Questions can still be open-ended (but much less broad) by probing more specifically. For example, sellers can also ask more specific open-ended questions like:

Salesperson: *"To what extent is growth a factor in your business?"*

"What plans do you have to upgrade your existing technology?"

"How will the new regulations affect your company?"

Even though these questions are more specifically crafted, they are still open-ended, which means they are designed to get prospects and customers to openly share their thoughts, feelings, and concerns.

Closed-ended questions are narrow in scope. Rather than trying to get prospects to take the conversation and run with it, closed-ended questions are intended to solicit very specific, short answer responses. Examples of closed-ended questions include:

Salesperson: *"How many users does your current system support?"*

"Do you own your existing equipment, or do you lease?"

"When does your maintenance contract expire?"

"Who will approve the final decision?"

In traditional sales training courses, salespeople are taught that open-ended questions are "better" than closed-ended questions, especially when you are trying to penetrate new accounts. On the surface, that seems to make sense; after all, we *do* want prospects to open up.

There's a slight problem with this thinking, however. While we would like prospects to openly share, the vast majority of prospects are reluctant to open up until the person who is asking the question has established his or her own credibility. Consider this, Why would you or anyone else choose to openly share your thoughts, feelings, and concerns with someone you don't know or trust—especially with a salesperson who you assume has near-zero credibility?

Secret #61   Open-ended questions are great tools for expanding relationships, but they don't help establish your credibility.

Suddenly, we find ourselves in another catch-22 situation. We want to ask open-ended questions because they are wonderful tools for expanding the conversation and building relationships. But until you establish credibility, you haven't earned the right to probe into the prospect's thoughts, feelings, and concerns.

Putting the Cart Before the Horse

Prospects will base their impressions on the statements you make. I guess that's why so many salespeople are out there trying to claim their own credibility. But if we look at it from a different angle, it's clear that prospects will also base their impressions on the questions you ask. This realization marks the beginning of another paradigm shift in Question Based Selling.

> **Secret #62**   Prospects will form impressions quickly—based on the
> statements you make, and the questions you ask.

I'm always a little amazed when cold calls start off with the salesperson saying, *"Hi Mr. Freese, my name is John Doe, and I'm with Financial Planners of America. What are your financial goals and objectives for the next five years?"*

I don't know about you, but I am reluctant to share my financial goals and objectives with someone I don't know. Even if the caller happened to be the best financial planner on Wall Street, I would still be reluctant to share my personal affairs—because at this point in the call, I don't know anything about John Doe. Instead, I would probably think to myself, *"Why should I tell you?"* and then quickly get off the phone.

By probing too deeply too soon, this salesperson misses an opportunity because he hasn't yet *earned the right* to ask questions that are so personal. Moreover, asking such broad, open-ended sales questions does little to help his credibility. To me, this salesperson sounds more like someone who is reading from a cold-calling script than a competent professional who is offering a valuable service.

> **Secret #63**   Prospects are reluctant to answer questions until the sales-
> person has proven that he or she is indeed credible.

Sellers can sound less competent by asking the wrong questions (as in this example). But interestingly enough, the opposite is also true. Sellers can raise their prospect's confidence by asking questions that demonstrate high levels of competence and credibility. We will show you how to accomplish this by *narrowing the scope* of your questions.

Narrowing Scope for Maximum Credibility

If you were a patient lying in a hospital bed and a physician came in to check your condition—not your family doctor whom you have known for twenty years, but a specialist who was called in to perform a specific procedure—wouldn't you begin to form an impression about the doctor's competence shortly after he entered the room? Most people would. They would become more or less comfortable depending on what the doctor said, and more specifically, what he asked. After all, there's no way to know whether this doctor got an *A* on the final exam in medical school or a *C*.

How would you react if the doctor came into your room and struck up a conversation by turning on a fake smile and asking, *"So...what are your medical goals and objectives for the next five years?"* Most of us would start to feel a little uneasy. We might even question his competence (or his sanity).

As a patient, I would want my doctor to be the consummate professional. I would want him to initiate an intelligent dialogue by asking questions that would bolster my confidence and show me that he knows what he's doing. I would want him to ask if I was allergic to any medications. I would want him to ask questions about symptoms that I've been experiencing and about my medical history. The more specific the questions, the better, since each diagnostic question would raise my confidence that his understanding of the problem would help produce the best solution.

Now let's apply the same principle to selling. Prospects want to know that they're dealing with a competent sales professional, right? (As opposed to someone who's following a script.) They want to have confidence that the salesperson can identify potential problems and provide valuable solutions. How can you give them this confidence? One way is by narrowing the scope of your questions—to convey higher levels of competence and credibility.

Ask a Series of Diagnostic Questions

Throughout Question Based Selling, one of the techniques we use to initiate sales conversations is to simply say, *"Can I ask you a question?"* If the prospect is even the least bit curious about whom you are or what you can do for them, they will answer yes. Now you have earned the right to ask a question. But rather than starting with one of the "standard" open-ended sales questions, QBS suggests that you use this opportunity to establish your own credibility by asking a series of short-answer, diagnostic questions.

Diagnostic questions are closed-ended and very specific. Because they are intentionally concise, they are easy to ask and easy to answer. Brevity at this stage in a sales conversation is critical because sellers typically have a limited window in which to pique their prospect's curiosity and establish credibility. That's why diagnostic questions are such valuable tools. Within the confines of a sales call, sellers can demonstrate high levels of competence and credibility by asking a series of intelligent, diagnostic questions.

When I sold Superservers for NetFrame Systems, I opened almost every sales conversation with the same list of diagnostic questions. It wasn't a trick to get someone to buy something they didn't need; rather it was an effective strategy that differentiated me from all the other salespeople who were also knocking on the prospect's door. I would look for an opportunity to say, *"Can I ask you a question?"* and then roll right into the following diagnostic questions.

Seller: *"How many file servers do you currently have installed?"*

Prospect: *"We have twenty-two servers downtown and seven in the annex."*

Seller: *"Is your network topology Ethernet or Token Ring?"*

Prospect: *"Ethernet."*

Seller: *"Are you using Microsoft NT or Novell?"*

Prospect: *"Microsoft."*

Seller: *"Version 3.X or 4.X?"*

Prospect: *"We just upgraded to release 4.0."*

Seller: *"How many network segments do you currently support?"*

Prospect: *"Two per server for a total of fifty-eight."*

Seller: *"And how many users?"*

Prospect: *"We currently have 550 users...but we're growing rapidly."*

If you timed this exchange, you'd see that this series of diagnostic questions took less than thirty seconds. That's a lot of information in a very short time. In addition to gathering valuable information about the account, this technique allowed me to demonstrate (via questions) that I knew something about file server hardware, network topology, operating system software, network infrastructure, and network management.

This is one of the best secrets of Question Based Selling. By demonstrating that you know how to ask intelligent and relevant diagnostic questions, you communicate higher levels of competence, credibility, and value. This automatically sets you apart from other sales callers who either claim their own credibility or sound like they're reading from a script.

Secret #64	When you demonstrate an ability to ask intelligent and relevant questions, prospects will automatically perceive a higher level of competence, credibility, and value.

You might think, why doesn't QBS just tell salespeople to ask closed-ended questions? It's because the term "closed-ended" sends a mixed message.

For decades, sellers have been taught that closed-ended questions are detrimental to the sales process because they "close down" the conversation. In QBS, we say just the opposite. When salespeople try to "open" a conversation by posing the traditional open-ended sales questions, very few prospects will actually open up. On the other hand, the more credibility you earn by asking diagnostic questions, the more prospects will *want* to engage.

Narrowing the scope of your questions is an effective way to establish credibility early in your sales conversations. Once you are perceived as credible, you earn the right to *broaden the scope* of your questions to uncover the prospect's needs—by probing their thoughts, feelings, and concerns. We'll talk more about broadening the scope of your questions later in the chapter.

> **Secret #65**   If a prospect who is curious also believes that you are credible, then uncovering needs and presenting solutions is easy.

Crossing Industry Boundaries

Some sales techniques are industry specific—but not this one. It applies to virtually any industry because it solves a universal problem. Whether you're selling computers, pharmaceuticals, advertising space, office furniture, financial services, cars, insurance, or employee benefits, you are presumed to be valueless until proven credible. Let's look at some real-life examples to show you how salespeople in different industries can establish their credibility using diagnostic questions.

Selling Office Furniture

When I trained the leading office furniture supplier in the Midwest, I was asked to help solve a familiar problem. Although much of their business was in multimillion-dollar contracts with major corporations, the company's sales force was still having trouble overcoming the typical skepticism that is often displayed toward salespeople. Frankly, they had the very same credibility problem that was described earlier, and asking the same old open-ended sales questions was only making it worse.

In the QBS training, I showed these salespeople how to differentiate themselves by narrowing the scope of their questions. Together we created a list of diagnostic questions that was specific to their business and their results were immediate. Now, they kick off their sales conversations with questions like:

1. Do you currently use systems furniture or free standing?

2. Is your office environment traditional or contemporary?

3. Do you prefer steel or a wood-grain finish?

4. How many office employees are in your company?

5. In how many locations?

6. Do you own your office space or lease?

If you sell office furniture to large corporations, the question you really want to ask is: *"What's the biggest facilities issue you currently face?"* If you start there, however, most prospects will instantly tune you out for all the reasons we've mentioned thus far. But with a very small investment (usually twenty to thirty seconds at the beginning of a sales conversation), someone who sells office furniture can differentiate themselves by asking a series of diagnostic questions that helps establish their credibility. Doors that were previously closed to this client suddenly opened, and their sales organization was able to capitalize on more business opportunities than ever before.

Selling Insurance

Having worked with numerous insurance companies and individual agents, I've seen this technique offer similar benefits to those people who sell insurance. If that includes you, rather than jump ahead asking the traditional open-ended questions about a client's "goals and objectives," try opening the conversations with a series of diagnostic questions. Next time you meet with a new insurance prospect, first pique their curiosity and then say, *"Can I ask you a question?"* When they respond by saying yes, ask the following diagnostic questions:

1. Do you currently have a life insurance policy?

2. Was it provided by your employer or did you purchase it separately?

3. Is your existing insurance whole life or term?

4. How long has your current policy been in force?

5. How many people are in your immediate family?

6. When was the last time you reviewed your insurance needs?

In addition to establishing your credibility as a competent professional, diagnostic questions are designed to make the prospect think. With just a few quick questions, prospects often realize that their family situation *has* changed, their insurance needs *are* different, or they haven't reviewed their existing coverage in quite some time. This paves the way for you, as a competent insurance professional, to further explore those areas where the prospect may have a need.

It Even Works for Car Salesmen

This technique even works for what many people regard as the lowest form of salesmanship—the car salesman. I have nothing against car sales, but I think we can all agree that most people who walk into an automobile dealership picture the "typical" car salesman as pushy and overbearing. But that doesn't have to be the case. Car salespeople can establish their credibility by asking a series of diagnostic questions, just like anyone else. Here's a quick example of how a car salesperson could use this technique.

Seller: *"Welcome to ABC Motors…How can I help you today?"*

Prospect: (reluctantly) *"I'd just like to look around, thank you."*

Seller: *"Have you been to this dealership before?"*

Prospect: *"Once, a couple years ago."*

Seller: *"Then I should let you know that we just rearranged our entire inventory. Frankly, we've sold so many cars lately, we had to do something. How the cars are organized is a little confusing right now, but it should help in the long run. Would you like a quick overview to make looking around a little easier?"*

Prospect: *"OK, sure."*

- (Pause) -

At this point in the dialogue, the seller has accomplished something significant. By using a question based approach, he has discovered that the prospect is unfamiliar with the dealership. But rather than jumping ahead and trying to *sell* a car, this salesperson is performing a valuable service by identifying a problem (the prospect's unfamiliarity with the car lot), and then offering to help solve it. When the prospect accepts his offer, the salesperson has an opportunity to engage further—in this case, by asking a series of diagnostic questions to establish credibility and raise the buyer's confidence. You see, car buyers are averse to a salesperson's pushiness, not their competence. So, let's continue the dialogue.

Seller: *"First, can I ask you a question?"*

Prospect: *"Yes."*

Seller: *"Are you more interested in cars or trucks?"*

Prospect: *"Cars."*

Seller: *"Would you rather have two doors or four?"*

Prospect: *"Four-door is better."*

Seller: *"Is this car for personal use or business?"*

Prospect: *"A little of both, but I will definitely be taking customers out in it."*

Seller: *"Do you prefer sporty or traditional?"* (response)

"Does engine size matter?" (response)

"How about trunk space?" (response)

Seller: *"Here's an idea. What if I show you a few different options to get started, and then you can decide how to proceed from there?"*

Prospect: *"That would be great, thank you."*

As the salesperson establishes his credibility by asking diagnostic questions, the tone of the conversation changes. If this prospect is truly interested in buying a new car, the salesperson is proving through questions that he (or she) can be a valuable resource in the sale—which is very different from the impression people have when a car salesman first approaches with an outstretched hand and a Cheshire cat smile.

Use Diagnostic Questions to Open Your Presentation

Diagnostic questions are also useful for breaking the ice in your sales presentations. Sellers often penetrate new accounts through a primary contact and then schedule a presentation for the rest of the committee. Trouble is, you may have established your credibility with your primary contact in the account, but to everyone else on the committee, you are just another salesperson. They don't know you from Adam, which means you start your presentation with near-zero credibility. You also inherit the baggage of all the other salespeople who have come before. Consequently, presentation audiences tend to assume the worst—that you provide little or no value—until you prove otherwise.

How can you establish credibility with your presentation audience? The same way you establish credibility in an initial sales call—by proving that you know how to ask intelligent and relevant questions. I use this technique every time I kick off a presentation. Knowing that people in the audience who don't know better are going to be skeptical, I want to change their perceptions and I want to change it early in the presentation. So whether I'm the keynote speaker at a national sales meeting or leading a QBS sales training program, I always open my presentation with diagnostic queries like:

Presenter: *"How many people in the audience call on new prospects?"*

"Raise your hand if you leave lots of voice-mail messages."

"Keep your hand up if it's tough to get prospects to call back."

"Do you find that it's difficult to get to the right person?"

By asking questions that people identify with, I am letting the audience know that we're going to be dealing with important issues that are critical to their success. In addition to establishing my own credibility, this technique also helps to pique the audience's curiosity so they'll want to hear more. (We'll talk more about building value in your sales presentations in chapter 14.)

Characteristics of a Diagnostic Question

Crafting effective questions is somewhat of an art, but there are some basic guidelines that will enable you to ask better diagnostic questions and implement this technique in your own unique sales environment.

Start with the Bigger Picture

I like to open with a question that inquires about the bigger picture. Essentially, this paves the way for me to follow up with other more specific diagnostic questions. Going back to the example where I was selling Superservers, the first question I always asked new prospects was, *"How many file servers do you currently have installed?"* Since NetFrame's bread and butter was reducing the number of file servers a customer had to manage, this question got right to the heart of the matter. If the prospect didn't have any file servers, there was no reason to continue the conversation. If they did have file servers, however, then their response would lead right into my next diagnostic question, which was: *"Is your network topology Ethernet or Token Ring?"*

> **Secret #66**   Starting with the bigger picture allows you to probe more deeply into more specific areas.

The same thing happened when the car salesman asked, *"Are you more interested in looking at cars or trucks?"* Whichever way the prospect goes, the salesperson can easily roll right into the next question, which in the example was, *"Would you rather have two doors or four?"*

Offer Your Prospects a Choice

When an optometrist gives an eye examination, he puts a pair of test lenses in front of a patient's eyes, adjusts the strength of those lenses, and then asks, *"Is this better or worse?"* Offering a choice is a diagnostic technique that enables the doctor to zero in on the best solution for the patient.

If you look back, you will notice that many of the diagnostic questions we used in the previous examples offer the prospect a choice. *Is your insurance whole life or term? Is your current office environment traditional or contemporary? Do you own office space or lease?* Offering a choice makes your questions easier to answer, which is particularly important at the beginning of a sales conversation when you don't yet have the prospect's full attention or their trust.

Variety Is the Spice of Life

Insert some variety into your diagnostic questions. I say this for three reasons. First, if your questions aren't interesting, it's very difficult to engage new prospects in productive conversation. "Sales robots" don't sound credible, so your questions should be both relevant and interesting.

Secondly, the diagnostic process is a divide-and-conquer strategy. By narrowing the scope of your questions, you are helping to break a large and often intimidating decision down into its component parts. This is a very effective technique because it enables prospects to systematically work through a series of smaller decisions in order to come to the larger conclusion.

> **Secret #67** For most prospects, it's easier to make decisions on smaller components of a sale than to tackle the larger purchase in its entirety.

Last, but certainly not least, mixing up your diagnostic questions gives you multiple avenues in which to explore an opportunity further. In the NetFrame sale, I intentionally asked a variety of questions about computer hardware, network topology, operating system software, and number of users. This opened the door for me to pursue multiple areas where my product could offer a unique advantage.

To Be Perceived as an Expert, Ask Expert Questions

Early in the sales process, our objective is building credibility, to communicate an increased sense of competence and expertise. We're saying you can do this by asking intelligent questions. But I'll let you in on a little secret: you don't have to be an expert to ask expert questions.

A brand-new salesperson can take over a new territory and by the end of their first week on the job sound like a credible expert who's been selling for years. How? By learning what questions to ask and how to ask them.

Experts in every business ask very specific questions at certain times. In fact, they use the same questions in account after account because, while every prospect is different, most have similarities in terms of what they need. Therefore, if you want to sound like an expert, here are some steps you should take. Start by seeking out successful salespeople in your business. What questions do they ask? Make it a point to compile a list of their most frequently asked questions, and then take the time to memorize them. With a few hours of practice, you will be able to rattle off those same questions and convey a similar level of expertise. This doesn't replace the need to understand your product or industry. I'm simply making the point that perceived credibility isn't just a function of what you know, it's also a function of the questions you ask.

Be Careful Not to Qualify Too Early

Qualifying your prospect opportunities is important, but don't get hung up on trying to qualify an opportunity in the first thirty seconds of the call. That's why I recommend not starting with questions about the prospect's budget, their time frame for making a decision, or anything else that might cause them to pull back. Once you have established your credibility, and prospects are ready to openly share their thoughts, feelings, and concerns, you will have lots of opportunities to expand the conversation and qualify the account.

Broaden the Scope to Expand Relationships

Credibility is an asset that does wonderful things for salespeople. Most importantly, it earns you *the right* to expand the scope of your sales conversations. But you must be ready to take advantage of this opportunity. As prospective buyers become more willing to openly share, you must be ready to broaden the scope of your questions—to find out more about their needs and their motivations for making a decision that will favor your product or service.

> **Secret #68** By establishing credibility, salespeople earn the right to broaden the scope of their sales conversations.

Closed-ended questions are excellent tools for building credibility, but they aren't particularly effective for building relationships. That's because they are too narrow. For example, if you ask a prospect, *"Is performance the most important issue in your evaluation?"* and the prospect says no, what then? Do you guess again, asking, *"Is reliability the most important issue? What about cost effectiveness?"* In addition to feeling uncomfortable, having to guess puts you in a position of weakness, which is one of the quickest ways for an otherwise competent salesperson to compromise his or her credibility.

> **Secret #69** Closed-ended questions are great credibility building tools, but you can't build a house if your *only* tool is a hammer.

There's more to broadening the scope of your questions than just reeling off a sequence of open-ended questions, however. To develop the opportunity, you'll want to ask questions that uncover the prospect's needs—needs that can be successfully addressed by your product or service offering. That's what we'll talk about next in chapter 9. There, you'll learn how to escalate the focus of your questions to expand relationships, uncover needs, and increase the value of your sales conversations.

Summary

Narrowing the scope of your questions will help you establish more credibility than anything else you can do. By asking intelligent questions, you let prospects know that you are a cut above everyone else who is also competing for their time and attention. This credibility will give you an opportunity to probe more deeply into their thoughts, feelings, and concerns, so you can uncover more needs and put yourself in a position to provide greater value.

Chapter 9

ESCALATE THE VALUE OF YOUR QUESTIONS

To provide solutions, sellers must first uncover a need. That's one of the reasons questions are so important. But needs development is a double-edged sword. We want to successfully uncover needs that will fuel the sales process, but we don't want prospects to feel "pumped" for information. In this chapter, we show you how to accomplish both of these goals by escalating the focus of your questions.

"Focus" is the second of three attributes that characterize strategic questions in QBS. In addition to managing "scope," escalating the "focus" of your questions will uncover greater needs and increase the value of your sales conversations.

By establishing credibility, you earn the right to *broaden the scope* of your questions. This allows you to expand relationships and uncover needs. We talked about this in chapter 8. Open-ended questions are very effective tools for bolstering your sales conversations, but that doesn't mean we want prospects to ramble on and on without direction. This is a hard lesson, and it's one that I learned many years ago as a neophyte salesperson.

I had always been taught it was critical to get the prospect talking. In theory, that meant asking open-ended questions to build rapport, which would hopefully pave the way for a business relationship. With that in mind, I called on the senior vice president in one of my largest prospect accounts.

The secretary showed me into his office, which was lavishly furnished with mahogany paneling and designer furniture. On the walls were numerous awards, intermixed with original oil paintings. Although I was a little nervous, he seemed quite relaxed and willing to spend time with me. Since this was my big chance, I decided to break the ice by asking a few open-ended questions about his background.

Most people love to talk about themselves, and this executive was no exception. He told me about his college years at Harvard. Then he told me about his two tours of duty in Vietnam. I listened intently—as I had been taught. Forty-five minutes went by and I knew details about his family, his medical condition, where he lived, and his career. I thought it was going well; that is, until the secretary popped in to say, *"Your next appointment is here."*

> **Secret #70**   Small talk might be good for building rapport, but it isn't nearly as valuable as BIG TALK—focusing on key business issues.

We had spent the better part of an hour talking about his life, but not about his company's needs or my solutions. I had succeeded in getting this senior executive to open up, but I had failed to point the conversation in the right direction. As a result, I missed an opportunity to have a productive discussion about mutual business objectives. I learned that while it is important to ask probing questions, it's even more important to ask the right questions at the right time. This is critical if you want to increase your probability of success and decrease your risk of failure.

Asking the Right Questions

Asking questions to uncover needs is hardly a new idea. There are eighty-seven sales books on my office shelves that all say you have to ask questions. In fact, most sales managers and sales trainers will quickly tell you that questions are the key to qualifying new prospect opportunities and identifying buyer motivations. Even the Bible says, *"Ask and ye shall receive."* As a result, salespeople go out into their respective territories asking questions in order to create business opportunities that otherwise wouldn't exist.

The problem is, asking questions in a random fashion is unproductive. Questions *are* important, and used properly, they can absolutely enhance your interactions with prospective buyers and further the sales process. But questions can also kill a conversation. Asking too many questions can make prospects feel pumped for information, and asking questions too aggressively can make them feel as if they're being interrogated.

> **Secret #71**   A fine line exists between asking productive questions and "pumping" your prospects and customers for information.

In Question Based Selling, asking questions is *not* a random process. We don't just suggest that you should go out and ask questions. Instead, we've developed a multi-faceted questioning strategy. Managing the scope of your questions is important because it establishes your credibility and gives you an opportunity to build relationships. It's equally important to increase the value of your sales conversations by escalating the focus of your questions.

Strategic Questioning Is a Process

The Declaration of Independence clearly states that *all men are created equal.* But it doesn't say anything about the equality of questions. That's because all questions are *not* equal; depending on where you are in the sales process, some questions are significantly more valuable than others.

While I do agree that there is a certain art to asking the right questions at the right time, successful questioning is a strategic process—one that goes far beyond telling salespeople to go out and ask open-ended questions. In Question Based Selling, we characterize this process by stratifying the different types of sales questions, according to their mutual value, into four unique categories.

If you dissect a sales conversation, you will notice that the questions being asked probe to uncover one of the following: the *status* of the opportunity, an *issue* the prospect may have, the *implications* of that specific issue, or whether a potential *solution* provides value. Because each of these sales questions has a different strategic *focus*, we categorize them as either *Status Questions, Issue Questions, Implication Questions,* or *Solution Questions.*

Once we have categorized the different types of questions being asked, we must also look at how these questions are being delivered. In QBS, it's our belief that strategic questions, asked in the proper sequence, cause prospects to feel more comfortable, so they become more open to sharing their thoughts, feelings, and concerns. This is important because we want to gain a detailed understanding of their specific needs.

What's the proper sequence for asking sales questions? I'm glad you asked. One of your goals in conversations with prospects should be to ask questions that earn you the right to probe further. I say this because it's unrealistic to expect that you will gain a complete understanding of the prospect's needs with a single question. Consequently, it makes sense to ramp up your sales conversations by starting with questions that are easy to ask and easy to answer. That's what we accomplished in chapter 8—asking short-answer, diagnostic questions to establish credibility. Of course, once you have earned the right to probe further, you'll want to escalate the focus of your questions to increase the value of your sales conversations.

> **Secret #72**   To increase the value of your sales conversations, you need to escalate the focus of your questions.

The diagram below shows each of the four different types of questions escalating in value from *Status Questions* (lowest in value), to *Issue Questions*, *Implication Questions*, and *Solution Questions* (highest in value).

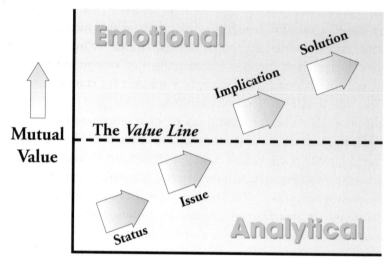

Escalating the "Focus" of Questions

If your objective is to uncover prospect needs, then Issue Questions are more valuable than Status Questions. You can't begin to solve a problem until you uncover key issues. Similarly, it's important to uncover the implications of an issue in order to justify the need for a solution. And more implications create a greater urgency to find a solution. That's why Implication Questions are so valuable. Lastly, Solution Questions transition the focus of the discussion from the prospect's needs to the benefits of your solution. This escalation strategy works because asking more valuable questions tends to generate more valuable sales opportunities.

Emotional vs. Analytical

It's important to escalate the focus of your questions because strategic decisions are made emotionally, rather than analytically. You can see this depicted in the previous diagram as QBS's escalation model is divided into two sections: Emotional and Analytical. In other words, after the attorneys, consultants, engineers, and accountants have all submitted their detailed analyses, decision makers still have to "feel" that they are making the right decision in order to pull the trigger.

> **Secret #73**   Most purchase decisions are emotional, and prospects have to *feel* that they are making the right decision.

Status Questions and Issue Questions are analytical in nature. On the previous diagram, they fall below the *Value Line,* which means they aren't designed to find out what prospects are thinking or feeling. While these questions are great tools for information gathering, escalating the focus of your questions is what enables salespeople to uncover the emotional nuances that will ultimately drive a purchase decision.

Implication Questions and Solution Questions are emotional in nature, and as you can see from the diagram, they rise above the Value Line. These are the probing questions that salespeople really want to ask—to uncover the prospect's thoughts, feelings, and concerns. After all, an emotionally driven discussion is where you will find out what is actually motivating your prospects to move forward, or what might be holding them back.

Perhaps you are wondering, *"If emotional questions are so much more valuable than analytical questions, then why not jump ahead?"* We discussed this earlier in chapter 6. Sellers can absolutely jump ahead in the sales process, but doing so only increases their risk and reduces their probability of success. Instead, QBS follows a logical progression. We teach you how to ask enough Status Questions to earn the right to probe more deeply into the prospect's issues. Once you begin to uncover issues, you earn the right to ask about various implications of the issues you have uncovered. And finally, once you've identified one or more opportunities to solve a problem or satisfy a desire, you earn the right to close with Solution Questions, which essentially ask: *"Mr. Prospect, if our product or service provides a solution for the issues we just discussed, would you be willing to take the next step?"*

To successfully escalate the value of your questions, you must understand the role each question plays in the needs development process. We will dedicate the balance of this chapter to understanding those roles.

Status Questions

What's a Status Question? A Status Question is a question that probes for specific pieces of information that will help reveal the current

"status" of a prospect opportunity. Status Questions are the typical starting point in most sales conversations. These questions should look familiar because the diagnostic questions we introduced earlier in chapter 8
were Status Questions that probed for specific pieces of information
about the status of an opportunity.

Examples of Status Questions are abundant, but for continuity's sake,
let's look at some of the same diagnostic questions we used earlier. After
piquing the prospect's curiosity, we asked a series of (diagnostic) Status
Questions to establish credibility. For selling Superservers, we asked:

1. *"How many file servers do you currently have installed?"*

2. *"Is your network topology Ethernet or Token Ring?"*

3. *"Are you using Microsoft NT or Novell?"*

4. *"Version 3.X or 4.X?"*

5. *"How many network segments do you support?"*

6. *"And how many users?"*

Each of these questions is designed to uncover information about the
"status" of the prospect opportunity. The same was true when we listed a
series of diagnostic questions that a life insurance salesperson could ask to
establish their credibility. Those questions included the following:

1. *"Do you currently have a life insurance policy?"*

2. *"Was it provided by your employer or did you purchase it separately?"*

3. *"Is your existing insurance whole life or term?"*

4. *"How long has this policy been in force?"*

5. *"How many people are in your immediate family?"*

6. *"When was the last time you reviewed your insurance needs?"*

Once again, these questions are designed to uncover facts and information; but because they are narrow in scope, they are very effective tools
that you can use to establish credibility. You could try to initiate your sales
conversations with open-ended Status Questions, but I don't recommend
it. Prospects generally aren't ready to open up until they perceive that a
salesperson is credible. Frankly, you'll have lots of opportunities to broaden
the scope as you escalate the focus of your questions.

Status Questions Are Low in Mutual Value

Status Questions *do* play a crucial role in sales conversations, but we have to recognize that Status Questions are low in mutual value. Ask yourself: how much value do prospects gain from answering Status Questions? The answer is: they get no value because they already know the status.

> **Secret #74** Status Questions are low in mutual value because prospects aren't learning anything new. They already know the status.

This doesn't mean that we shouldn't ask Status Questions. It simply means that sellers must recognize that questions that are low in mutual value are merely stepping stones to more in-depth conversation. It also means you have to be careful not to ask too many Status Questions, as prospects quickly become bored and impatient with a one-sided conversation. Instead, make it a point to ask enough Status Questions to establish your credibility, and then move on to *Issue Questions.* That's where you will begin to uncover needs that will fuel the sales process.

Issue Questions

Issue Questions facilitate the first stage of problem solving. They move beyond the status of an opportunity to uncover potential issues that are in need of viable solutions. Examples of Issue Questions include:

Seller: *"What's the most significant business issue you currently face?*

"What would you like to accomplish with this type of product?"

"To what extent is growth a factor in your business?"

"What other challenges do you foresee?"

Issues Questions are broader in scope, because once we establish credibility, we want prospects to openly share. We want them to identify potential issues, problems, concerns, and desires, but we also want them to expand the conversation by telling us why those issues are important.

To What Extent Is _____ Important?

In almost every sales situation, the first Issue Question I ask is: *"To what extent is _____ important?"* Just fill in the blank with a relevant issue that is important to the prospect, and you have successfully escalated the focus of your questions. The reason I open with this particular question is simple. Asking "to what extent" provides a seamless transition between Status Questions and Issue Questions. It's specific enough to be diagnostic, yet broad enough to generate an in-depth explanation about why the issue is important. The net result is, prospects will open up sharing their thoughts, feelings, and concerns about issues that you can help solve.

> **Secret #75**   Asking, *"To what extent is _____ important?"* is a technique that uncovers needs and encourages people to expand their responses.

Asking "to what extent" is also a *risk* avoidance strategy. I could have asked, *"Is cost savings important to your business?"* The only problem is, prospects could easily mismatch this question because it sounds rhetorical. Rather than risk sounding "canned," I would prefer to ask, *"To what extent..."*

Probe for Gold Medals and German Shepherds

When probing for issues, it is important to remember the motivational differences we talked about in chapter 4. While some people are motivated by rewards (*gold medals*), others are motivated by aversion (*German Shepherds*). This same concept should also change the way you probe for needs.

The key is asking Issue Questions that probe for *gold medals* and *German Shepherds* (both). For example, are your prospects more interested in state-of-the-art technology (*gold medal*) or eliminating system downtime (*German Shepherd*)? Similarly, you'll want to know if your prospects are more interested in reduced operating expenses (*German Shepherd*) or increasing revenues (*gold medal*). These are very different buying motivations. But as we pointed out in chapter 4, most prospects are motivated by a combination of *gold medals* and *German Shepherds*, which gives salespeople who are willing to probe for both an opportunity to uncover twice as many needs.

> **Secret #76**   By probing for *gold medals* and *German Shepherds*, you have an opportunity to uncover twice as many needs.

Probing for both *gold medals* and *German Shepherds* helps salespeople uncover more needs, which gives them an opportunity to provide even greater value, and more easily justify a favorable purchase decision.

Use the Herd Theory to Raise Key Issues

Part of our responsibility as salespeople is helping prospects recognize their own needs. Some prospects will respond to your probes with a robust list of issues and concerns. Others will be more reticent, which makes expanding the conversation that much more difficult. If you have ever interviewed a cautious prospect, then you know what I mean.

Rather than pounding your prospects to get them to articulate their needs, you might try leveraging the Herd Theory. Prospects tend to be much more responsive when they find out that other people have similar needs or are already finding value in your solutions. Letting prospects know, for example, that other accounts are trying to address issues like security, management, warranty, support, and product availability. Once you plant the seed by citing other prospects who have (or have had) certain issues, prospects will often recognize that they too have similar needs.

Urgency Sells!

We know from earlier discussions that complacent people aren't going to buy. That's because they are complacent. They are already satisfied with the status quo, and by definition, their issues aren't serious enough to justify taking any action. The opposite of complacency is urgency, and it has the opposite effect on the sales process. The greater the need, the more likely your prospects will feel an urgency to find a solution and make a buying decision.

> **Secret #77**   Greater needs cause prospects to feel a greater sense of urgency for finding a solution and making a purchase.

People aren't going to buy just because a problem or a desire surfaces as an issue. Rather, they buy when these issues become detrimental enough, or opportune enough, to justify a purchase. That's why it's critical to uncover the implications of issues that get raised by asking *Implication Questions*.

Implication Questions

Once a prospect acknowledges an issue as being important, salespeople must probe further to understand *why* the issue is important. When I was selling computer systems, for example, system downtime was an important issue—one that most people wanted to avoid. But *why* was it important? Was it because end users would complain every time the system went down?

Was it that downtime prevented the company from entering new orders or servicing its existing customers? Was management getting upset? Was downtime costing the company money? If so, how much money?

Implication Questions are designed to get prospects to think about the implications of an issue, because it's the implications that will ultimately justify the decision. This is how you can emotionally transition your sales conversations. While Status and Issue Questions probe for facts and information, Implication Questions probe further into the prospect's thoughts, feelings, and opinions to find out what might happen if a pending issue isn't properly addressed.

Here's a quick example of an Implication Question.

> **Seller:** *"What would happen if your computer system went down and was unavailable for an entire day?"*

Imagine the responses you might get. When you ask Implication Questions about issues that are important to your prospects, they will explain vividly why their issues are critical. But don't leave it up to your prospects to think of all the reasons to buy your product or service. Invariably, they will fail to raise some key points that could help justify your solution. Therefore, you should probe for implications that will raise the prospect's awareness to even greater heights, and make their issues larger and more urgent.

> **Seller:** *"Have you ever calculated how much money every hour of unscheduled downtime is costing your company?"*
>
> *"How does system downtime affect your customers?"*
>
> *"How does management feel about recent system problems?"*
>
> *"What would happen if your data was lost completely?"*

As more and more implications are identified, prospective buyers will feel a greater sense of urgency to buy your solution—and we would much rather they have five, ten, or even twenty reasons to make a favorable decision, not just one or two. Hence, the value of Implication Questions.

Secret #78   The more implications you uncover, the easier it is for prospects to justify a favorable purchase decision.

Although system downtime was the issue we expanded in the previous example, the same technique applies whether you're selling medical supplies, real estate, financial services, advertising space, pharmaceuticals, or insurance. It also applies to each and every issue that gets raised. By probing further, you're essentially asking, *"Mr. Prospect, if (issue) becomes a problem, what effect will that have on the different areas of your business?"*

Issue Questions & Implication Questions Work Together

To increase the value of a sales conversation, QBS teaches salespeople to open with Status Questions. This is an effective technique because asking relevant status questions helps establish your credibility and earns you the right to ask Issue Questions. The underlying strategy is sound. Once you are perceived as valuable, you can escalate the focus of your questions to uncover needs. It's like graduating from high school in order to move onto bigger and better things.

The relationship between Issue Questions and Implication Questions is different. Rather than uncovering a bunch of issues and then moving on to ask about the implications of those issues, a back-and-forth strategy is more effective. This means asking a series of Implication Questions to expand each one of the prospect's issues as they get raised. This process is depicted by the graphic on the right.

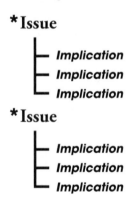

To uncover needs in QBS, we use a simple formula. Every time you uncover an issue, you should probe further by asking Implication Questions to understand the prospect's thoughts, feelings, and concerns about that particular issue. You will want to know how each issue affects their business and how they may be affected personally. The objective of this technique is to expand the issues that get raised, so prospects will feel a greater sense of urgency to find a solution and make a decision. This back-and-forth strategy will also help you accomplish your objective of uncovering multiple aspects of an issue to give your prospects multiple reasons to move forward in the sales process.

Once you have successfully expanded an issue, the process repeats. Uncover another issue, and then expand it by uncovering the implications of that issue. There's no need to make this difficult, however. To uncover the first issue, you simply ask, *"To what extent is (Issue 1) important?"* When it's time to move on to the next issue, simply ask, *"What about (Issue 2)? To what extent is (Issue 2) important to your business?"*

Use Global Questions to Develop the Need

What I'm describing is a process of building relationships by enriching and deepening your sales conversations. We want to ask questions that make people feel comfortable enough to openly share their thoughts, feelings, and concerns, but we don't want to ask so many questions that prospects feel *pumped* for information. That's where *Global Questions* come in.

What's a Global Question? Basically, a Global Question is a way to say, "*Tell me more.*" But since we don't have the right to "tell" our prospects and customers what to do, it's always better to ask.

Examples of Global Questions include:

"How do you mean?"   *"What else?"*

"What happened next?"   *"And then what?"*

"Like what?"   *"How does that work?"*

You'll notice that with Global Questions, there is no subject within the question itself. That's because the Global Questions are designed to expand the context of the existing conversation. For example, to expand a comment or statement your prospect makes, you simply ask, *"What else?"* or *"What happened next?"* Using this technique, you are essentially paying them a compliment by showing that you are interested in what they said or what they have asked. Essentially you are inviting them to please continue.

Global Questions are easy to deliver, and they are some of the most productive questions you will ever ask—especially if you are trying to encourage prospects to open up and talk about the emotional aspects of a problem or an upcoming purchase decision. To illustrate, suppose you wanted to find out just how important the issue of security was to a prospect's business. Then, you might ask:

Seller: *"To what extent is security important to your business?"*

Prospect: *"Security is very important."*

Seller: *"How do you mean?"*

The salesperson in this example uses a Global Question to probe further and find out why the prospect feels security is important. In a real life conversation, you can actually feel the tone of a conversation shift when you show additional interest. What's more, Global Questions are extremely practical—much more so than having to concoct a sophisticated-sounding question every time you want to probe for additional information.

You might be surprised to know that the single most effective question I used as a salesperson, and still use today, is the Global Question, *"How do you mean?"* This question is effective because it's extremely nonthreatening. When you ask, *"How do you mean?"* people automatically open up. In fact, whenever you use this Global Question, you can expect at least two paragraphs of additional information from prospects, customers, coworkers, or anyone else. Even though this question is "grammatically challenged," it is one of the most effective ways to find out what people are thinking and feeling.

> **Secret #79**   Asking, *"How do you mean?"* will give you great insight into what other people are thinking and feeling.

Be careful, though. Asking, *"How* do you mean?" is very different than asking, *"What* do you mean?" *"What* do you mean?" causes some people to get defensive. When people feel their opinion is being challenged, they tend to close up—which is counterproductive in a sales conversation. This may seem like a trivial distinction, but the difference between "what" and "how" could mean the difference between a budding relationship and a lost opportunity.

Focus on Your Areas of Strength

Using strategic questions to uncover a prospect's needs gives you tremendous latitude in directing your sales conversations. This is an important point because very few products enjoy superiority in every area, and you will want to focus your conversations on those areas where you provide the most value. For example, if your competitive advantage is quality, you will want to find out *to what extent* quality is important to the prospect. Likewise, if your competitive strength is providing cost effective solutions, you'll want to find out *to what extent* your prospects are interested in saving money. I'm not suggesting that you should avoid other issues. I'm merely suggesting that it never hurts to tip the scales in your favor by focusing on your areas of strength.

Solution Questions

Solution Questions are valuable closing tools. After you've uncovered your prospect's needs and the implications of those needs, Solution Questions are used to secure the next step in the sales process. This is how you change the focus of your sales conversations from a discussion of issues and problems to a discussion about the benefits that will come from having the right solution.

Solution Questions help balance your sales conversations. On one hand, we want to increase the prospect's sense of urgency. (That's why we use Implication Questions—to make the issues that get raised even larger.) On the other hand, we don't want prospects to feel so overwhelmed by the magnitude of a problem that they divert their attention elsewhere. Instead, we want them to be excited about solving the problem. That's where Solution Questions come in. They help prospects recognize that positive emotions like satisfaction and relief are just around the corner from their current levels of frustration, pain, and concern.

What are Solution Questions supposed to look like? I'll illustrate by creating a quick example. Let's say that during your initial meeting with Mr. Jenkins, the assistant director at one of your largest prospects, you successfully uncover several issues and the implications of those issues. You feel that you can offer some real solutions, so to move the opportunity forward, you would ask a Solution Question like:

Salesperson: *"Mr. Jenkins, if I could show you how to solve each of the issues we just discussed, would you be willing to take the next step?"*

What's the next step? That depends on what you are selling. The next step might be a technical meeting with a certified engineer, or a presentation to the decision committee. Perhaps it would make sense to schedule an executive meeting. Whatever the next step in your sales process is, Solution Questions are excellent closing tools that use the potential value of your offering to secure the prospect's commitment to engage further.

Secret #80   Solution Questions motivate prospects to move forward by focusing their attention on solving the problem.

Solution Questions are also great qualifying tools. If your prospect is not willing to move forward, then something is wrong. After all, why would a qualified prospect willingly participate in an in-depth discussion about their issues and the implications of those issues, but then not want to hear more about your solutions?

Make the Next Step Their Idea

Prospects don't want to be "told" and they certainly don't want to be pushed. It's always been my belief that buyers cannot be forced to take the next step in the sales process, so there's little point in trying to push them. As we said in chapter 2, the harder you push, the harder your prospects and customers will push back. That's why it's smart to make closing their idea.

In chapter 7, QBS introduced you to one of the fundamental principles of engagement. We said that prospects who are curious will choose to engage, while prospects who are not curious won't. This same principle applies when asking Solution Questions. If your prospects are curious, they will *want* to find out more about how your solutions address their specific needs. How can you make prospects curious? By asking Solution Questions that give prospects *a glimpse of value* for how they can improve their existing condition.

Another Opportunity to Be Creative

Solution Questions are usually hypothetical. Essentially, you're posing a question to your prospects that asks, *"If we can show you how to solve your outstanding problems, would you like to know more about the solutions we offer?"* Another way to get prospects to focus on benefits rather than problems is to ask them to visualize the perfect solution. You can easily accomplish this by asking:

Seller: *"Mr. Prospect, in your mind, what would the ideal solution to this problem look like?"*

– or–

"If money was no object in your decision, what would you do to solve this problem?"

One caution: be careful not to ask Solution Questions too early in the needs development process. The reason? You have to get prospects to open up before you can close. Solution Questions end the discovery process because they dangle your potential solutions out in front of a prospective buyer asking, *"Would you like to know how our products or services can add value?"* Asking Solution Questions too early puts you at risk because you will end up moving forward before you have uncovered enough needs (and implications) to justify a favorable decision. (Of course, this is a moot point if you properly develop the need before dangling your solutions.)

Summary

Asking sales questions isn't without irony, however. Faced with the pressure and anxiety that often accompanies a sales call, inexperienced salespeople sometimes panic when prospects seem standoffish or reluctant to answer Status Questions. Not wanting to upset the prospect further by asking even more questions, sellers jump prematurely into their sales pitch. In the strategic sale, this is a mistake because it's impossible to present valuable solutions without first developing a need.

What these sellers fail to realize is that important prospects appreciate being asked important questions. They want to talk about their issues, problems, and concerns, because they do need valuable solutions. Once you understand this, you can literally watch prospects perk-up as you escalate the focus of your questions, thereby raising the value of your sales conversations.

> **Secret #81**   Prospects are motivated to respond when they recognize that by helping a salesperson, they're actually helping themselves.

People love to talk about themselves. They also love to talk about issues that are important to them. Using the techniques and strategies we outlined in this chapter, you can help prospects satisfy their own needs by engaging them in more productive sales conversation. It's truly a win/win situation.

Chapter 10

HOW TO SOLICIT MORE ACCURATE FEEDBACK

Disposition is the third and final attribute that characterizes strategic questions in QBS. It refers to the tone of your questions. Most sales questions are delivered with a certain degree of positive hopefulness, because the salesperson is hoping to receive a positive response. But just the opposite happens, as "hopeful" questions are more likely to generate cautious and less accurate responses.

In this chapter, you will learn how to solicit more open, honest, and accurate feedback from your prospects, customers, friends, and coworkers—by neutralizing the disposition of your questions.

Early in the sales process, prospective buyers are cautious and reluctant when responding to questions, mostly because the salesperson hasn't yet earned enough credibility to gain their trust. Later on in the sale, prospects may still be cautious and reluctant when responding to questions—but now it's because they don't want to say something that would either jeopardize themselves or be detrimental to their relationship with you.

This creates a problem for salespeople because prospects who are cautious or reluctant aren't likely to provide open, honest, and accurate feedback. Rather than tell you exactly how they feel, they hold back. As a result, it's very difficult to know exactly where you stand in the sale, and your ability to manage the sales process is significantly impaired.

Accuracy Is the Objective

Accurate information is one of your most valuable assets in the sale. It's critical to know where the prospect stands and what else needs to occur to complete the transaction. Accurate information is also important because if a transaction is not going to happen, you want to know so you can refocus your efforts on something else that's more productive.

It's always valuable to know about things that are going well, but it's critical that salespeople know when something is wrong. Particularly in the strategic sale, many of the decision factors that will influence the outcome of a sale are constantly changing. That means the status of your opportunity is always in a state of flux. Sometimes, a sale will take a turn for the better. Other times, problems are brewing within an account, and it's imperative that the salesperson know exactly what's happening. In Question Based Selling, we've adopted the premise that the only way sellers can effectively manage a sale is to recognize potential problems or issues as they arise.

How can sellers be aware of potential problems when they arise? It would be easiest to suggest that salespeople should just ask their prospects for an updated status. But guess what? Most prospects are reluctant to share bad news, and most salespeople aren't particularly good at asking for it.

> **Secret #82**   Prospects are reluctant to share bad news, and most sales-
> people aren't particularly good at asking for it.

Unfortunately, when sellers don't have complete and accurate information, they sometimes blame their prospects, thinking that the prospect should have been more forthright. In QBS, we take the opposite tack. Instead of blaming prospects, we find that the quality of the information you receive is more a function of the questions you ask. To show you what I mean, let's take a look at what happens when a salesperson asks "hopeful" questions.

Do You Ask Hopeful Questions?

Asking questions in sales is a risky proposition—particularly the hard questions, where salespeople are trying to qualify an opportunity or secure a prospect's commitment to move forward. What if the prospect says no or, *"We're going to purchase your competitor's product."* What if they raise an objection you can't resolve? With the potential for bad news lurking on the other side of every question, probing the status of an opportunity can be an intimidating task.

Let's be honest. Most salespeople don't want to hear bad news. They don't want to find out that an opportunity may be slipping away or that their investment in time, effort, and energy may have been wasted.

> **Secret #83**   The risk of failure and the possibility of hearing bad news makes the "hard" questions in sales very difficult to ask.

As a result, salespeople who are averse to hearing bad news tend to bias their questions toward the positive. Rather than probing for information, they probe for positive information. And rather than soliciting open, honest, and accurate feedback, they deliver questions with a positive tone, hoping to avoid an unfavorable response. It's as if they're saying, "*Mr. Prospect, please spare my feelings by telling me what I want to hear.*"

For example, if a salesperson was trying to close an important deal by the end of the month, he might ask: "*Mr. Prospect, are we still in good shape to complete this deal by the end of the month?*" You will notice that this salesperson is not asking for bad news. Rather, he is very specifically asking if the sale is still "in good shape."

Another salesperson might come at it from a different angle by saying, "*Our solution looks really good, doesn't it?*" Or, "*Are you happy with the information we've provided thus far?*" Some might even ask: "*Are you as excited as we are about entering into a business relationship?*"

These are all "hopeful" questions. You can hear the hopefulness in the wording of the question and the way in which it's being delivered. In each of these questions, the salesperson is obviously hoping to hear a positive response. They are hoping to be "*in good shape*" to complete a sale by the end of the month. They are also hoping that their solution "*looks really good,*" and that the prospect is "*happy with the information*" that has already been provided. The last salesperson is even hoping that the prospect is "*as excited as they are*" about entering into a business relationship.

> **Secret #84**   Salespeople who bias their questions positively are hoping that prospects will tell them what they *want to hear*.

In QBS, we say these questions are positively *dispositioned*. This means they have a built-in tone that is biased toward the positive. People ask positively dispositioned questions when they are hoping for good news or when they are feeling some risk. You can even watch someone who asks a positive question bob their head up and down with a certain puppy-dog hopefulness, as if to encourage the other person to give a more positive response.

Do you ask hopeful questions? If so, you are limiting the value and depth of the responses you will receive.

The fact that salespeople are reluctant to ask for bad news is understandable—after all, who wants to invite trouble, especially when things seem to be going well? But have you ever thought about why prospects are reluctant to share? It's one of the great ironies of selling. When a prospect senses that you are hoping for good news, they are more likely to respond cautiously and diplomatically, rather than openly and honestly. As a result, you end up getting incomplete and less accurate information.

Being the Bearer of Bad News

No one likes to deliver bad news, particularly when the message being conveyed is not what the other person wants to hear. For example, suppose you are invited to your friend Linda's house for dinner. After a five-course meal, it's obvious that Linda is very proud of her accomplishment, but you thought the food was terrible. If, at the end of the evening, Linda, in her most hopeful tone, asks, *"How was everything?"* would you be completely honest? Most of us wouldn't, because we would not want to hurt Linda's feelings. Frankly, we would rather sidestep the issue or make up something, because it's very difficult to be totally honest when the whole truth is *not* what the other person wants to hear.

> **Secret #85**   Most people would rather sidestep a difficult issue, or make up a convenient excuse, than be the bearer of bad news.

Prospects are often faced with this type of situation when they are dealing with an energetic salesperson whose livelihood depends on hearing good news. It's very possible that the prospect will not be ready to complete a transaction by the end of the month. Perhaps the budget was cut, or the company is leaning toward a competitor's product. Whatever the reason, if bad news is brewing, prospects are reluctant to share when they know it's not what the salesperson wants to hear.

Salespeople Don't Handle Rejection Well

In addition to protecting our delicate egos, prospects have also learned (through experience) that salespeople don't handle rejection well. When an opportunity seems to be headed south, rather than thank prospects for their time and graciously bow out, salespeople are trained to persist. I remember listening to a sales training cassette early on in my career where the trainer's motto was, if you're going to lose a sale, you might as well go down in flames.

Almost every prospect you call on has had to deal with a salesperson who wouldn't take no for an answer. *"What do you mean you're not going to buy our product? I've worked on this deal for months! Let's schedule another presentation or meet with the committee again."* When the prospect turns them down, the seller goes over their heads, calling their boss or anyone else who will listen. As a result, prospects have been conditioned to play it close to the vest, rather than sharing their thoughts and concerns with an over-zealous salesperson who might go berserk at the first sign of rejection.

Soliciting Open, Honest, and Accurate Information

Soliciting feedback from your prospects and customers isn't difficult. What's difficult is soliciting open, honest, and accurate feedback. This means knowing the total picture, which includes positive information as well as any potential problems, pending bad news, or constructive feedback.

The question is, if problems or issues are brewing in one of your prospect accounts, do you want to know about it? If your answer is yes, then a simple change in your strategy will make it OK for prospects to openly share both good news and bad. As a result, you'll receive more open, honest, and accurate information.

> **Secret #86**   If you want open, honest, and accurate responses, then you need to make it OK for prospects to openly share.

How can salespeople make it OK for their prospects to openly share? By neutralizing the disposition of their questions. Rather than ask hopeful questions in the hopes of receiving a positive response, this QBS technique of neutralizing the disposition of your questions will enable you to have a more productive sales conversation by replacing hopefulness with accuracy.

Neutralize the Disposition of Your Questions

Neutralizing the disposition of your questions is easy. Simply offer the prospect a choice to respond either positively or constructively. For example, in an earlier illustration the salesperson asked, *"Mr. Prospect, are we still in good shape to complete this deal by the end of the month?"* As is, this question is biased with a certain positive hopefulness that encourages prospects to not share openly and honestly. To ensure a more productive response, I would much rather neutralize the disposition of this question, by asking,

"Are we still in good shape to complete this deal by the end of the month, or do you think something might cause it to be delayed?"

By repositioning the question, I am giving this prospect a chance to agree that either yes, we are in good shape to complete the deal by the end of the month, or no, something might cause it to be delayed. In essence, I have invited the prospect to share the whole story, which includes good news as well as any potential problems or concerns.

This technique can be applied to everyday life. Whether you're posing questions to your prospects, your boss, or even to your spouse, you will get a more accurate response if you give them the opportunity to answer either positively or constructively. Below are some sample neutral questions.

To a Prospect: *"Ms. Prospect, would it be possible to meet later this week…or would that put a burden on your schedule?"*

To Your Spouse: *"Honey, do you feel like making dinner tonight…or is that too much to ask after a long day with the kids?"*

To Your Boss: *"Would it be OK for me to take a week's vacation during the holidays…or no?"*

As you may be noticing, neutral questions are not hopeful in their delivery, nor do they urge a more positive response. Instead, neutral questions are designed to solicit open, honest, and accurate feedback by making people comfortable enough to share their thoughts, feelings, and concerns.

Introducing the Negative

A question is neutralized when you introduce the negative. This is not a defensive strategy, however. In fact, just the opposite. By asking prospects for both good news and bad, you take the pressure off by inviting them to give you an accurate response. It's a terrific way to let people know that you are a professional who is more interested in dealing with the needs of your customers, rather than someone who's just pursuing his or her own interests.

Neutralizing the disposition of your questions is actually easier than you might think. Just add four letters (*o, r, n, o*). By appending the phrase *"or no"* onto the end of any positive question, you automatically invite the other person to share both good news and bad. Perhaps you noticed this technique moments ago in the example where the employee asked, *"Would it be OK for me to take a week's vacation during the holidays…or no?"*

Introducing the negative into your sales questions doesn't guarantee a favorable response. That's fine because we're not trying to manipulate prospects into saying yes. The truth is, you may *not* be in good shape to get the deal by month-end, or it may *not* be OK to take vacation during the holidays. But the only way to know exactly where you stand is to have a complete and accurate status—and neutralizing the disposition of your questions *does* guarantee more open, honest, and accurate information.

Secret #87   Having an accurate read on your sales opportunities gives you a strategic advantage over your competition.

Competent professionals aren't afraid of hearing bad news, and they don't ask questions positively, hoping to generate a more favorable response. Instead, they would rather deal with important business issues by introducing "the negative" as an integral part of their questioning strategy, as opposed to beating around the bush with a less direct approach.

The Emotional Rescue

Critics of this technique could argue that "neutralizing" the disposition of your questions gives the prospect an "easy out." I disagree. Your prospects already have an out. Unless you represent a monopoly, people you call on are well aware that they are under no obligation to buy from you.

But consider this. We have already talked about neutral questions, and how they make prospects feel more comfortable about sharing *bad* news. Neutral questions are good because they give sellers a chance to discover any problems or issues that may be brewing within one of their prospect accounts. When *good* news is brewing, however, it's a whole different story.

People are reluctant to share bad news when they know it's not what the other person wants to hear. On the other hand, sharing good news makes people feel great. So guess what happens when you neutralize the disposition of your questions? Actually, two things. First, if there are any problems brewing, you will find out about them. Secondly, if there's good news, prospects will not only share the good news, they will be emphatically positive. In QBS, we call this reflexive behavior the *emotional rescue.*

By definition, the emotional rescue is a mismatch. But rather than asking positive questions and having prospects push back against the positive, you can leverage the negative disposition of your questions to let those same prospects rescue you. Let's take an example. Earlier, we rephrased a sample closing question (and neutralized its hopefulness) by asking: *"Are we still in good shape to complete this deal by the end of the month, or do you think something might cause it to be delayed?"* If this deal is at risk of being delayed, the neutral disposition of this question invites the prospect to share any bad news. We talked about that. But if the opposite is true, and you are in "good shape" to get the deal, prospects will quickly rescue you by saying: *"No, no...everything is fine! The order is being approved. Don't worry. I'm all over it."* I don't know about you, but this is the kind of emotional support I like to receive from prospects.

> **Secret #88**   Inserting the negative into your sales questions causes positive responses from prospects to become emphatically more positive.

Talk about irony! For all this time, people have been asking hopeful questions positively in the hopes of receiving a more positive response. Lo and behold, the opposite happens. When you insert "the negative" into your questions, people will jump to your emotional rescue.

Test it out for yourself. Walk up to someone and say, *"Excuse me, but am I interrupting?"* Then listen carefully to see how they respond. More often than not, they will rescue you saying, *"No...no, it's OK. I was just getting ready for an appointment. What can I do for you?"*

You will see this technique used several times in QBS, particularly in chapter 12 when we talk about calling new prospects. I use it all the time. Whether I'm calling a business contact or a friend, I always open the call off by saying, *"Hi Jim, this is Tom Freese. Did I catch you at a bad time?"* Notice the disposition of my question. There's a high probability that Jim will rescue me by saying, *"No...no, this is fine. What's up?"*

Of course, Jim might say, *"Tom, I'm sorry but this is not a good time. I've got a bunch of people in my office."* That's good information to have because if Jim is busy, blindly plowing ahead with the call would have created an awkward situation. I'd rather know right off the bat that it's a bad time, so I can ask, *"When should I call you back?"* When Jim tells me what time to call back, now I have an appointment.

The emotional rescue is *not* a manipulation tactic to get people to buy something they don't need. And please, don't even think about approaching your prospects and saying, *"You don't want to buy any of this crap, do you?"* in the hopes that they will rescue you. That is *not* how this technique works.

Neutralizing the disposition of your questions is a strategy for making people feel more comfortable. It takes the edge off and makes it easy for prospects and customers to respond openly, honestly, and accurately. It also makes the "hard" questions easier to ask, because when you know that you are going to get a more productive response, your risk (in asking) is significantly reduced.

> **Secret #89**   By making it easy for prospects and customers to respond, the "hard" questions become much easier to ask.

It all boils down to one simple question, would you rather have prospects and customers invite you in or hold you at arm's length? In other words, since we know that mismatching is an instinctive behavioral tendency, would you rather have prospects pushing back against the positive in your questions, or rescuing you from the negative? I would much rather be rescued; and therefore, invited in—which is why I neutralize the disposition of my questions.

Humbling Disclaimers

Using *humbling disclaimers* is another way to get prospects to openly share. What's a humbling disclaimer? A humbling disclaimer is an assertion that precedes a statement or question for the purpose of injecting humility and procuring a more productive response. That's a mouthful, I know.

Humility is a very attractive human quality. Sellers can effectively leverage this quality by neutralizing their questions, using humbling disclaimers to lower the prospect's defenses. Examples of humbling disclaimers include:

Salesperson: *"I'm not sure how to ask this, but…"*

"Without being too forward, can I ask about…"

"At the risk of getting myself in trouble, would you mind if…"

"I don't want to ask the wrong thing, but…"

Humbling disclaimers give other people in the conversations a chance to rescue you before you even deliver the question. Again, I encourage you to test it out for yourself. In your next sales call, when you want to ask about something delicate (like the prospect's budget) simply precede your question with a humbling disclaimer. Something like, *"I don't mean to push, but can I ask you about the budget for this project?"* Before you even make it to the real question, your prospect will be reassuring you, saying *"No…no, it's OK…you can ask about the budget."* Bingo!

> **Secret #90**   Humbling disclaimers give other people an opportunity to "rescue" you before you even deliver the question.

Humbling disclaimers also help to soften your questions. Besides making prospects feel more comfortable, humility lets them know that you are not just another high pressure salesperson who won't take no for an answer.

Being Humble Doesn't Mean You Should Apologize

When you make a mistake, in life or in business, you should apologize. But you should not have to apologize for doing your job as a salesperson. I make the point to distinguish between using humility as a conversational tool and apologizing unnecessarily.

One of my former office mates used to begin every sales call with an apology. He would start off the call by saying, *"Hi Ms. Prospect, my name is Jeff and I'm with XYZ Company. I'm really sorry to bother you, but I wanted to see if I could get just a few minutes of your time to talk about...."*

Prospects form their impressions very quickly, and opening your sales calls with an apology is not the message you want to be sending. If you want to be perceived as a competent professional, then it's important to act like one, which does not include begging, groveling, or doing anything else that will reduce your credibility or disparage yourself as being unimportant.

Asking the Hard Questions

As the sale progresses, you will come to a crossroads where it's time to ask the prospect if they are ready to move forward. For salespeople who do not want to hear bad news, these closing questions are very difficult to ask.

We'll talk more about closing sales in Phase III of the QBS methodology, but for now, I want to make the point that hopeful questions are counterproductive when you are trying to close. Especially when you are nearing the end of the sales process, you must know exactly where an opportunity stands. That's why I always make it a point to ask questions in a way that invites the prospect to openly share. Here are some examples of closing questions that I would ask:

Seller: *"Is it a fair question to ask your impression?"*

"Mr. Prospect, are we at risk of losing this business?"

"If you were the salesperson on this account, what would you be doing differently?"

By inviting prospects to openly share, you may find out that you are *not* in good shape to get the sale. Some people view this as bad news. To me, it's an opportunity to make a conscious decision about how best to proceed, either by addressing the outstanding issues, or cutting your losses and real-locating your selling resources elsewhere.

You can also use "the negative" to smoke out any issues or objections that are preventing an opportunity from moving forward. As we said ear-lier, some prospects are reluctant to share their problems and concerns, especially with a salesperson. That's why I ask questions like:

Seller: *"Something is holding you back, isn't it?"*

"Is it just me, or is something bothering you about this proposal?"

"What other concerns do you have?"

Negative dispositioning allows salespeople to be very direct without being overly aggressive. This is a quality your prospects (and your sales manager) will greatly appreciate. Even you will be amazed at the openness and the value of the responses you receive.

Ask Prospects to Predict the Outcome of the Sale

Another way to find out where you stand in the sale is to ask your prospects to predict the outcome of the sale. Essentially, you invite them to become part of the process by helping to accurately assess the status of an opportunity. But rather than revert to the "hopeful" approach, it's much more productive to ask questions that will produce open, honest, and accurate responses; questions like:

Seller: *"Mr. Prospect, my boss keeps asking when this sale is going to close. I'd much rather be accurate than optimistic, so should I tell him that we are in good shape to complete the deal by the end of the month, or should I tell him not to get his hopes up?"*

"Realistically, what are the chances your management will approve this deal before year-end?"

"If you were a betting man, would you say this deal is getting ready to close, or would you say we're at risk?"

All of these are great trial closes, and unless a prospect is intentionally stringing you along, they'll come forward with information that will tell you exactly where you stand in the sale.

Also Good for Building Champions

Neutralizing the disposition of your questions also serves as a great tool for developing internal champions. There are people out there who will love the solution you have proposed. But since most prospects have not had any formal sales training, they won't know how to position the value of your product or service to others who need to sign off on the decision. Before their boss or someone else on the decision committee puts them on the spot, you may want to ask some tough questions to see how they respond. This will tell you how much additional coaching they need. For example, I always make it a point to ask questions like:

Seller: *"What will you do if your boss says the price is too high?"*

"What if someone on the committee wants to delay the project?"

"What if they ask about different maintenance options?"

If your champion has the answers to these questions down pat, this exercise will boost their confidence. But if they hesitate, you can work with them to reinforce key points that support a decision for your offering.

Secret #91   Negative dispositioning gives sellers an opportunity to see how well champions will handle the "tough" questions.

Summary

Competent sales professionals aren't afraid of hearing bad news, and they don't ask positive questions in the hopes of receiving a more "positive" response. Instead, they want to know exactly where they stand in the sale and what else needs to occur to complete a transaction. That's why complete and accurate feedback is so important. By learning how to neutralize the disposition of your questions, you will solicit more accurate responses from prospects and customers. This will boost your sales and give you a strategic advantage over your competition.

Part Three

Implementation: Putting Methods into Practice

Part 3 of *Secrets of Question Based Selling* is where the rubber meets the road. Thus far in QBS, we've talked about strategies for increasing your probability and reducing your risk; we've given you the tools to engage more prospects in more productive sales conversations; and we've shown you how to manage the *scope, focus,* and *disposition* of your questions. Now, it's time to take an in-depth look at the QBS sales process to see how a question based approach can help you penetrate new accounts, get to the right people, build value in your sales presentations, and ultimately close more sales faster.

Strategic questions play an important role in the implementation of the QBS methodology. In addition to piquing interest, establishing credibility, and uncovering needs, strategic questions are powerful tools that you can use to navigate the sale. They put you in control of the sales process by allowing you to set the pace, content, and direction of your conversations. They also help you to find out where you stand in the opportunity so you can determine what else needs to occur to bring the sale to fruition.

Come with us now as we show you how to implement QBS's techniques and strategies into a proven sales model that will enable you to put this methodology into practice.

Chapter 11

NAVIGATING THE QBS SALES PROCESS

To achieve your goals in the profession of selling, you must have a proven and repeatable sales model that produces consistent results. Your model must lead qualified prospects and customers through the sales process, and it must effectively lead them toward the desired result.

In this chapter, we introduce you to the QBS sales process. As a proven and repeatable sales model, the QBS approach will show you how to accomplish your goals using the most powerful tool in sales—the strategic question.

I have always believed there's no such act as *selling*. Salespeople don't just walk into their offices in the morning, sit down at their desks, and begin "selling." While it is true that we *do* tend to wrap everything in our daily routines together and call it selling, we make the point in Question Based Selling that selling is not an activity...it's a process.

You can't just start selling. You can, however, start making sales calls to generate qualified leads. You can also solicit referrals, send correspondence, and call new prospects to engage them in productive conversations about what they might need. And as an opportunity progresses, you can work with your prospect to demonstrate solutions, handle objections, justify the purchase, and consummate a mutually beneficial transaction.

From a methodology perspective, there is a huge difference between "selling" and identifying the specific sales steps, activities, and events that need to occur in order to motivate qualified buyers to move forward in the sales process and toward the desired result.

> **Secret #92**   In QBS, "selling" is not an activity…it's a process.

Without exception, the most successful salespeople are the ones who follow a consistent and repeatable sales process. Rather than just trying to sell a product or service, they take the time to identify each of the component steps that will lead to a successful sale, and then they organize those steps into a proven success formula that's both easy to understand and easy to implement. Now the question is, what should your specific sales process look like?

The Evolution of a Sales Process

To get our arms around the sales process, we must first identify the component steps that are necessary to have a successful interaction with a qualified prospect. If this was a live QBS seminar, I would grab a marker and ask you (the audience) to help me compile a typical list of sales steps onto a flipchart. Here's a list that was created during a recent QBS program.

Identify Leads	Follow-up	Demonstration
Qualify	References	Site Visits
Initial Meeting	Handle Objections	Negotiate
Presentation	Proposal	Close

After identifying the components of your sales process, the simplest way to organize these steps is chronologically. This creates a linear sales model.

The linear model is one way of representing the sales process. It gives salespeople a mental image of the events and activities that must occur, and the order in which they occur, from the beginning of the process to the completion of a sale. The diagram below depicts a linear sales model.

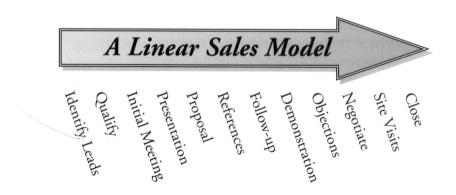

A Linear Sales Model

Identify Leads · Qualify · Initial Meeting · Presentation · Proposal · References · Follow-up · Demonstration · Objections · Negotiate · Site Visits · Close

Particularly in the strategic sale, a linear sales model loses some of its luster when we begin to realize that it's only two-dimensional. Essentially, it's a sequential list of sales events and activities plotted against a time line—and while this does help to identify possible next steps, the linear sales model does not prioritize the importance of individual events. It also does not account for the fact that prospects are different and every sales situation is unique.

Another way to characterize the sales process is to make the presentation of value the central event. The typical salesperson feels most comfortable when talking about the value of their product or service, so it's easy to gravitate to the idea that presenting features and benefits is the watershed event in the sale. Of course, this changes our image of the sales process from a linear model to one that revolves around a central event (as pictured). But in most strategic sales, the presentation of value is not the most important event. It's just one of many steps that must occur for an opportunity to move closer to a mutual business transaction. In fact, you'll find in Question Based Selling that the *Presentation* phase of the sales process doesn't require nearly as much time, effort, or resources as the *Interest Generation* phase or the *Closing Steps* phase.

Introducing the QBS Sales Process

As the sales process continues to evolve, we recognize that it's important to identify each of the component steps in the sale, but it's also important to consider the issue of resource allocation—where to spend your time, effort, and resources to maximize the greatest return on your effort. In QBS, we give consideration to these factors by taking a more holistic view of the sales process and breaking the larger sale down into three distinct phases. These phases are: *Interest Generation, Presentation*, and *Closing Steps*.

Successfully engaging new prospects, presenting solutions, and closing sales is not as easy as one, two, three, however; and we certainly don't want to trivialize or oversimplify the strategic sale. That's why the QBS process model includes two other unique characteristics: an hourglass-shaped outer shell, and an embedded sales funnel. By characterizing the sales process in this way, QBS gives salespeople a blueprint that's generic enough to implement across a wide range of industries and customer scenarios, yet specific enough to implement with consistent and repeatable success.

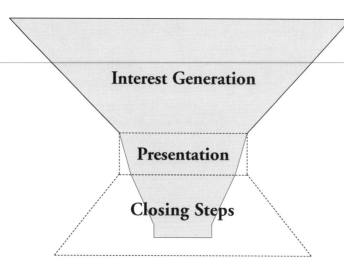

The hourglass shape represents the distribution of effort in each of the three phases in the QBS sales process. Unless you're selling a commodity, the majority of your time, effort, and resources will be spent in the *Interest Generation* and *Closing Steps* phases. It sometimes takes months of positioning and persistence to break into a brand-new prospect account and get them to agree to sit through a sales presentation. It can be just as time consuming to work with prospects to justify a purchase and bring it to closure.

The *Presentation,* on the other hand, is a one-time event. And while it's a very important event, the presentation itself usually represents a much smaller investment in time, effort, and resources. Most salespeople spend only a small fraction of their time delivering presentations, compared to all the time they spend generating interest and closing sales.

Secret #93   Most of your invested sales effort is spent generating interest and moving prospects forward toward closure.

In addition to its hourglass shape, the QBS sales process also features an embedded sales funnel. No matter how well a territory is organized, sellers cannot escape the fact that selling is ultimately a numbers game. A large pool of targeted accounts will yield some lesser number of qualified opportunities; and, depending on your qualifying criteria, the actual number of prospects who are ready, willing, and able to make a decision will naturally funnel down to an even smaller number of closable transactions.

This narrowing of opportunity doesn't mean you're doing a bad job. It simply means that not every prospect you call on is a qualified lead. Some prospects won't have needs. Others won't have the money, the authority, or the sense of urgency to make a buying decision.

This funneling effect creates an interesting phenomenon with respect to resource distribution. In the top of the funnel, in the *Interest Generation* phase, the amount of effort invested (by a salesperson) is diluted across a broad number of prospect opportunities. At the bottom of the funnel, roughly the same amount of sales effort is concentrated on a smaller number of qualified deals. This means a salesperson's invested effort *per prospect* increases dramatically as an opportunity moves forward in the sales process. This is particularly significant later in QBS when we talk about moving opportunities toward closure and securing the prospect's commitment to buy.

Moving the Opportunity Forward

Whether a prospect enters the sales process on their own or you initiate contact via a sales call, it's up to you to pique their interest and keep them engaged. I make the point about keeping them engaged because very few strategic sales are consummated during the initial conversation. It's rare that a prospect becomes so interested that they make a purchase decision on the spot. It's more likely that prospects who become interested will want more information. They'll want to see a detailed presentation or talk with customers who are already using your product or service.

But engaging potential buyers is only the beginning of the journey. We must also move them forward in the sales process. This means that we must generate enough interest in Phase I (*Interest Generation*) to move qualified prospects on to Phase II (the *Presentation*). Once we are in Phase II, we must accumulate enough value to motivate them to move forward into Phase III (*Closing Steps*).

> **Secret #94**   Sellers must accumulate enough value to get their prospects to *want* to move into the next phase of the sales process.

Phase I: Interest Generation

Everything that happens at the beginning of the QBS sales process is designed to generate interest—to pique the prospect's interest and get him or her to want more information about the value you offer. That's why we call it *Interest Generation*. In Phase I, prospects enter the sales process as the result of interest generation activities like initial sales calls, trade shows, seminars, mass mailings, and special promotions. The initial phase of the QBS sales process is represented by the top of the embedded sales funnel.

Our objective in Phase I is simply to generate enough interest to move potential buyers onto Phase II. How do you generate interest? The three ways we have discussed so far in Question Based Selling include: making prospects curious (chapter 7), establishing credibility (chapter 8), and uncovering needs that will fuel the prospect's sense of urgency (chapters 5 & 9). We also showed you how to leverage the Herd Theory in chapter 3 to increase your ability to motivate prospects to *want* to move forward.

Since our objective in Phase I is motivating prospects to move forward into Phase II, one might view Phase I as the least important part of the sales process. Don't let yourself fall into this trap. Your success in sales will likely be determined by your ability to pique the prospect's interest, uncover needs, and establish credibility—all of which occur in Phase I.

> **Secret #95**   Salespeople who are the most effective in Phase I typically have the largest pipelines and the greatest sales results.

Phase II: The Presentation

People often think of the sales presentation as a formal event, but it doesn't have to be. Depending on the product, some sales are geared more toward a one-on-one presentation—like when an insurance agent sits down with an individual prospect to discuss a new policy. In most corporate sales, the presentation is usually accompanied by some degree of pomp and circumstance to make an impact on the audience and to differentiate the message.

The presentation is the pivot point of the sales process. Once you have generated enough interest to get prospects into Phase II, the sales presentation is your opportunity to educate them on the value of your solutions so they will want to continue forward into Phase III (*Closing Steps*).

Phase III: Closing Steps

Phase III of the sales process is where buyers and sellers come together to agree on the terms and conditions of a sale, and wrap up the business transaction. In QBS, we take the position that you can't force prospective customers to buy a product or service they don't really want. Instead, they must conclude that the value of your product or service is great enough to justify its cost. How prospects arrive at this conclusion is often determined by what transpires after the sales presentation.

The steps that are required to close a sale will depend on the opportunity. Some buyers will want proof—references or testimonials that support key points that were made during the presentation. Other prospects, especially those who focus on the monetary aspects of a decision, might be more interested in seeing financial projections that will justify the purchase.

Ultimately, your objective in Phase III is closing the sale. That means securing the prospect's commitment to choose your product or service. While this sounds straightforward, it's a little ironic that your ability to close sales in Phase III usually depends on how effective you were at generating interest in Phase I, and presenting your solutions in Phase II.

Who Controls the Process?

As much as you might wish it would, the sales process does not move forward by itself. It needs a catalyst—someone who can control the process and make sure opportunities are headed in the right direction.

Who controls the sales process? The answer to this question depends on what you believe. Some people choose to believe that the customer is always right. They rationalize that since the customer has the need, the budget, and the authority to make a decision, they should also control the sales process.

While I do agree that customers ultimately control their own destiny, I will argue that it's problematic to assume that they should control the sales process. Here's why. If you assume that *the customer is always right*, then you have to assume they already know everything about your product or service. You also have to assume that they fully understand their own problems and know how best to proceed in addressing them. If this were truly the case, why would anyone ever need a salesperson? Obviously, these assumptions are incorrect. Not only that, assuming that the customer is always right leaves salespeople in the undesirable position of having to ask what to do next, rather than leading prospects through the sales process toward a mutual exchange of value.

> **Secret #96**   If you believe the old saying, *the customer is always right*, then you forfeit your opportunity to add value.

Expecting customers to control the sales process opens a salesperson up to significant risk. If the buyer is inexperienced and doesn't know how best to proceed, then your opportunity can quickly get off track. If you are dealing with an experienced buyer, relinquishing control of the sales process invites them to concoct a long list of to-dos and action items that may not move you any closer to making a sale. In either case, you don't want to put yourself in a position where prospects tell you to jump, and you then have to ask, *"How high?"*

When Larry Dawson first started selling communications equipment to small- and medium-sized businesses in the Southeast, he didn't want to be perceived as too aggressive. Some of Larry's accounts were candidates for upgrading their existing systems. Others were first-time buyers. But because Larry was timid about taking control of the sales process, he asked questions like: *"What would you like me to do next?"* He put himself at the mercy of prospective buyers, many of whom wanted to find out just how high Larry was willing to jump. As a result, here's how some of Larry's conversations went:

Larry: *"What would you like me to do next?"*

Prospect: *"Well…first, I need a list of twenty local references who all have the exact configuration that you proposed."*

Larry: *"Twenty? Are you sure you need that many?"*

Prospect: *"Yes! …and I want you to prepare a detailed cost justification document for the board of directors.*

"…and I also want your proposal broken down by cost center and resubmitted by this Friday.

"…and I need a detailed price list showing the maximum discounts we can expect.

"…and I want a document that shows how your solutions compare to other competitive products.

"…and…and…and…and…and"

Like many other sellers who have tried this approach, Larry has good intentions. He wants to be attentive to the prospect's needs and responsive to their requests. The only problem is, by asking the prospect to control the process, Larry extends an open invitation for them to create a long list of action items that may have him chasing his tail for weeks.

Buyers *do* need direction from salespeople. At the very least, they need clues that will show them how best to proceed. As a salesperson, you're the expert. You have the skills and experience to help identify potential problems and you can give prospects a vision for how those problems can be addressed. So rather than ask prospects: *"What would you like me to do next?"* it's critical that salespeople take a proactive role in the sales process, to help lead prospects through those steps that must occur to successfully complete a sale.

> **Secret #97**   Buyers need direction from sellers, or at the very least, clues that will show them how best to proceed.

In reality, prospects don't *always* understand their own problems, and they certainly don't *always* know how to proceed in addressing them. Moreover, every prospect is different, and every sale is unique. That's where you (the salesperson) have an opportunity to add value—by taking a leadership position and helping prospects uncover needs, investigate alternatives, and evaluate the benefits of your proposed solutions.

The Paradox of Control

Suggesting that salespeople should control the sales process creates an interesting paradox. As you know, sellers don't have the right to *tell* prospects what to do, but, as we just explained, it isn't particularly effective to ask prospects what should happen next. Effective salespeople can, however, control the process by leading prospects toward the desired result using questions, rather than trying to push them forward with statements.

> **Secret #98**   Top performers control the sale (using questions) while average performers let themselves be controlled by the sales process.

Asking questions enables you to manage your sales conversations in much the same way a handheld remote allows you to control your television or VCR. If you would like to know the status of one of your prospect's accounts, simply ask a question that solicits accurate feedback. If you want to expand the discussion, ask a question that broadens the scope of the conversation, or solicits additional detail. To switch topics or further clarify a point, you can easily change the focus of a conversation by asking questions. We could go on and on looking at examples. The point is, questions are strategic tools that enable you, the salesperson, to control your conversations and more effectively navigate the sales process.

Using Questions to Soften Your Suggestions

You can't just *tell* prospects they need to see a presentation, but you can absolutely *ask* them if they would like to know how other customers have increased their revenues and decreased their expenses by using your product or service. Likewise, you can't just *tell* prospects to check references or escalate a recommendation to the appropriate decision maker, but you can certainly *ask* them if it makes sense to act on these suggestions as the next step in the process of evaluating your solution.

Questions are valuable tools for managing the sales process because they soften your suggestions. This enables salespeople to be more assertive without making prospects feel pressured or pushed.

> **Secret #99**   Questions allow sellers to offer ideas and raise aspects of a decision that prospects might not otherwise consider.

This idea of leading prospects through the sales process using questions has a wide range of implications. Suppose, for example, that several key people in the decision were unable to attend your recent sales presentation. Given the competition, you realize that educating everyone is critical to maintaining a leadership position in the account. Instead of demanding equal time, why not ask a question that leads your prospect toward the desired result? You could ask:

Salesperson: *"Mr. Prospect, several people on the committee were not able to attend last week's presentation. Does it make sense for us to educate these people—so they will be up to speed when it's time to review the details of our proposal?"*

Prospect: *"Yes, that probably would make sense."*

Salesperson: *"Could we schedule a follow-up event to include everyone who was unable to attend the first presentation?"*

After the salesperson in this example raises a problem, he states the benefits of solving the problem, and then asks a question that suggests how best to proceed. This seller is controlling the sales process by making valuable suggestions, even though the buyer still has *the final say* in whether or not they wish to move forward. It's a win-win situation.

How Strategic Questions Work

Asking questions has always been an integral part of selling. Frankly, it's the only good way to establish credibility, gather information, and uncover needs. Well-crafted questions can help move opportunities forward in the sales process. But while sales trainers (and sales managers) are quick to stress the importance of questions, they often ignore the stresses of asking them.

Since I started studying questions and their effect on the sales process, I've discovered an interesting phenomenon. Some salespeople, particularly those with limited experience, are timid about asking questions. They worry that their questions will be viewed (by prospects and customers) as a sign of weakness, as if *having to ask* indicates their lack of intelligence or capability. Think about it this way: haven't you ever felt stupid or inadequate because you didn't already know something and had to ask for help?

This creates another paradox. Salespeople need to ask questions to establish credibility, gather information, and uncover needs. We've talked about this at length. But if questions make them feel inadequate or incompetent, then *having to ask* would actually undermine their own credibility by demonstrating a lack of knowledge. Can you see the dilemma?

This paradox confuses salespeople about the role of questions in the sales process, which leads us to ask, Are questions putting salespeople in a position of weakness or a position of strength?

He Who Asks the Questions Has the Power

Make no mistake, asking questions puts you in a position of strength. No matter how squeamish you might feel about asking them, questions will ultimately drive every conversation you will ever have. In fact, rather than feeling nervous about asking questions, Question Based Selling helps salespeople realize that *he who asks the questions has the power.*

Here's a little anecdote to show you what I mean. Suppose you are diligently working at your desk, when someone suddenly knocks on your office door. "*Come in,*" you say, not expecting anyone in particular. Much to your surprise, in walks the president of the United States, followed by an entourage of government officials and Secret Service agents. The president greets you with a hardy handshake, and you graciously exchange pleasantries.

After the initial shock of the situation, you pull yourself together long enough to realize that you have the opportunity of a lifetime—a chance to talk with the president of the United States. But rather than trying to impress him with something you could say, you decide to ask him a question.

Fortunately, your brain happens to be "on," and despite all the hoopla, you deliver a wonderfully articulated question that even impresses the Secret Service agents who are milling about the room. Upon hearing your question, the President pauses for a moment to collect his thoughts, and then he begins to respond.

Here's my point. When the president of the United States begins to respond to your question, who is answering to whom? In this case, the president of the United States, arguably the most powerful man in the world, is answering to you. At that very moment in the conversation, you have control because it was *you* who asked the question.

> **Secret #100**   He who asks the questions has the power in sales conversations.

Asking questions puts you in a desirable position with respect to your sales conversations. It puts you in control. By asking questions, you can control the subject of your sales conversations. You can also control the pace and depth, depending on what questions you ask and how you ask them.

If your prospects are asking all the questions, then they are controlling the sales process. Does that mean it's bad for prospective buyers to ask questions? Not at all. In QBS, we want prospects to be curious so they will ask for additional information. But, you can still maintain control of your conversations by using the QBS technique of answering a question with a question.

Answer a Question with a Question

When someone asks me, *"How much do you charge for QBS training?"* I always answer their question with a question of my own. I say, *"Which QBS program are you interested in?"* Now, who's controlling the conversation? Answer? Whoever asked the last question—in this case, me.

Some people might argue that answering a question with a question is a deflection strategy, a method of dodging the original question in the hopes of deflecting the prospect's attention onto something else. That's not the case in Question Based Selling, however. Rather than dodging the prospect's questions, we are simply trying to find out *why* they are asking so we can know how best to respond.

> **Secret #101**   When people ask questions, it's important to know *why* they're asking in order to know how best to respond.

There are countless examples of this. One of your prospects might ask, *"What advantages does your product have over other solutions?"* Instead of jumping into an explanation of features and benefits, I would recommend asking, *"How familiar are you with our products?"* This gives you a chance to find out whether they simply want more information, or are challenging your proposal—which would dictate two very different responses.

The easiest way to find out why a prospect is asking a question is to respond with a Global Question. We first introduced this technique back in chapter 9. A Global Question is designed to get the other person to elaborate on something they've said, or asked. Essentially, Global Questions allow you to say, "*Tell me more.*" Try it. The next time one of your prospects or customers asks you a question, ask them back, "*How do you mean?*" Odds are, they'll provide a lengthy narrative which will give you valuable insight about how best to position your response. Using Global Questions to understand the prospect's perspective is a valuable strategy whether you are responding to inquiries at the beginning of a sale, or handling objections at the end.

The only caveat is that your questions must pass the *Four-Year-Old Test.* It may be cute when little Johnny incessantly asks, *Why?... Why?... Why?...,* but it's a lot less cute when a professional salesperson asks a mindless barrage of questions. The moral is: don't sacrifice quality for quantity. Every question you ask should add value in the conversation by uncovering additional information, or clarifying something that's already been said.

The Second Law of Thermodynamics

In addition to controlling the sales process, salespeople must also ask questions to gather information. It's part of qualifying an opportunity, uncovering needs, and understanding the competitive environment. To accomplish these objectives, however, information must flow freely and easily from the buyer to the seller.

In high school physics, many of us learned (and some even remember) the Laws of Thermodynamics. If you don't remember your physics, the Second Law of Thermodynamics states that heat flows naturally from high concentrations to low concentrations (from hot to cold). To demonstrate this phenomenon, open a window in the middle of winter. Heat will escape from the higher concentration inside your home to the lower concentration outside.

The same principle applies to sales conversations. If you humble yourself long enough to show prospects that you don't know everything, you may be surprised to see how readily information flows from the person who has it (the prospect), to the person who wants it (the salesperson). How can salespeople humble themselves? One way is to use humbling disclaimers, saying things like "*I'm confused,*" or "*Am I missing something?*" followed by a summary of the points you want to better understand. The point is, if you are willing to ask for help or admit that you don't already know everything, people are quick to offer assistance. Contrast this with the perceived arrogance of someone who positions themselves as a know-it-all. Of course, prospects are going to clam up because they will feel like they were in a position where they could not contribute any additional value.

Ironically, the flow of information from high concentrations to low is initiated by silence. If you want other people to respond productively, you have to be willing to ask questions and then shut up. The resulting silence creates a natural vacuum in the conversation, and this vacuum automatically puts the onus on the other person to respond.

> **Secret #102** After a salesperson delivers a question, the flow of valuable information is initiated by silence.

Unfortunately, silence makes some salespeople very uncomfortable. As a result, they jump into the conversation to fill the silence with noise. You must resist this temptation, however, because if you don't fill the silence with noise, your prospects will fill it with valuable information.

Summary

The most effective salespeople in every industry are the ones who realize that one of their greatest assets is their ability to find out information they don't already have. Even the most knowledgeable sellers still have to ask questions because every prospect is different and every sale is unique. Once we understand that questions do allow us to control our own destiny, we can shift or focus to executing the specific sales steps—starting with the initial sales call, which is what we cover next in chapter 12.

TURN YOUR COLD CALLS INTO LUKEWARM CALLS

Nobody likes cold calls. Salespeople don't like to make them, and potential buyers don't like receiving them. Nonetheless, sellers must contact new prospects to uncover new sales opportunities, and cold calls are the primary way to do that.

But who says your initial sales calls have to be "cold"? By applying the QBS techniques that we've introduced thus far, you can leverage curiosity, credibility, momentum, and a greater sense of value, to "warm up" your sales calls and significantly enhance your results.

Most selling opportunities begin with a sales call. While some potential buyers might just show up on your doorstep because they have already recognized an opportunity to improve their existing condition, most won't. And when they don't show up on their own, it's your responsibility to initiate contact and create business opportunities that otherwise wouldn't exist.

Initiating contact is a difficult challenge, however. Whether it's on the telephone or in person, decision makers are constantly being barraged by sales callers who are either trying to introduce a new product or unseat an existing vendor relationship. Even if prospects wanted to entertain every sales call that comes in, there's simply not enough time in the day to do so.

As a result, the average success rate when contacting new prospects is very low, typically between 2 and 5 percent. That means out of every hundred sales calls, the average performer can expect to generate only a small handful of opportunities. The other 95 to 98 percent of these calls end in rejection—which, as we talked about in chapter 1, makes it that much more difficult for sellers to stay motivated.

> **Secret #103** Show me a salesperson who says they *like* making cold calls, and I'll show you someone who would really rather not.

If you already have an existing relationship that you can leverage, or some other entry into a targeted prospect account, your probability of success will increase significantly. Having an "in" relieves much of the tension, anxiety, and nervousness that accompanies an initial sales call. If you don't already have an existing relationship, the alternative is cold calling—contacting potential buyers to introduce yourself, your company, and your product, in an attempt to create a spark of interest that will make them want to engage further.

Nobody Likes Cold Calls

Most prospects view a cold call as an unwelcome interruption rather than a valuable use of their time. We have to realize that key people at important prospect accounts are already busy with meetings, events, and managing their daily business. So when the telephone rings and an overeager salesperson dives headfirst into his or her spiel, most prospects are neither excited or impressed.

The problem with cold calls is, they're *cold*. When a prospect picks up the telephone or answers the door, and they don't know you from Adam, they are naturally reluctant to engage. It's a predictable reaction. Remember, we said earlier that salespeople begin the sales process with near-zero credibility; therefore, if prospects aren't yet curious, and you don't already have a relationship to leverage, it's likely that your cold calls will be poorly received.

Nonetheless, the initial sales call is a watershed event in the QBS sales process. If the first contact goes well, you will have an opportunity to engage new prospects in productive sales conversation. This starts you down the path toward uncovering their needs and presenting your solutions. If the initial sales call goes poorly, however, you're out. That's the bottom line. That's also where QBS comes in, by showing you how to increase your probability of success when making initial sales calls. Read on!

Warm Up Your Cold Calls

Early in my own sales career, I made countless cold calls. "Smiling and Dialing" we used to call it. With a prospect list and a telephone, I held onto the belief that persistence was the key. So I called each of the prospects on my list, again and again, assuming they would be impressed by my tenacity.

But my results were mediocre, and I got more frustrated with every call. As it turned out, the prospects I was pursuing were getting frustrated as well.

The people I called weren't as impressed with my persistence as I had hoped. Instead, they were put off by it. I was doing everything I could to penetrate the account and schedule an appointment, but they were doing everything they could to get off the phone. Every call was a battle and I was obviously losing the war. Something had to change.

What changed was my approach to the initial contact. Since my cold calls didn't seem to be working, it didn't make sense to continue with the same old strategy of blindly lobbing calls into prospective accounts. Once I realized it was the "coldness" of my initial contacts that was causing the problem, I decided to change my approach to increase the "warmth" of my sales calls. As a result, I significantly increased my results when contacting new prospects.

How can you increase the warmth of your sales calls? That's what the rest of this chapter is about. You'll learn how to increase your effectiveness by applying the QBS methodology to pique the prospect's curiosity, establish your own credibility, uncover needs, build relationships, and secure the prospect's commitment to take the next step in the sales process.

> **Secret #104** When calling new prospects, the rule of thumb is: the "warmer" the call, the greater its probability of success.

Contacting new prospects is just as important now as it ever was. But that doesn't mean your initial sales calls have to be cold. Instead, QBS teaches salespeople how to make "lukewarm" calls. After all, you will only get one chance to make a first impression, so it might as well be a good one.

A Microcosm of the Sales Process

In chapter 11, we introduced a sales process model that breaks the larger sale down into its component parts. While our ultimate goal is closing more sales, you must succeed in the smaller components of a sale (generating interest, uncovering needs, and presenting solutions), before you can ask prospects for their commitment to buy. Accomplishing these smaller steps will lead to completing the larger sale.

The same is true in the initial sales call. If your objective on the call is getting an appointment or securing some other commitment to engage new prospects in the sales process, then you must first pique the prospect's interest, uncover needs, and let them know that you provide valuable solutions. In that sense, lukewarm calling is a microcosm of the larger sales process.

In QBS, we use a divide-and-conquer strategy to break the initial sales call down into its component parts. Perhaps you've heard the old saying, *the only way to eat an elephant is one bite at a time.* We make the same argument here. The only way to consistently succeed in the initial sales call is to execute the call one step at a time. That means accomplishing a series of smaller objectives to achieve the larger goal.

> **Secret #105** In the strategic sale, the larger goal of making the sale is achieved by accomplishing a series of smaller successes.

The lukewarm sales call that we'll describe throughout the rest of this chapter has four unique stages: *Introduction, Discovery, Value Proposition,* and *Closing on Next Steps.* This model serves as a blueprint for conducting the actual call and for qualifying the opportunity. Does the prospect have a need? Do they have a sense of urgency? Do they have the authority to make a decision? Who else needs to be involved? This blueprint will look familiar because it follows the Conversational Layering Model that we introduced earlier in chapter 6. This model is also versatile enough to apply in virtually any sales situation, yet specific enough to implement with predictable results.

The 4 Stages of a Lukewarm Sales Call

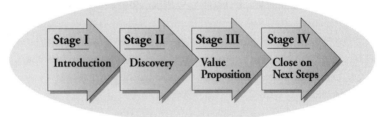

Some people ask if it's really necessary to have such a detailed strategy for the initial contact. The answer is no, it's not. Anyone can make cold calls, and it takes almost no skill whatsoever to transform a large number of sales leads into a sparse number of prospect opportunities. But if you want to significantly increase your sales results, then you will need to penetrate significantly more accounts. That's what you will learn how to accomplish in this chapter. By understanding how each component of the lukewarm call works, you will be able to engage more prospects in more productive sales conversation.

STAGE I
Introduction

The telephone rings and your prospect answers, *"Nick Hansen."* For salespeople, this is the moment of truth—the beginning of the initial sales call, where all the butterflies in your stomach must fly in formation. Whether the prospect picks up the telephone or answers the door, it's time to execute and it's do or die.

The lukewarm sales call begins with the *Introduction* stage. Although the *Introduction* is the shortest of the four stages, lasting only 15 to 40 seconds, it's a mistake to discount the significance of an effective opening. Our objective in the *Introduction* stage is very straightforward. We are simply trying to get "one foot in the door," in order to secure a few minutes of the prospect's time and attention. While this may sound easy, experienced salespeople are keenly aware that the beginning of the initial sales call is one of the highest hurdles in the sales process. In reality, salespeople know that it will take thirty, forty-five, or even sixty *minutes* to uncover needs and communicate value, but once the prospect realizes you are a salesperson, it's more likely that you will only have thirty, forty-five, or sixty *seconds*. Cautious prospects form their impressions very quickly, and as a salesperson, you aren't likely to get a second chance. Therefore, how you choose to manage this window of opportunity will likely determine whether your call ends abruptly or you succeed in getting in.

> **Secret #106** Very few sales are consummated during the initial sales call, but this is where many sales opportunities are lost.

The first stage of the lukewarm sales call (*Introduction*) is divided into three sub-steps. Each of these component steps and their effect on the successful execution of your initial sales calls is explained below.

Identify Yourself and Your Company

When you contact new prospects over the telephone, you may get through to their voice-mail system. When this happens, I recommend using one of the curiosity strategies that was outlined earlier (in chapter 7) to generate a return call. If the prospect answers the phone directly, however, then it's critical that you identify yourself and your company right up front.

Seller: *"Hello Mr. Prospect, my name is Jane Whitman and I'm with Pharmacom Products Corporation."*

This salesperson is very straightforward and to the point. She identifies herself and her company, and rather than trying to open the call with some clever line or juicy enticement, she lets her prospects know (up front) who they are dealing with. Some sellers attach a tag line to their opening to give prospects more information about the nature of the call. This is particularly effective when prospects wouldn't otherwise recognize you or the name of your company. Here's an example of what that sounds like:

> Seller: *"Hello Mr. Prospect, my name is Jane Whitman and I'm with Pharmacom Products Corporation, the leading manufacturer of pharmaceutical supplies in North America."*

Not only should your words be straightforward, your physical conduct should be as well. When you meet prospects in person, look them in the eye, extend your hand, and confidently state your first and last name. Prospects will follow your lead. They too will reach out their hand and reciprocate by saying their first and last name. Now, you have automatically put yourself on a first-name basis with the potential buyer.

The beginning of a sales call is typically *not* a good time for small talk, however. Opening with questions like, *"How are you today?"* or *"How's your day going?"* may seem nice, but you might as well say: *"I'm trying to get you to like me so I can sell you my product."* Remember that many other salespeople are also calling and asking how the prospect is doing. So keep it brief and to the point. There will be lots of time for chitchat once you establish a credible relationship.

Use Humbling Disclaimers to Minimize Your Risk

To some degree, making sales calls is a matter of personal style, but I can tell you that I use one particular QBS technique to open almost every call. I open with a humbling disclaimer (chapter 10). Whether I'm calling new prospects or existing customers, I identify myself and my company first, and then ask: *"Did I catch you at a bad time?"*

Some salespeople are reluctant to ask this. They worry that this question will give prospects an easy out. But as we stated earlier, your prospects already have an "out." Prospects and customers are well aware that they don't have to buy from you. Frankly, they don't even have to take your calls.

Asking if it's a "bad time" actually puts you in a very strategic position. The person you're trying to reach might be on another call or in the middle of a meeting; in which case, they'll respond by saying, *"Yes, this is a bad time. I have several people in my office."* But you mustn't despair. If a prospect is truly unavailable, you wouldn't have secured their time or attention no matter what you said. But asking if it's a "bad time," gives you an opportunity to follow up with: *"When should I call back?"* In most cases, the prospect will name a time when they expect to be more available. Now you have an appointment.

What happens if you ask, *"Did I catch you at a bad time?"* and your prospect says, *"No…no, this is fine. What can I do for you?"* Prospects don't like to deliver bad news, but they are often quick to rescue you by inviting you to please continue. This gives you exactly what you wanted—an invitation to proceed with the call. In addition to being polite, this approach is extremely respectful of the prospect's situation, which increases the likelihood that they will give you a few minutes.

What If the Prospect Asks: "What's This About?"

Some prospects will jump in after your opening blurb and ask, *"What's this about?"* This question often puts sellers on the defensive. Understandably, the prospect is trying to cut to the chase to decide whether the call is a valuable use of time or just another nuisance. Unfortunately, salespeople who get intimidated tend to jump ahead into their sales pitch. This usually sends the call into a tailspin because as we said previously (chapter 5), sellers cannot effectively present a solution until they first uncover a need.

Rather than jumping ahead to position your value of your product or service, try leveraging their curiosity. The next time one of your prospects jumps in and asks, *"What's this about?"* you respond by saying, *"We solve a very important problem that most companies have."* Few prospects will pass up the opportunity to ask, *"What problem do you solve?"* Now you have an invitation to engage the prospect further.

Associate to Create a Sense of Familiarity

After you identify yourself and your company, it's important to let the prospects know *why* you're calling. But that doesn't mean jumping ahead into a litany of generic-sounding features and benefits that sounds like:

Seller: *"Mr. Prospect, our company prides itself on maintaining the highest quality standards in the industry. We have the best products and the best service, and I would like to have an opportunity to solve your problems with our valuable solutions."*

This may sound good to a salesperson, but to the prospect, it sounds more like Charlie Brown's teacher: *"Mr. Prospect, our company prides itself on*

...wah...wah...wah. We have the best...wah...wah...wah, and I would like to have an opportunity to...wah...wah...wah." As we pointed out earlier, if this is what your prospects hear, they will probably respond by saying, *"No thanks, we already have enough...wah...wah...wah."*

A salesperson should have a valid reason for calling, one that piques the prospect's interest so they will *want* to engage further. While many initial sales calls are "cold," QBS's lukewarm calling strategy is intended to lower the prospects' defenses by creating a sense of familiarity (an association) that lets them know you have already made it past the gatekeeper.

> **Secret #107** Prospects are more likely to engage and share information with a salesperson who is already "plugged-in."

Have you ever noticed that it's easier to find a new job when you already have a job? Likewise, it's easier to get a date when you already have a boyfriend or girlfriend. We can draw a similar conclusion when trying to penetrate new prospect accounts. It's much easier to get to the key person if it appears that you are already engaged in the account. You can create this sense of familiarity (to warm up your sales calls), by leveraging any number of techniques that were introduced earlier in Question Based Selling, including: *Personal Endorsements, Associative References, Herd Momentum,* and *Glimpses of Value.* Keep in mind that we're still in Stage I of the luke-warm sales call, which usually lasts between fifteen and forty seconds.

Personal Endorsements

Chip Graddy sells financial services for Northwestern Mutual Life in Atlanta. During the past eight years, his sales results have skyrocketed, and he has become one of the company's top producers. Chip's success is largely attributable to his ability to leverage personal endorsements. Chip has mastered the use of mutual contacts to create a sense of familiarity that warms up his initial sales calls. Here's a sample dialogue:

Chip: *"Hi Steve, this is Chip Graddy of Northwestern Mutual Life. Did Fred Thompkins let you know I'd be calling?"*

Prospect: *"I think he mentioned it."*

Chip: *"Fred is a good friend of mine, and he's also a client. He speaks very highly of you and suggested that you would be a great person for me to get to know. Do you have a few minutes?"*

Chip knows that first impressions mean a lot. If the endorsement comes from a credible source, most prospects will take a few minutes—if for no other reason than out of respect for their friendship with the person who gave the referral. This technique can do wonders for your credibility, and it's also a good way to pique the prospect's interest.

Associative References

Some sales trainers are adamant about calling the decision maker first. You have to get to the right person, they insist! That means cold-calling some very important people. Personally, I would rather have a valid reason for calling than give important prospects the impression that I'm just another cold-caller. So in Question Based Selling, we take a different approach.

We talked about this in chapter 7. Rather than starting with the highest-level decision maker, you can initiate a dialogue with purchasing, marketing, or some other area of the business first. This gives you an opportunity to create an *associative reference*. Now, when you call the high-level decision maker, your opening sounds less like a sales call and more like someone who's already plugged into the account. Here's an example:

Salesperson: *"Hi, Ms. Prospect. My name is Don Smith, and I'm with XYZ Company, the leading provider of office automation systems in Dallas. Ms. Prospect, I just got off the phone with Doris in purchasing…and I have a question. Do you have a minute?"*

Most prospects will take this call for two reasons. First, the salesperson in this example is making it easy for the prospect to engage. After giving a valid reason for the call, the salesperson is only asking for "a minute" of the prospect's time. Everyone can spare a minute. Secondly, this approach is designed to pique the prospect's curiosity by leveraging an associative reference. In this example, if the prospect wants to know what's up with Doris in purchasing, then you will get some of their time and attention. Remember, at this point in the call, you're just trying to get one foot in the proverbial door.

Herd Momentum

Another way to warm up your sales calls is to use *herd momentum*. You've heard the phrase, "guilt by association." The Herd Theory gives salespeople an opportunity to establish *credibility by association*—by letting prospects know that "everyone else" is already moving in a certain direction.

Salesperson: *"Our products are currently being used by companies like Delta Airlines, IBM, General Motors, Lanier Worldwide, Nations-Bank, Monsanto, Lockheed, Citicorp, International Paper, Compaq, TRW, Coca Cola, Westinghouse, and the federal government…just to name a few.*

"On May 17, we are hosting a seminar to demonstrate how we have already helped many other customers solve some of the same issues that you currently face."

As prospects become curious about what the rest of the herd is doing, salespeople will have an opportunity to engage them in a more in-depth discussion. This helps transition your conversation into the next stage of the lukewarm sales call (*Discovery*).

> **Secret #108** Associative references won't close the sale, but they can give you an opening to execute on a strategy that will.

Glimpses of Value

You can also warm up your sales calls by giving prospects a *glimpse of value*. This early in the call, you haven't *earned the right* to ask lots of questions. But you can absolutely dangle a few enticing benefits out in front of your potential buyers to see if they would like to hear more. Some people call it "selling the sizzle, not the steak." Here are some examples:

Seller: *"Would you like to know how to significantly reduce your cost of goods sold with one simple change in strategy?"*

"If we could increase your revenue by 45 percent, would you be interested in hearing more about our new products?"

One of my best clients, International Network Services (INS), started as a network services company based in the Silicon Valley in 1991. They have since enjoyed explosive growth in the U.S. and around the world. One of the strategies INS used very effectively to penetrate new accounts was dangling a glimpse of value in front of their prospects. They would say:

Seller: *"Give us your most difficult networking problem, and if we can't solve it within a reasonable time frame, our time and effort will cost you nothing."*

For those decision makers who were wrestling with a host of technical problems, this was a valuable offer. Who wouldn't want to resolve their most difficult networking issue? Frankly, the INS salesperson was putting the prospect in a position where they had nothing to lose and everything to gain. INS, on the other hand, gained an opportunity to qualify and penetrate more new accounts. This positioning also gave them an opportunity to expand the engagement by demonstrating real value in terms of on-site expertise, technical capability, and measurable performance increases.

The Transition into Stage II (Discovery)

In Stage II, the direction of the initial sales call changes—from an introductory mode into an information gathering mode. The transition between Stages I and II is where sellers often lose control of their calls, however. In many cases, salespeople have been taught to press on whether the prospect wants to or not. QBS takes the opposite approach. Rather than trying to force a conversation, we recommend putting yourself in a position that earns you the right to engage further and uncover the prospect's needs in Stage II.

The easiest way to set up this transition between the *Introduction* and *Discovery* stages is to ask one of two questions. After you have identified yourself and your company, and you have communicated your reason for calling, simply ask: *"Are you the right person to talk with about _____?"* If you are selling office equipment, for example, you would ask, *"Are you the right person to talk to about upgrading your office equipment?"* If you sell surgical supplies, you would say, *"Are you the right person to talk with about medical supply purchases?"*

Their answer is either going to be, *"Yes, I am the right person,"* or, *"No, I'm not."* If the person on the phone is not the "right person," this does not mean you have failed in the call. Many times, the wrong person will go out of their way to help you get to the right person. Of course, this gives you a terrific opportunity to leverage a new associative reference by saying:

Seller: *"Hi, Mr. Prospect, I just got off the phone with Joe Sandler in the Minneapolis office and he said you would be the right person to talk with about _____. Do you have a minute?"*

If, on the other hand, your prospect concedes that he or she is indeed the right person, then you automatically gain their implied permission to proceed with the *Discovery* stage of the call.

> **Secret #109** Whenever someone agrees that they are the *right person*, you automatically earn the right to probe further.

The other question you can ask to set up the transition between Stages I and II of the initial sales call is: *"How familiar are you with ABC Company?"* This is different than asking, *"Have you heard about..."* or *"Are you familiar with ABC Company?"* Asking prospects if they have "heard about," or if they "are familiar with," your company is problematic because if they say yes, their response essentially shuts the door on your opportunity to educate them further. If instead, you ask prospects "how" familiar they are with your company or products, very few will claim absolute knowledge. That gives you an opportunity to educate them.

"Can I Ask You a Question?"

The most effective way to transition your calls from Stage I (*Introduction*) to Stage II (*Discovery*), is to simply say to your prospect: *"Can I ask you a question?"* As we pointed out earlier, this is one of those questions that elicits a predictable response. When you say, *"Can I ask you a question?"* 99 percent of the people you ask will automatically say, *"Sure."* Now you have their permission to proceed.

> **Secret #110** By securing your prospect's permission to proceed, you can expect more productive responses to your probing questions.

Some sales trainers might argue that it's unnecessary to ask prospects if you can ask them a question, but I haven't met a customer yet who didn't appreciate the gesture. In fact, asking people if you can ask them a question not only earns you the right to proceed, it's also a terrific way to eliminate some of the nervous tension that's often present at the very beginning of a sales call.

What If the Prospect Asks You a Question?

Prospects sometimes put salespeople on the defensive by asking them a question at the beginning of the call. But guess what? We want prospects to ask questions. We want them to be curious, and we want them to want additional information about the solutions we offer. If your prospect asks a question, don't be nervous. Be excited, and then let their question be your invitation to engage them further in a discussion about their needs and your value.

STAGE II
Discovery

Congratulations! You have made it past the most difficult part of the initial sales call (Stage I). By piquing the prospect's interest and securing their permission to proceed, you now have an opportunity to ask questions, to establish credibility, and most importantly, to "discover" potential problems or desires that will fuel the sales process. That's why Stage II is called *Discovery*.

Because it's still early in the call, however, you must resist any temptation to start spewing features and benefits. Until you know what your prospects need, you cannot effectively position the value of your solution. Hence the importance of asking good discovery questions.

Narrow the Scope for Credibility

Having earned the right to ask questions, let's ask ourselves, what's the best way to proceed in the call? You could start by asking some of the more traditional open-ended sales questions, like: *"What are your goals and objectives?"* or, *"Tell me a little about your business."* These are certainly good questions, but if you remember, QBS recommended back in chapter 8 that it's more effective if you open with a series of short answer, diagnostic questions—to establish your credibility. Realizing that salespeople begin the process with near-zero credibility, *narrowing the scope* of your questions allows you to demonstrate a higher level of competence and credibility, which helps differentiate you from the other forty or fifty sales callers who are also trying to penetrate the same account.

> **Secret #111** Prospects who don't like cold calls will gladly open up once you differentiate yourself as a competent professional.

By demonstrating that you know how to ask intelligent and relevant diagnostic questions, prospects will automatically assume that you can provide valuable solutions. Diagnostic questions also help to uncover information that will qualify the opportunity. If you sell employee benefits packages to large corporations, for example, you might ask the following series of diagnostic questions:

1. *How many employees does your company have?*

2. *What percentage of your work force receives health benefits?*

3. *Does your current health plan offer an HMO or PPO?*

4. *What about life insurance, disability, and dental coverage?*

5. *Who is your current benefits provider?*

6. *When is your benefits contract up for renewal?*

If you sell computer equipment and supplies, you might ask:

1. *Is your current I/S environment centralized or distributed?*

2. *Is your network operating system Microsoft or Novell?*

3. *Are you using version 3.X or 4.X?*

4. *How many end users do you support?*

5. *Do you develop your own software or buy applications?*

In QBS, we recommend that you work through a series of five or six diagnostic questions to let prospects know that you *do* understand their business. This allows you to establish credibility quickly, which is critical at this point because it's still early in the call. Of course, once you establish your credibility, something magical happens. Curious prospects, who also believe that you are credible, begin to open up. They share information, and they ask to hear more about your products and services.

Broaden the Scope for Relationships

Narrowing the scope of your questions establishes your credibility so you can *broaden the scope* of your questions to uncover needs and build relationships. Effective probing is more than just asking a bunch of open-ended questions, however. You also need to *escalate the focus* of your questions to raise the value of your sales conversations.

Escalate the Value of Your Questions

We made the point in chapter 9 that some questions are more valuable than others. There, we showed you how to escalate the *focus* of your questions to increase their intrinsic value in the conversation. This process begins with Status Questions which probe the "status" of the opportunity. Status Questions are diagnostic in nature, which allows you to initiate conversation, gather information, and most importantly, establish your credibility. Status Questions are easy to ask and easy to answer, which makes them a good starting point in the sales call. But as we pointed out, prospects have a limited tolerance for Status Questions because they are low in mutual value. Your prospect already knows the status. Therefore, you'll want to ask enough Status Questions to establish credibility in the call, and then escalate the focus of the conversation, asking Issue Questions and Implication Questions that will uncover key business issues and the implications of those issues.

Issue Questions don't have to be complex and they don't have to challenge the intellectual depths of your prospects to be effective. In fact, it's best to keep it simple, by asking, "*To what extent is _____ important?*" Now, just fill in the blank with a relevant business issue and you can very effectively probe the needs of any prospect in any industry.

> **Secret #112** The most effective way to uncover prospect needs is to simply ask, "*To what extent is _____ important?*"

Prospects don't respond well to rhetorical questions, so stay away from questions like, "*Is quality important?*" or "*Is cost important?*" Of course quality and cost are important! Instead, you want to understand *why* these issues are important. Asking, "to what extent," is valuable because it helps uncover implications that will justify a favorable decision later in the sale. For specific examples of Implication Questions, refer back to chapter 9.

Expand Responses with Global Questions

Some prospects will take the ball and run with it, giving you in-depth responses to your questions. With others, you will have to work harder to get them to open up. That's where Global Questions are particularly useful.

If you remember, Global Questions were introduced earlier as tools for expanding your sales conversations. They also helped reduce any risk that prospects would feel that you are asking too many questions or probing too deeply. Essentially, Global Questions offer a very polite and respectful way to say, "I'm very interested...so please tell me more."

Some of the most common Global Questions include:

> *"How do you mean?"*   *"What else?"*
> *"Like what?"*   *"And then what?"*
> *"What happened next?"*   *"Why is that?"*

Global Questions offer a compliment to the prospect's ego because you are letting them know that you are interested in their opinion, and you would like them to please continue. This sentiment is likely to generate a significant amount of additional input from qualified buyers.

Clarifying Vague-O-Nyms

Another technique that you can use to expand your sales conversations is to clarify any *vague-o-nyms*. What's a vague-o-nym? You probably know what synonyms are—different words that have the same meaning (i.e., big and large). Homonyms are words that sound the same but have different meanings (i.e., hair and hare). Antonyms are opposites, like up and down. So what's a vague-o-nym? A vague-o-nym is a word (or phrase) that is so vague that it's impossible to know what the other person means without additional information.

Sales managers tear their hair out when salespeople use vague-o-nyms to report the status of an account saying, *"The deal is going to close soon."* Most sales managers will immediately ask, *"What do you mean by soon?"* In many cases, the salesperson is just telling the sales manager what the prospect told them. A similar lack of information exists whenever prospects say things like: *"Your product costs too much,"* or *"Quality is one of our biggest concerns."*

Vague-o-nyms don't give you enough information. How soon is "soon?" For some prospects, soon might mean the close of business on Thursday. For others, soon might mean a couple of months, or it might signal that a prospect is having trouble overcoming a budget problem or some other obstacle in the sale. And while we're at it, how much is "too much," and what does a prospect mean when they say that quality is one of their "biggest concerns"?

The *Discovery* stage of the initial sales call is a good time to clarify vague-o-nyms as they come up, which gives you an opportunity to better understand the prospect's needs and their buying motivations. For example, if a prospect says, *"We have recently experienced significant problems,"* you should immediately ask for clarification with questions like: *"What kind of problems? What do you mean by significant? When did these problems occur?"* (though maybe not in a rapid fire delivery!). Here are a couple other examples where the salesperson has an opportunity to clarify vague-o-nyms.

Seller: *"Mr. Prospect, you mentioned that you were looking for some creative solutions. What did you mean by creative?"*

"When you said you want your new computer system to be easily expandable, what did you mean?"

Colloquial English is an imperfect language, and as such, it's chock full of vague-o-nyms. What does this mean for salespeople? It means that you should assume nothing because everyday words and phrases can have very different meanings, depending on the context in which they are used and the biases of the people involved.

> **Secret #113** The meaning of everyday words depends on the context in which they are used and the biases of the people involved.

This idea of clarifying vague-o-nyms makes some salespeople nervous because they wouldn't want their prospects to think they aren't listening. Fortunately, clarifying the prospect's vague-o-nyms gives you an opportunity to demonstrate that you were actually listening so intently that you want to understand exactly what the prospect means. It also gives you an opportunity to probe further by asking additional questions.

The Transition into Stage III (Value Proposition)

Our objective in Stage II is information gathering. We want to uncover enough needs to fuel the sales process, and we want prospects to feel comfortable enough to openly share. Once you have accomplished these goals, it's time to transition the call into Stage III (*Value Proposition*).

Stage III is your opportunity to communicate the value of your product or service. But it's important to recognize that just because you are ready to present value doesn't necessarily mean your prospects are ready to listen.

How can you make sure your prospects are ready to listen? The answer is, by making them curious enough to want more information about how your product can address their specific needs. Prospects must *want* to be educated further. Therefore, to successfully transition the call into Stage III, it's easiest to keep it simple, by asking, *"Would it make sense for me to take a minute and bring you up to speed on our products?"* Prospects who were willing to share their issues will surely want to hear more about the solutions you offer.

Stage III of the lukewarm sales call is the *Value Proposition*. This stage marks the beginning of your opportunity to educate qualified prospects. It's also where you'll start to build value in your product or service offering.

For people who sell over the phone in a telemarketing capacity, Stage III of the initial sales call becomes the product presentation. When a prospect is interested, and they have a need for what you sell, this stage of the call is your opportunity to communicate the value of your solutions. You will learn more about positioning value in chapter 14, "Building Value in the QBS Presentation."

In most strategic sales, the initial sales call is just the first step in a longer process, and it wouldn't make sense to try and close the sale over the phone. Instead, you should be trying to secure a commitment where the prospect agrees to participate in the next step in the sales process, whether that's a meeting, a presentation, a proposal, or a product demonstration.

Provide a Thumbnail Sketch

Top performers in sales are masters of their message. When they have an opportunity to give a full-blown presentation, they provide a complete and detailed account of how their product or service works, and they explain how their proposed solution will address the prospect's needs. When they have limited time, however, they can very effectively condense these same value messages into a *thumbnail sketch.*

Positioning value in Stage III of the lukewarm sales call is somewhat of a balancing act. We want to give potential buyers enough information to get them excited about our solutions, but we also want to leave some "meat on the bone" so they will have a reason to engage further.

> **Secret #114** Providing too much information, too early in the process, makes it too easy for prospects to say, "*No, thanks.*"

The initial sales call offers a limited time window in which to communicate your value. You must be clear, concise, and impactful. Brevity counts. Tom Peters makes this point in his book, *The Pursuit of WOW*, where he says that given the pace of today's business environment, successful business people should be able to articulate their entire value proposition in twenty-five words or less. Can you do that for the product you sell?

Put Your Best Foot Forward

I like to think of Stage III as an "infomercial." It's your opportunity to rant and rave about the value of your product or service. By letting prospects know you can significantly improve their existing condition, you cause them to want more information; and when they want to know more, it's easy to schedule an on-site meeting or a product presentation.

> **Secret #115** Salespeople can rant and rave about their products without sounding arrogant. They sound arrogant when they start ranting and raving about themselves.

The goal in Stage III is to put your best foot forward. Essentially, you want to match the value of your solutions to the needs you uncovered in Stage II. You also want to position *gold medals* and *German Shepherds* (both) so you maximize your opportunity to motivate prospects. After you get prospects interested, you will have an opportunity to substantiate your claims of value in a more detailed presentation.

Another Opportunity to Leverage the Herd

The Herd Theory can be used very early in your sales calls to pique a prospect's interest, and it can also be leveraged in Stage III to communicate value. Because prospects are naturally cautious, The Herd Theory gives them a sense of comfort, knowing that many other customers have already blazed the trail to success.

Seller: *"Mr. Prospect, you mentioned that you wanted to increase the efficiency of your business while reducing expenses. I'm not surprised to hear you say that because that's what other customers like Exxon, IBM, BellSouth, Bank of America, Norfolk Southern, General Electric, Westinghouse, Southern Railroad, Ford Motor Company, and Coca-Cola are already doing."*

Whether it's at the very beginning of the sales process or later on, the Herd Theory is a momentum play. The fact that "everyone else" is already moving in a certain direction implies that something about your offering must be valuable. Now the question is, do your prospects want to know more? If so, then it's time to move on to Stage IV of the call.

STAGE IV
Close on
Next Steps

As in the larger QBS process, once you have successfully generated interest, uncovered needs, and communicated value, it's time to close. In the lukewarm sales call, closing means securing the prospect's commitment to take the appropriate next step(s) in the sales process.

Stage IV is much more than just scheduling additional events, however. It's also an opportunity to manage your prospect's expectations and expand the scope of engagement to include other people who will play a role in the final decision. Additionally, Stage IV of the lukewarm sales call is a good time to develop potential champions—people who will help ensure that subsequent sales events go well.

So, how do you close the initial sales call? Let me show you.

Seller: *"Mr. Prospect, I can go on and on telling you about the value of our product...but here's the problem. There's no good way to show you how the product actually works over the telephone. That's why, with most customers, we set up a meeting, demo, or presentation so you can understand how our product will address your specific issues. Would that be valuable?"*

This closing dialogue incorporates a number of strategic phrases. Two of the most critical occur in the very first sentence:

"Mr. Prospect, I can go on and on talking about the value of our product... but here's the problem."

Here, the salesperson interrupts his own Stage III value proposition to let the prospect know that he could go *"on and on."* The salesperson's inference that there is so much more to say about the product entices prospects to want to engage further. But instead of going on and on over the telephone, the seller raises a problem, and in so doing, he sets up the actual close.

"There's no good way to show you how the product actually works over the telephone."

The salesperson here is essentially saying that a different venue is needed to satisfy the prospect's desire for additional information. This is a reasonable conclusion, since very few products can be adequately explained via telephone. This positioning actually adds to the salesperson's credibility because the seller is now helping the prospect solve a problem by working with him to figure out how best to proceed. This lays the groundwork for the salesperson to suggest an alternative path.

"That's why, with most customers, we set up a meeting, demo, or presentation so you can understand how our product will address your specific issues."

Once again, we're closing on a familiar phrase—asking prospects if they want to know how "our product" can address "specific issues." The salesperson is basically suggesting that unless there's a better way, the prospect should take the direction that we already know is productive. *"Would that be valuable?"*

What If the Prospect Says Yes

If the prospect says yes and accepts your invitation to take the next step in the sales process, then you have accomplished the primary objective of the initial sales call. But don't hang up yet, because there's still some work that needs to be done to properly close the call.

> **Secret #116** The prospect's acceptance of your offer to engage further marks the beginning of your sales effort, not the end.

Closing the call is your opportunity to secure the prospect's commitment. It's also your opportunity to set the prospect's expectations so that the next step in the sales process is destined to succeed. To ensure your success, however, you should always make it a point to help prospects think through the logistics of subsequent events, and you should work with your contacts in the account to expand the audience to include other key players. Also, to help your champions look good in front of their peers and their manager, I encourage you to cover the following points before wrapping up the call and moving on.

Ask Who Else Needs to Be Involved

Most strategic sales involve more than one person. For sellers, that means the person you originally contact in the account may not be the person who ultimately signs off on the purchase. Particularly if your next step in the sale is a presentation, you will want to expand the audience to include everyone who will have a role in the purchase decision. Some salespeople just assume that the right people will automatically show up at the next event. This is a mistake. Instead, you should make it a point to ask, *"Who else needs to be involved?"* We will talk more about getting to the "right person" and getting the right people involved in chapter 13.

Scheduling the Actual Event

The best time to schedule the next event is when you're closing the call. Be sure to pick a date that's far enough into the future to allow everyone to synchronize their calendars, but not so far off that prospects will say, *"Can you refresh my memory and tell me why we scheduled a meeting?"* It's also important to avoid dates that conflict with regularly scheduled staff meetings, the decision maker's vacation plans, or a national holiday.

Offer a Range of Dates

Most sellers work closely with their internal champions to schedule the next event—a product presentation, for example. Once you select a tentative date, the champion goes off to see if that date works with their boss and other members of the decision committee. When multiple people are involved, there is often a scheduling conflict. So, your champion comes back and says, *"We need to choose another date."* As soon as you pick another date, somebody else has a conflict; and you end up trying to schedule against a moving target.

Going back and forth to accommodate everyone's schedule can be a very frustrating experience for your internal champions, and it can also dampen their enthusiasm. To avoid this, offer a range of dates. If you want to schedule an event in April, for example, let your prospect know that as of right now, you are available on April 9 or 10, or during the following week. This gives your champion an opportunity to target a range of dates which will eliminate much of the back and forth hassle. Be sure to let your champion know that you need an answer ASAP, so you can work around other clients. It's a nice way to give them first choice, but this positioning also creates a sense of urgency, because they realize you can't be expected to hold tentative dates open indefinitely.

What If the Prospect Says No

QBS's lukewarm calling model increases your probability of success, and it also decreases your risk of failure. By the time you make it to Stage IV in the call, scheduling the next step in the sales process is usually a foregone conclusion. Very few prospects will become curious in Stage I, share their needs in Stage II, listen to your thumbnail sketch in Stage III, and then *not* want to hear more about the solutions you offer. If you are going to be rejected, it will usually occur much earlier in the call. Nonetheless, prospects still might say, *"No, thanks."* In that case, I would look for a reason to re-engage at some point in the future, rather than persist until the prospect gets upset, and the longer term opportunity goes down in flames.

Nobody likes being rejected—we've talked about this several times. Most salespeople would rather move on to some other task than dwell on the negative after a prospect says no. But just as we learn from our successes, there is also an opportunity to learn from rejection.

It's critical to understand why your prospects are saying no. If you are having difficulty in the initial moments of your calls, then you may want to revisit your curiosity and credibility strategies. If prospects seem to be losing interest after you provide a thumbnail sketch, you may want to reevaluate your transition strategy. In either case, I have always encouraged salespeople and sales managers to actively track their losses because we often learn more from our failures than we do from success—and one small adjustment in your approach might become the differentiating factor in your next sale.

Summary

I no longer make cold calls, and I recommend that you don't either. In addition to being universally despised, cold calls usually produce unimpressive results. To succeed in sales, however, you still must penetrate new prospect accounts and create business opportunities that otherwise wouldn't exist. That's exactly what you will accomplish with a little creativity and some solid QBS techniques—to "warm up" your sales calls and significantly improve your sales results.

Chapter 13

GETTING TO THE "RIGHT PERSON"

The question of whom to target in the sale is an ongoing debate in the world of sales training. Some sales trainers say it's better to start high in the organization and work down. Others feel it's better to start lower and work your way up the decision-making ladder. In either case, the key is getting to the right person—the one who can actually make a buying decision.

In this chapter, we'll talk about the best place to start, but more importantly, we'll show you how to get to the "right person," once you penetrate the account.

So far in this book, we have talked about many different aspects of the strategic sale. We've talked about uncovering needs and positioning value. We have also introduced numerous strategies and techniques for generating prospect curiosity, establishing credibility, leveraging momentum, and soliciting more accurate feedback. All of these things can significantly enhance your sales effectiveness, but only if you are dealing with the right person in your prospect and customer accounts.

Identifying the "right person" within your targeted prospect accounts is easier said than done, however. Every sale is unique, and the person (or people) who actually make decisions will vary from account to account. In some accounts, the president of the company will take a hands-on approach and want to be intimately involved with every aspect of the decision. In other accounts, senior managers will delegate decisions to lower levels of authority.

Earlier in my career, when I was selling Hospital Information Systems, the chief financial officer always played a role in the decision because he or she would ultimately have to sign the check. But between hospitals, the CFO's role in the sale would vary dramatically. Some CFOs became personally involved with everything from identifying the evaluation criteria to negotiating the terms and conditions of a contract. These CFOs were the true decision makers. In other hospitals, the CFO would assemble a committee that would represent the different hospital departments in a formal evaluation process. The committee would then submit a recommendation back to the CFO for approval. Were the people who served on these committees decision makers? You bet. Even if they didn't actually sign the check, their opinions and recommendations were integral to the final decision.

Corporate culture plays a role in how buying decisions are made. So does the personality profile of the person who has the authority to make a purchase. While some people choose to micromanage every decision, others are willing to solicit input from, or delegate responsibility to, someone else. For example, some marketing executives will only trust their own instincts when evaluating a proposed advertising campaign, while others will rely heavily on input from others to evaluate an idea or make a decision.

> **Secret #117** While some prospects micromanage every decision, others are more likely to solicit input from, or delegate responsibility to, someone else.

Away from the corporate environment, how decisions are made still depends on the individual prospect. Real estate agents can certainly attest to this. With some couples, the husband clearly has greater influence and he will ultimately determine the outcome of the sale. With other couples, it's the wife who will make the buying decision. In many cases, the husband and wife will each influence certain parts of the decision. The husband might have greater influence when it comes to the yard and structure of the house, while the wife may be more concerned about closet space, bathrooms, and decor. I'm not trying to be sexist here. I'm merely pointing out that different people make decisions differently.

What does this mean for salespeople? It means that sellers can no longer assume they know who will actually make the decision in any given account; and just because the vice president (or the husband) was the decision maker in the last sale, doesn't mean it will happen that way in the next.

Top-Down or Bottom-Up

It's easy to assume that the decision maker in a corporate sale must be the person with the greatest influence. That would mean the person with the biggest title or the one who is highest on the organizational chart. In addition to controlling the purse-strings, they also have the authority to determine priorities and set direction. In fact, the higher you go in an organization, the more authority the person you call on will have.

This idea that you'll find greater decision-making authority at the top of the organization has made it fashionable to train salespeople on using a top-down approach—contacting the very top officer in a company first. Some sales trainers base their entire strategy on making the "top officer" the central figure in the sale. While that may be good in theory, it's often an impractical approach because the top officer isn't always the right person.

If you sell copiers to small businesses, for example, it absolutely makes sense to "call high," because the owner or president of the company is usually the only one who has the authority to make a buying decision. Likewise, if you sell pharmaceuticals or medical supplies, you should call on doctors (directly) for the same reason. But if you are selling copiers, and you want to penetrate large corporate accounts like Westinghouse or Coca Cola, does it really make sense to initiate the sales process by calling the CEO? Of course not. Most large accounts have many layers of decision-making authority and starting too high ends up being a low percentage play.

I'm not against calling "high" in new prospect accounts, and the fact is, I have closed numerous sales that began with the top officer in a company. Top-down selling does work—but I have also sold millions of dollars worth of products and services in prospect accounts where the opportunity started with someone much further down in the organization. This has led me to conclude that bottom-up selling works too.

> **Secret #118** Some of the most exciting sales opportunities begin with someone other than the very important top officer.

When contacting new prospects, there are some definite advantages to calling high. But there are also some risks. Understanding both the benefits and the risks will help you determine how best to proceed when penetrating new accounts.

The Benefits and Risks of Calling High

The most significant benefit of calling high is power. If someone high in the organization likes what you say, they have the power to set up a meeting or schedule a presentation. They also have the power to make sure all the right people are in attendance. And, if the "big kahuna" likes what you have to offer, they have the power to pull the trigger on a purchase.

Calling high can also create some powerful associative references—an idea that we first introduced back in chapter 7. If you contact someone high in the organization, and they refer you to someone lower, you can leverage your new associative reference to say, "*I just got off the phone with Mr. Peterson,* (vice president of finance) *and he suggested I contact you. Do you have a minute?*" This gives you a very nice opening to initiate a productive dialogue with the "right person."

Ted Ranft, who sells professional services in Philadelphia, has been very successful using a variation of this technique. Ted targets someone high in the organization, knowing full well that his call is going to be intercepted by their voice-mail system. Then, Ted leaves a detailed voice-mail message, followed by this request, "*Can you, or someone on your staff, please call me back?*"

Senior managers are very busy people and they are always looking for ways to delegate action items. By leaving this message, Ted is actually inviting the senior manager to forward this voice mail on to someone else—presumably, a subordinate. As a result, Ted almost always receives a return call. If your boss forwarded a message and asked you to follow up, wouldn't you return the call? This technique is effective because it leverages the power of someone at a higher level to help the salesperson penetrate new accounts.

> **Secret #119** High-level contacts have the authority to make a decision, or the ability to bring together the people who can.

What are the risks of calling high? Actually, there are several. While high-level contacts typically have greater decision-making authority, they are significantly more difficult to reach. As you get higher in an organization, gatekeepers become more stringent. They have to be tough, because people in positions of authority are being pulled in multiple directions. They are also being bombarded with sales calls. Even if you succeed in getting past the gatekeeper, a senior manager may be so far removed from the details that they don't recognize the existence of a problem. Consequently, they wouldn't see a need for your solution. And even if they do recognize the problem, high-level managers simply cannot afford to personally involve themselves in each and every decision their organization makes.

Another risk of calling too high is political fallout. If a senior executive doesn't see a need for your product or service, or they are already pursuing another solution, they can quickly kill your opportunity by saying, *"No thanks."* Sure, you could still call someone lower in the organization, and you may even succeed in penetrating the account, but you will eventually have to come back to the big boss who has already said no.

If a high-level executive *does* like your offering and agrees to take the next step in the sales process, you may face a different challenge—the risk that lower-level people in the organization will resent you for circumventing their authority and going straight to the top.

The Benefits and Risks of Calling Low

There are advantages to calling low in an organization as well. The biggest advantage is lower-level people tend to be more accessible. This doesn't mean they aren't busy. It just means they are more likely to pick up the telephone when you call, or be available to meet with you. This is a tremendous advantage for salespeople. Before I meet with a corporate executive, for example, I try to talk with someone lower in the organization first. This gives me a chance to do some reconnaissance work and collect valuable information about their current business environment. People at lower levels typically have more time for detail, and they're almost always closer to the problems that need to be solved.

Calling low in an organization also gives you an opportunity to develop internal champions. We know most people like to look good in front of their peers and management, so if we can garner the support of people at lower levels, we can leverage them as advocates to help take our value messages much higher in the organization. It will always be true that internal champions have more credibility than a salesperson who's just trying to break into an account.

Lower-level contacts also make good associative references. Call it reverse name dropping. It can be a very effective, for example, to leave a voice mail with a senior manager saying, *"Mr. Prospect, my name is Tony Simpkins and I'm with Unified Systems, Inc. I just got off the phone with Frank in distribution...and I have a question. When you get a chance, could you please call me back?"* Most higher level managers will return your call because they'll want to know what's up with Frank in distribution.

Calling low is not without risks, however. Perhaps the greatest risk is being told by someone at a lower level of authority not to call anyone else in the organization—particularly not their boss. Now you're blocked. You could ignore this mandate and call their boss anyway, but then you risk losing the support of a potential influencer, champion, or coach. Of course, if you heed their advice, then your proposal might not ever get the visibility it needs to be seriously considered.

> **Secret #120**   The greatest risk of calling low is being blocked by some-
> one who doesn't have the authority to make a decision.

Another risk of calling too low is that people at lower levels of authority may not see the bigger picture. If their sphere of influence is limited to certain job functions, they may not be in the loop on decisions regarding the company's strategic direction or the timing of an upcoming purchase. As a result, calling too low can result in incomplete or inaccurate information. Even if your contacts are aware of the bigger picture, it's very possible that you could threaten their security. Perhaps you will expose a weakness in their current job performance. Or, your product's ability to enhance productivity (or reduce overhead) might eliminate their job altogether. Needless to say, people who feel threatened are less than helpful, and they might even try to sabotage your selling efforts.

Strategic Decisions Involve Multiple Players

Purchase decisions for small items are typically made by a single person. For example, when a transaction involves products like cosmetics, radios, shoes, books, or office supplies, the actual buyer rarely needs someone else's approval in order to make a purchase decision. But when you are selling high-end solutions to large corporations, it's a different story. Very few large decisions are made by a single person.

Strategic decisions usually involve multiple players. Of course, we are talking about decisions that will impact multiple areas of a business over an extended period of time. To go back to an earlier example, purchasing a hospital information system is a very strategic decision, one that affects doctors, nurses, patients, employees, hospital administrators, and in some cases, the entire community. Similarly, when companies purchase database software, employee benefits packages, telephone switches, consulting services, manufacturing equipment, or commercial real estate, they are making strategic decisions that will have far-reaching effects on their business.

Strategic purchases are more complex, because each of the participants in the decision has his or her own agenda. Nurses who evaluate hospital information systems, for example, want user-friendly clinical systems that will enable them to provide better patient care. Department managers want capabilities that will reduce their administrative workload. Meanwhile, the "ever frugal" accounting department may be satisfied with fewer bells and whistles, in order to reduce the acquisition cost of the system. At some point, the hospital's decision committee will assimilate all of this input, weigh it against the decision criteria, and make a recommendation.

When multiple players are involved, it's unwise to focus on any one individual in the hope that they alone will determine the outcome of the purchase. Instead, we want to focus on everyone who can influence the outcome of the decision. This includes *decision makers, influencers, executive sponsors, champions, coaches, informants, and anti-champions.* In order to help you identify who's who in your prospect accounts, here's a profile of each major player in the strategic sale.

The Decision Maker

As we said earlier, the decision maker in a prospect account can be difficult to spot. In many cases, the person who signs the check will also make the decision. Other times, the person who signs the check will delegate the decision to someone else. And it's also true that some people will *claim* to be the decision maker even though they are not.

In simplest terms, the decision maker is the person in the account who will ultimately "pull the trigger" on the decision to purchase. They have the authority to accept or reject your proposal, and they are held accountable for the decisions they make. But just as no man is an island, few decisions are made in a vacuum. Most decision makers solicit input from other sources. In doing so, they are influenced by the opinions, biases, and recommendations of people around them.

> **Secret #121** Not everyone can *pull the trigger* and make a decision, but lots of people can *pull the plug* on your opportunity to sell.

As salespeople, we definitely want to target the decision maker within our prospect accounts, but we also want to work closely with those people who will influence the outcome of the purchase decision.

Influencers

Influencers are people that decision makers listen to. While influencers can't actually make the buying decision, they will definitely affect the outcome of your sales by providing input and information that will sway the decision one way or another. That's why they're called "influencers."

These people are important to identify, because of their effect on the opinions of other people within the account. Especially when a recommendation is being issued by a committee, influencers can garner the votes of other people to create a powerful voice in the final decision.

> **Secret #122** Key influencers are able to *influence* opinions and create a very powerful voice in the final decision.

One caution though. Don't be fooled into believing that the most vocal participants in a decision have the greatest influence. It's more likely that the person who sits quietly and listens carefully wields the biggest sword. Sellers also have to be aware that influencers can affect the outcome of an opportunity in more than one direction. A key influencer who likes your product or service can help you immensely, while an influencer who either dislikes your offering, or supports some other alternative, can negate your sales efforts from inside the account.

The Executive Sponsor

When a decision is made by the top officer in a prospect account, the decision maker and the executive sponsor are one and the same. But as we said before, larger companies have to delegate decision-making authority because the top officer cannot be intimately involved in every purchase.

Most delegated decisions have an executive sponsor—a senior manager who doesn't actively participate in the detailed evaluation, but who does approve the final decision before the purchase takes place. The executive sponsor is generally the ranking officer in the part of a business that is most directly impacted by a pending decision.

It's very difficult to sell an executive sponsor without first securing the support of the decision maker and any key influencers. In fact, executive sponsors usually don't like a top-down approach. That's because they rely on the diligence and expertise of their subordinates to investigate potential alternatives and present the best solution. It is valuable, however, to find out as much as you can about the executive sponsor, so you can appropriately package your solution for easy approval.

Internal Champions

One thing that separates top salespeople from the rest of the masses is their ability to develop internal champions. An internal champion is someone in the account who wants your product or service offering so much that they are willing to help you secure a favorable decision.

Internal champions become your inside salespeople. They are the ones who are willing to support your proposal and fight to overcome objections that get raised. They also have an emotional stake in the solution, and in many cases, they want the sale to happen as much as the salesperson does.

How do you build internal champions? The answer is, by making your victory in the sale their victory as well. Champions are people who have something to gain if your product or service is selected and something to lose if it is rejected. For salespeople, the trick is figuring out who will benefit if your proposed solution is chosen.

Let's remember that advocate relationships are developed. Very few prospects have ever attended a sales-training course. Therefore, they will most likely need your help to sell your solutions internally. But one thing is for sure: internal champions *do* want to look good in front of their peers and their manager. So, it's to your advantage to teach them how to effectively position your proposal. This is an investment that will pay you back many times over, as your internal champions become an extension of your own selling efforts. One other point, the more authority your champions have, the greater impact they will have on the outcome of a decision.

Coaches

Coaches won't fight for your solution like an internal champion would, but they can absolutely give you valuable advice and direction about how best to proceed in the sale. Ultimately, coaches want you to succeed in the sale, but they are not in a position to actively promote your solution.

Your coach may be someone who is directly involved with the decision, or your coach may be an independent third party working in the account. At NetFrame Systems, for example, we often partnered with third-party leasing companies to finance the sale. Not surprisingly, we shared information and coached each other about how to succeed in the account. Other vendors and outside consultants can also be valuable coaches. In reality, it's amazing how much coaching you can receive if you are just willing to ask for it.

Informants

Some people can assist you in the sale, even if they are not in a position to champion your solution or coach you on how best to proceed. We call these people informants. What they can do is provide you with valuable information that will help plan your next move. As an example, administrative assistants and executive secretaries make great informants, although it's amazing how many salespeople just blow these people off as being unimportant. Instead, you should try to develop relationships with informants because they often have valuable information that will help you more effectively navigate the sale. They may know something about your competition, or about the status of the budget. They may also know when the decision maker will be back in his office and what's on the agenda for the next staff meeting.

Informant relationships are based on trust. Hence, the more credibility you establish with a potential informant, the more information you will receive.

Indifferents and Anti-Champions

There are other people in the sale who aren't decision makers, influencers, executive sponsors, champions, coaches, or informants, but who are still important to know and understand. These people fall into one of two categories: indifferents or anti-champions.

People who are indifferent couldn't care less about the outcome of a decision. Either they're not impacted by the purchase, or they are too busy fighting other fires to dedicate any emotional bandwidth to your sales cycle. Trying to cultivate a relationship with someone who is indifferent may have some long-term benefit, but you should definitely limit your investment of time, effort, and resources in the shorter term.

Anti-champions are the people you have to watch out for. They are the ones who will speak out against your proposed solution, whether they favor a competitive offering or just want to maintain the status quo. How much time should you spend with anti-champions? Some sellers attempt to turn them around by proving that their proposed solution is indeed better. I usually don't. If they are truly anti-champions, direct confrontation just fuels additional debate and disagreement. Instead, I try to neutralize the anti-champion's negative influence by getting them to agree that both solutions are viable options. Then, once they do agree that my solution is indeed viable, I work through my internal champions to position my proposal as the best alternative.

> **Secret #123** The best way to neutralize an anti-champion is to get them to agree that both solutions are viable alternatives.

Knowing Who's Who in the Decision

When a salesperson first calls on a new account, they may know a few names and titles, but until they actually engage the prospect, it's impossible to know who's who in the decision making process. As we've said, every prospect is unique and just because someone played an important role in your last sale, it doesn't mean a person at the same level will be a key player in the next.

The actual decision maker might be the president of the company. Perhaps the decision will be made by a vice president, director, regional manager, supervisor, or a technical analyst. In some cases, an on-site consultant will make the decision. Identifying the actual decision maker is only part of the puzzle, however. To maximize your effectiveness, you must also identify the other key players, including influencers, potential champions, coaches, informants, executive sponsors, and anti-champions.

In a complex sale, the director of operations may choose your product after being influenced by several key department managers. But when the recommendation is presented to the president (the executive sponsor), suddenly there is resistance from the internal auditor—your anti-champion in the account—who is more familiar with a competitor's product. When you sell complex products to large corporations, any number of political and economic subtleties can affect the outcome of a decision. But one thing is sure, anyone who doesn't understand the value of your product or service will ultimately vote against it. That's why it's critical for salespeople to understand how decisions are made and who needs to be involved.

> **Secret #124** Anyone in an account who doesn't understand the value of your product or service will ultimately vote against it.

How can salespeople know who needs to be involved in a decision? By asking questions that will not only reveal the key players, but also their role in the evaluation, selection, and approval process for your proposed solution. That's why I always make it a point to ask the following questions:

Seller: *"Are you the right person to talk with about _____?"*

If this sounds familiar, it's because this was one of the initial questions we posed in the lukewarm sales call in chapter 12. It's a great question because you are asking the person to either accept responsibility for a particular function of the business, or refer you to someone else.

Seller: *"Who else needs to be involved?"*

Since most strategic decisions do involve multiple players, it's critical to find out who else will need to be involved in the decision. To reduce the risk of getting blocked by someone lower in the organization, I purposely phrase the question this way. Even if my contact wants to limit access to other people in the account, this phrasing will usually produce a response that lets me know who the key players are, in addition to giving me some valuable information about how decisions are typically made.

Seller: *"Who will ultimately sign off on the purchase?"*

This question will uncover the decision maker and the executive sponsor. It may also initiate a discussion about the various steps a recommendation must go through to be approved.

Seller: *"Is there anyone who might oppose this proposal?"*

Who knows…you might be able to smoke out any anti-champions. At the very least, this question will help you identify potential opponents to your proposed solution.

Probe for Champions and Coaches

In addition to finding out who fills the various roles in a decision, I also want to find out whether the person I'm talking to would be willing to help me as a coach or a champion. It can be a little awkward to come right out and ask, so I use the following questions to give prospects an opportunity to let me know where they stand in the sale.

Seller: *"How do you feel about the proposal that's on the table?"*

Essentially, you are asking the prospect how they plan to vote. Those people who oppose your solution will either be antagonistic or tight-lipped. Prospects who support your offering, however, will often step forward with some valuable information about where your proposal currently stands in the evaluation process, and how you should proceed in the sale.

Seller: *"How would you handle this situation if you were in my shoes?"*

People love to give advice. We talked about this in chapter 11. If you are willing to ask, it's amazing how much help you will receive. Personally, I have always contended that your best coach in the account is the person on the other end of the telephone. In addition to knowing the status of the sale, they also know the political climate within the account. Anyone and everyone can help you in some way, if you are just willing to ask.

> **Secret #125** When making calls, your best coach in an account is the person on the other end of the telephone.

The Best Place to Start

Question Based Selling doesn't advocate a top-down approach *or* a bottom-up approach. Instead, we take the position that, in the vast majority of new prospect opportunities, it's virtually impossible to know how decisions are made until you actually penetrate the account.

So, rather than trying to guess who the "right people" are, I recommend that sellers target multiple contacts within their prospect accounts. Where it's appropriate, call prospects at a high level, even if your chances of getting through are somewhat limited. But you should also contact lower levels too, in an effort to build grass roots support for your product or service. Then, once you get in (at whatever level), you can leverage your contacts within the account to identify the right people, uncover needs, and move the sales process forward.

Cross Reference the Information You Receive

One of the challenges salespeople face when talking to more than one person within an account is conflicting information. Because people tend to view things differently, you are likely to receive different information from a high-level manager than you would from a technician. It's easiest to assume that people in positions of authority are always right, but we have to be careful not to discount the value of the information we receive from other sources. When you do receive conflicting information, it's important to find out which version of the truth is correct. In QBS, we call this cross referencing.

Cross referencing is a questioning technique that's designed to validate the accuracy of information you receive. Essentially, you pose the same questions to different contacts in the account and then compare their responses. If the information you receive from two or more sources is consistent, then that information is probably accurate. If, however, the information you receive from different sources does not match, then further investigation is required. Chances are good that one of the answers is accurate—you just don't know which one until you do some follow-up.

> **Secret #126** When multiple people give the same response, the information you are getting is probably accurate.

Cross referencing gives you an opportunity to uncover some of the political subtleties within your prospect accounts. Using this technique, you will find out who is likely to help you make a sale, and who is likely to lead you down a dead-end path. This knowledge will help you more effectively position your solution and navigate the sales process.

Summary

Getting to the right person in your prospect accounts is critical to your success in sales. So is understanding all the different influences that will affect the purchase decision. Whether you're selling computer systems, medical supplies, life insurance, financial services, or employee benefits, every account is unique, and different people will take on different roles. Your job is to successfully identify those people who will affect the decision, so you can effectively manage the outcome of the sale. Once you know who's who in the decision, the next step is getting them involved in the sales process, so you can build value in the QBS presentation. That's what we cover next.

Chapter 14

BUILDING VALUE IN THE QBS PRESENTATION

Phase II of the QBS sales process is the presentation. Once you have generated enough interest to motivate prospects to want to engage further, the sales presentation is your opportunity to communicate the value of your product or service.

This chapter isn't about presentation skills like voice inflection, how to use a slide projector, or the proper way to gesture to an audience. Instead, we focus more on the strategic aspects of the presentation—how to leverage curiosity, credibility, and momentum to differentiate yourself and your solutions.

After you have successfully generated interest and uncovered needs in Phase I of the QBS sales process, the logical next step is educating your prospects on the value of your product or service. This is usually done in the context of a sales presentation—where sellers have an opportunity to match the benefits of their solutions to the prospect's specific needs.

Back in chapter 11, we introduced the three phases of the QBS sales process. In Phase I, our objective was generating enough interest to motivate qualified prospects to move forward into Phase II. Now that we have made it to the presentation, there are three strategic objectives we want to accomplish in Phase II. First, we want to communicate enough value in our solutions to justify a favorable purchase decision. Second, we want to increase the prospect's sense of urgency so they will want to purchase our solution sooner rather than later. Lastly, the sales

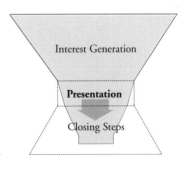

Phase II: Presentation

presentation provides sellers with an excellent opportunity to identify and cultivate potential champions who can be groomed to carry our flag as the decision moves toward closure.

The sales presentation also gives you an opportunity to teach qualified prospects the three *how's* of QBS: *how to buy, how to sell,* and *how it works.* Some prospects will have a clear picture of the criteria they want to use when evaluating potential solutions. Other prospects won't have any idea what to look for, or how to choose between competing vendors. Rather than let them fend for themselves, QBS recommends taking a proactive role in the sales presentation to teach prospects *how to buy.* This means working with prospects to establish decision criteria that will lead them to the right solution—more specifically, to your product or service.

QBS also recommends that sellers take a proactive role in teaching the prospect *how to sell.* If your presentation goes well, you'll want those people who attended to promote your solution to others in the organization who also need to sign off on the purchase decision. The presentation is an excellent opportunity to teach these people how to position the value of your offering.

The third *how* is teaching your prospects *how it works.* This is the main thrust of your presentation—educating attendees about all the features and benefits your solution provides.

> **Secret #127** The value you build in the sales presentation is what ultimately justifies a favorable purchase decision.

The format of a sales presentation can vary dramatically depending on the product you sell and the audience you're selling to. In smaller sales, where your first call is typically face-to-face, the Phase II presentation is often an extension of the initial sales call. If you sell pharmaceutical supplies to doctors, for example, and you've waited ninety minutes to be seen, you had better be ready to deliver a presentation right then and there. If you sell life insurance, brokerage services, or advertising space, prospects expect the initial sales call to lead directly into a presentation of value. Frankly, with some prospects, you may not get a second chance.

When selling to individual buyers, the presentation phase of the sales process tends to be less formal and more relaxed. That's OK, because in a one-on-one sale, we want prospects to feel comfortable and be in an environment where they can freely ask questions. This way, you can tailor your value messages to the uniquenesses of each specific buyer.

> **Secret #128** When selling to individual buyers, the presentation phase of the sales process tends to be less formal and more relaxed.

For larger corporate sales, the Phase II presentation is much more strategic. It's also significantly more complex. Once you pique the interest of someone in the account, whether it's on the phone or in a personal meeting, the presentation is generally scheduled as a separate event. This gives everyone who will be involved in the decision, or who needs to know about your product or service, a chance to participate. Managing this level of complexity will be our focus throughout the rest of the chapter.

Essentially, we want everyone who will be involved in the purchase to attend the presentation. As we said earlier, anyone who does not understand the value of your solution will ultimately vote against it. But your success in the presentation isn't as simple as convening an audience and then telling them about the value you offer. In addition to having good content, you must also secure the audience's time and attention, and you must overcome the same credibility issues you faced in the initial sales call.

Challenges Salespeople Face in the Presentation

At the beginning of the sales process, salespeople have near-zero credibility. When we first pick up the telephone to initiate contact with a new account, we inherit all the negative biases and prejudices that prospects have formed as the result of having to fend off a steady stream of pushy and over-zealous salespeople. Again, we are guilty until proven innocent.

These same prejudices carry over into the Phase II sales presentation. While you may have already established some good contacts in the account, other people who show up at your presentation may be seeing you for the very first time—in which case, they're likely to see you as just another salesperson who has near-zero credibility.

To illustrate the challenge, let's suppose that you sell manufacturing equipment to large corporations, and along comes a promising new prospect. Carol Williams, the director of operations, is so impressed with your product that she invites you in to present at next month's project committee meeting. It's a wonderful opportunity, because they have a very specific need and you have a terrific solution.

Like any good salesperson, you understand that preparation is the key to success; therefore, you go into reconnaissance mode. Using your network of industry contacts, you find out who will be in the audience, what the various hot buttons are, and what questions might get raised. Essentially, you want to be ready so you can avoid being blindsided in the presentation by something you are not prepared to address.

Then comes the actual sales presentation. Your champion in the account (Carol) says a few words of introduction, and it's your show. It's also do or die. Unfortunately, this is where many sellers make a costly mistake. They assume that because they are there to make a presentation, they should jump right into an explanation of product features and benefits. For the same reasons we recommended against jumping ahead in Phase I, we recommend you don't jump ahead in your sales presentations either.

In chapter 6, we made the point that in order to present solutions, you must first accomplish each of the prerequisite steps in the Conversational Layering Model. The same is true in a sales presentation. Here, your prerequisites include piquing the audience's curiosity, establishing your own credibility, and uncovering needs that will justify your solution. If you press on with the presentation without first accomplishing these prerequisites, you are setting yourself up for failure.

Conversational Layering

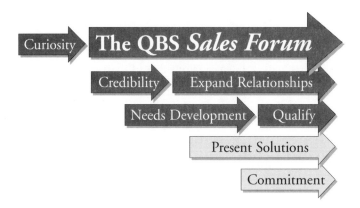

Going back to our example, Carol Williams may be the only person in your audience who is ready for you to jump into an explanation of how your product works. She wants to hear more about your product because she has already formed a positive impression of you, and she is curious to find out how your solutions will satisfy her needs.

Contrast Ms. William's level of readiness with that of the rest of the attendees. Everyone else comes into your presentation cold. They don't know you from Adam—in which case, they aren't curious, you aren't credible, and they may or may not recognize the existence of a need. In fact, many of them just sit there with their arms folded against their chests, glaring at you as if to say, *"Can we get this over with? I've got other important things to do."*

Can you blame them? If yours is the fifth, tenth, or twentieth sales presentation they've had to sit through so far this month, who knows how many other salespeople have already tested their patience. Moreover, the odds that they'll be impressed are stacked against you, because only a small fraction of sales presentations ever generate value for the attendees. Most prospects say that they get something out of 20 to 25 percent of the presentations they attend, but the other 75 to 80 percent just waste time. No wonder some people are biased against you before the sales presentation even starts.

> **Secret #129** Just like the initial sales call, sellers begin the presentation with *near-zero credibility*.

With the exception of the person who sponsored the presentation, everyone is starting from scratch. You haven't yet piqued their interest, you have near-zero credibility, and you inherit all the negative baggage from other salespeople who have preceded you. You may have experienced this yourself if you have ever presented to an audience where some people were nodding in agreement, while everyone else was just sitting there with a glazed look. The moral is, just because you've been invited to present doesn't mean everyone in your audience is ready to listen. And if they aren't yet ready to listen, then plowing forward with your presentation is not only a bad strategy, it's a recipe for disaster.

In Question Based Selling, we want everyone who is going to be involved in the decision to attend the presentation. We also want them to listen attentively. For this to occur, we must adopt a more strategic approach in Phase II. That means accomplishing each of the prerequisite steps in the Conversational Layering Model before you start positioning the value of your product or service.

Breaking the Ice

The beginning of a presentation sets the tone for the rest of the event. In that vein, it's particularly important for your sales presentations to get off to a good start. Audience participants will form their impressions quickly, and you want their first impression to be a good one.

When I present, I want people in my presentation audience to feel comfortable; but more importantly, I want them to be mentally engaged and emotionally involved. This doesn't happen by itself. Given the hectic pace of today's business environment, people are bound to have other things on their minds, and if they aren't thinking about a previous meeting, they're thinking about their next one. That's why one of my foremost objectives at the beginning of a sales presentation is breaking the ice—getting the audience to focus their attention on what I'm about to present, and stop thinking about everything else.

To successfully break the ice in your sales presentations, QBS suggests a four step approach that consists of introducing the presenter and the audience, delivering an interactive opener, identifying the objectives in the presentation, and managing audience expectations.

Introduce the Presenter and the Audience

If you are presenting to a committee, it's always better to be introduced by someone from the audience, than to walk up and introduce yourself. But don't leave this to chance. If your contact in the account doesn't offer, you should ask them to kick off the event with some brief introductory words that explain why the meeting was called.

A well-planned introduction can significantly enhance your credibility. Since your contact in the account has a built-in incentive to make you look good, a little advance coaching can make them sound like one of your best references. This is a terrific way to kick off your sales presentations.

> **Secret #130** Your champions in the account have a built-in incentive to make you (the presenter) look good.

In addition to introducing *you* as the presenter, ask your champion to introduce the audience as well. Unless the size of the presentation audience is prohibitive, having someone (other than you) go around the room and attach names with faces offers a number of strategic advantages.

First, it reduces your risk. To be effective, sellers need to know who's in the audience. The problem is, it sometimes feels hokey or uncomfortable to ask people to introduce themselves. So let the person who kicked things off handle this function. They are usually happy to do so, and it reduces any risk of creating a "hokey" first impression.

Secondly, introducing the audience tends to create instant interaction. As people go around the room giving their "name, rank, and serial number," you can interject comments or ask specific questions about their areas of responsibility. This gives you an opportunity to bond with people in the audience before the presentation begins. In addition to increasing the number of "friendly faces" in the room, this technique makes it easy to emphasize key points and target your remarks during the actual presentation.

Lastly, fostering interaction at the beginning of a sales presentation is likely to yield some valuable information about how the decision will be made. If you want to know who the decision makers, influencers, and potential anti-champions are, then listen carefully. The politics of a decision will generally unfold during the pre-presentation banter.

Deliver an Interactive Opener

After the introductions, it's show time. Interestingly, there are as many opinions on how to begin a presentation as there are presenters. Some presenters like to kick off their presentations with a joke or a funny story. Others choose a more serious approach and dive right into the issues. In QBS, we favor an interactive approach—where the salesperson gains control of the audience, kicks off the event, and points the presentation in the right direction. To illustrate, here's an example of what I might say to deliver an interactive opener:

Seller: *"Hello everybody, and welcome. I appreciate your making the time to join us today. My name is Tom Freese, and I started QBS Research, Inc., the company that developed Question Based Selling. For years, we've been working with some of the world's leading sales organizations, including: IBM, General Electric, Lanier Worldwide, Compaq, AT&T, Motorola, and Hewlett Packard (just to name a few), teaching their salespeople how to leverage the most powerful tool in business to double their sales results.*

"To prepare for this presentation, I've talked at length with Steve Johnson (vice president of sales), and I have become somewhat familiar with your business model. But rather than assume that I already know everything, it might be better to ask. What would you like me to accomplish in this presentation today?"

(Then I pause and listen carefully.)

The effectiveness of this approach is buried in its subtlety. In just a few sentences, I have let the audience know that I have prepared in advance via my discussions with Steve Johnson. But I also gain a significant advantage by inviting them to participate in setting the direction for the presentation.

I could have opened with the traditional, *"My name is…, and here's my agenda for the presentation,"* but I intentionally shy away from these canned openings. The reason is because phrases like "my agenda" are easily mismatched. Prospects do want to know you are prepared, but they may not be ready to buy into what *you* think is important, or even what Steve Johnson thinks is important. In fact, the only way to know what the audience actually wants or needs is to invite their input at the beginning of the presentation, rather than just plow ahead with your own agenda.

In the sample dialogue above, you'll notice that I start by thanking the audience. Right off the bat, I want them to know that I do understand their time is valuable, and that I intend to make their participation a worthwhile experience. It's a courtesy…so be gracious, but there's no need to thank the audience profusely as if they're doing you a favor by attending. After all, if you provide value, they have something to gain from your presentation.

Next, I introduced myself (again). Even if you were formally introduced by your contact or champion within the account, you should always make it a point to introduce yourself, your company, and anyone else that you may have brought with you for the presentation. This allows you to set the tone for the presentation and it gives audiences a taste of your personality and style.

> **Secret #131** When prospects identify with you personally, they're more likely to identify with your presentation and your solutions.

The opening of the sales presentation is also a great time to leverage momentum. In QBS, that means using the Herd Theory to rattle off a robust list of "herd" references. This gives audiences a sense of confidence and reassurance that other companies have tested, utilized, and are already benefiting from the solutions you are about to present.

What Would You Like Me to Accomplish in the Presentation?

At the end of my sample opening, I do the unthinkable. After admitting to the audience that I do know something about their business (but not everything), I ask, *"What would you like me to accomplish in this presentation today?"*

Some salespeople are hesitant to ask this question, but you shouldn't be. This is a great question. More importantly, it's a wonderful diffusion strategy. If we assume that most audiences are naturally skeptical of salespeople, then asking what *they'd* like to accomplish in the presentation is a huge deviation from the "standard" sales pitch. You might even be surprised at how this one question will make prospects perk up in their seats.

Of course, there are people who would argue that asking the audience for input at the very beginning of a sales presentation increases your risk. What if they bring something up you're not prepared to cover? Good point. But if someone in the audience wants to bring up an issue during the presentation, they will. The only question is, do you want to know about any potential obstacles up front, or would you rather be surprised later in the presentation?

The truth is, salespeople can be fully prepared and still ask for input at the beginning of their sales presentations. Doing so demonstrates a great deal of confidence and expertise on your part, and it also lets prospects know that you plan to tailor your presentation to make good use of their time.

> **Secret #132** An interactive opener lets prospects know that you plan to tailor *your* presentation to make good use of *their* time.

Depending on your relationship with the prospect, this may be enough to get your presentation off to a good start. But one other key component that will help to break the ice and point your presentation in the right direction is managing your audience's expectations.

Managing Audience Expectations

After years of presenting to all kinds of audiences, I have adopted a simple formula that sums up the relationship between the audience's expectations and your delivery. Happiness is the difference between expectations and reality. To put this formula in mathematical terms: $H = R - E$. When a sales presentation falters, it's usually because the presenter fails to live up to the expectations of his or her audience. Although we can't always control reality in the sales process, we can always manage the audience's expectations in the presentation. In fact, managing expectations is critical to your success in Phase II.

> **Secret #133** Happiness is the difference between expectations and reality. In QBS, we put this into a simple formula: $H = R - E$.

One of the best ways to manage audience expectations is to use presentation qualifiers. What's a presentation qualifier? It's a positioning question that's designed to secure the audience's buy-in, so you can get off to a good start in your presentations. For example, if you want to start off talking about the prospect's business issues in order to set the stage for the benefits you offer, you can manage the audience's expectations and secure their buy-in by saying:

> **Seller:** *"Because some people in the audience are more familiar with our product than others, we usually start off by overviewing the issues our product solves, and then talk more specifically about how the product works. Would that make sense for this group?"*

Most people will say, *"That's fine."* It's a predictable response. When your audience consists of people with different levels of expertise (which is usually the case), it's easy to get them to agree that it *does* make sense to start off with the bigger picture—in this case, talking about the prospect's needs.

Another qualifier that you can use to point your presentations in the right direction is:

> **Seller:** *"Would you rather have a canned sales pitch, or would it make more sense to focus on your specific business issues?"*

You already know what the answer is going to be. Prospects would much rather focus on their specific issues than sit through another generic sales pitch. But I always ask this question because it sets up my next move in the presentation. When the audience tells me that they would rather focus on their specific business issues, I automatically earn the right to ask questions that will establish my credibility and uncover their needs.

Use Diagnostic Questions to Establish Credibility

No matter how you slice it, credibility sells. It raises the intrinsic value of the material being presented, and it gives the salesperson tremendous leverage in guiding the audience toward a favorable decision. But as we pointed out earlier, sellers must establish credibility first in order to uncover needs and communicate the value of their product or service.

> **Secret #134** The greater your credibility, the more value prospects will attach to the information, ideas, and solutions you present.

What's the best way to establish credibility at the beginning of a sales presentation? Unfortunately, too many presenters attempt to "claim" credibility by *telling* audiences how great their company or product is. QBS does just the opposite. We establish credibility by asking questions. Using the same strategy we outlined earlier in chapter 8, we recommend *narrowing the scope* of your questions to demonstrate a higher level of competence and value.

After breaking the ice in your presentation, you should transition into a series of short-answer, diagnostic questions. In many cases, I ask the same questions I asked earlier in Phase I—only now, I am posing those questions to the audience. Just like before, when you demonstrate an ability to ask intelligent questions, you raise the prospect's perception of your credibility.

The difference is, the diagnostic questions you ask at the beginning of the presentation will confirm information that you already have. You want to come in prepared, but you also want the audience to form an impression that's favorable and highly credible. To illustrate, in the earlier example where you were selling manufacturing equipment to large corporations, you could start off your sales presentation with a series of diagnostic questions like:

Seller: *"Your company produces between twenty-five hundred and three thousand widgets each year, depending on demand, right?"*

Audience: *"Yes."*

Seller: *"And your current system runs on an IBM mainframe system that was originally installed in…1995?"*

Audience: *"Yes, a nineteen-month installation was completed in fall of 1995."*

Seller: *"…and how many end-users does the system support?"*

Audience: *"Approximately 265."*

Seller: *"Is your software home-grown or turnkey?"*

Audience: *"We purchased most of our current software packages, but we usually integrate them ourselves."*

If you did your homework, then you may already know the answers to these questions. But this is not an exercise in playing dumb. Dumb doesn't sell! Rather, this is a technique that allows you to convey a higher level of credibility with the larger audience. It also helps to validate the information you have. In some cases, you might find out that the information you collected earlier was incomplete or incorrect. This will help your presentation because you want to have complete and accurate information before the presentation begins.

Generally, you should ask enough diagnostic questions to establish your credibility (usually five or six), and then move on. Move on to what? If you remember from chapter 8, establishing credibility earns you the right to *broaden the scope* of your questions—to uncover prospect needs. These needs will ultimately serve as the foundation for every successful sales presentation.

Without Needs...There Are No Solutions

The presentation is the salesperson's opportunity to educate prospects on the value of their solutions. But there's a catch. In order to build value in the presentation, the audience must first recognize the existence of a need. If they do perceive a need, then you have an opportunity to deliver value. If they don't recognize their own needs, however, they will find very little value in the solutions you present.

To maximize the impact of your presentation, you want prospects to have multiple needs so they will feel a greater sense of urgency to have these needs addressed. By uncovering more needs, you will also give yourself the chance to present greater value. (Chapters 5 and 9 have more detail on increasing needs and escalating the prospect's sense of urgency.) Suffice it to say, if you can satisfy nine or ten needs in your presentation, then you give your prospects nine or ten reasons to make a favorable buying decision. In that way, you are making it easier for them to cost-justify a purchase.

> **Secret #135** The greater the prospect's need, the more value you will be able to deliver in the presentation.

Realize too that different people in your presentation audience have different needs, priorities, and objectives. Whenever people with differing responsibilities come together for a presentation, it's safe to assume there will be a variety of issues and concerns. This variety creates an interesting challenge for salespeople. If you want everyone to be on the same page with respect to your presentation, you must get everyone to buy into a common agenda—one that will address individual needs and satisfy the audience as a whole. That's exactly what you'll accomplish by building a *Mutual Agenda*.

Building a Mutual Agenda

Every sales presentation needs an agenda. The agenda serves as a road map for matching potential solutions against the prospect's needs. The only question is, whose agenda should you follow—yours or the audience's?

There's an old adage about presentations that says you should start by telling the audience what you plan to say, say it, and then summarize by telling them what you've said. Presentation skills courses have been teaching this technique for decades. As a result, salespeople are quick to whip out their prepared agendas and "tell" audiences what they are going to say.

There is an inherent problem with this approach. Opening a sales presentation with a canned agenda greatly increases your risk. Your champion in the account might nod in agreement because they were included in previous discussions and they already buy into the points you plan to cover. In a sense, they are emotionally ready to hear the solutions you want to present. But what about everyone else? Do they even recognize the existence of a need? Do they have the same issues? If they don't, then your pre-fab agenda will miss the mark before the presentation even starts.

Secret #136   Just because you know where you want to go in the presentation, doesn't mean the rest of your audience will want to go there.

My experience at NetFrame Systems (selling Superservers) taught me a lot about how to position a sales presentation. At the time, very few prospects had ever heard of a Superserver, so I was starting from ground zero when educating the audience. The "standard" NetFrame presentation was a two-hour affair, complete with eighty slides and a detailed chalk-talk discussion about how the product worked.

In layman's terms, NetFrame's product was a mainframe-type computer that was designed to drive a local area network. It was a great product, one that was able to solve a number of important business issues that large corporations had been wrestling with for years. Issues like:

- Growth/Scalability
- Data Integrity
- Maximum Uptime
- Network Management
- Cost Effectiveness
- Upgradability
- Better Support
- Increased Performance

Our success hinged on getting audiences to buy into this list of issues. If the audience *did* agree that growth, data integrity, uptime, etc., were important to their business, then building value in the presentation was relatively easy. If they did not agree that these issues were important, it didn't matter how robust our product was—they weren't going to buy.

The challenge was securing their buy-in. As in many other companies, NetFrame salespeople (including myself) were getting up and trying to tell audiences that *our* issues were critical to *their* business. We even attempted to strengthen our case using slides, charts, and testimonials that proved that the issues we solved should be important to them.

Ironically, the more emphatically we tried to "tell" prospects that our issues were important, the more they resisted. *"How can anyone refute the importance of issues like growth, uptime, or data integrity?"* I wondered. Nonetheless, they resisted. Whenever I tried to explain why a certain issue should be critical to their business, they would argue that their situation was unique, or that my suppositions didn't apply to them. In fact, the harder I pushed (to secure their buy-in on my list of issues), the harder prospects and customers would push back. As you can imagine, this resistance was not helping my sales presentations get off to a good start.

> **Secret #137** Telling prospects why an issue is important often causes them to *mismatch*, telling you why it's not.

The problem is, whenever salespeople try to *tell* audiences what their issues are, audiences tend to resist. They think to themselves, *"Who are you to tell us what's important?"* As a result, sellers often have difficulty securing the audience's buy-in that the issues they plan to cover in the presentation are relevant to their business. In QBS, we solve this problem by asking instead of telling.

Ask and Ye Shall Receive

Prior to the actual presentation, most salespeople already know what the key issues are. They've met with key contacts in the account and have encouraged them to share their thoughts, feelings, and concerns. But we want the entire audience to buy into these issues. This is easily accomplished by escalating the *focus* of your questions.

After you break the ice in your presentations and establish credibility by asking a series of diagnostic questions, you simply transition to the same Issue Questions that we introduced in chapter 9, asking:

Presenter (to audience):   *"To what extent is _____ important?"*

Now, just fill in the blank with one of the key issues you plan to address in your presentation and you'll be shocked at how quickly your audience will come alive. By giving them an opportunity to participate in defining the problems that need to be addressed, your audience develops a sense of ownership with respect to your presentation.

> **Secret #138** When a presentation audience helps to define the problem, it's easier to get them to buy into your solution.

Asking "to what extent" not only confirms the importance of the issues being raised, it also expands the discussion by allowing you to probe further and uncover the implications of these issues. Moreover, asking "to what extent" prevents your questions from sounding too rhetorical.

Building a Road Map for Success

Your presentation may already have an agenda that works. Through trial and error and real-life experience, presentations are meticulously crafted to maximize the salesperson's probability of success. The key is getting audiences to buy into that agenda—so you can cover certain business issues in a certain order. To get audiences to buy in, try making your agenda *their* agenda.

At NetFrame, growth was the first issue we wanted to address, so we asked, *"To what extent is growth an issue in your business?"* Everyone's technology environment was experiencing significant growth; therefore, this was a good topic to secure a consensus and start building the agenda for the presentation.

What happens next is critically important. If your audience responds by agreeing that growth *is* significant (which they will because you have done your homework), then you should go to the flipchart and write the word "Growth." By writing it down, you are confirming that the audience *does* think growth is an important issue—one that needs to be addressed in your presentation. Growth becomes the very first item on the agenda. Then, you simply move on to the next issue you plan to cover, asking:

Presenter: *"What about data integrity? If something were to corrupt your data, to what extent would that be a problem?"*

Audience: *"That would be a huge problem!"*

You can make the issues that get raised even bigger by asking Implication Questions that help people in the audience visualize scenarios that would dictate a need for your product or service. The goal is to emotionally involve each of the participants in some way, so be spontaneous and broaden the conversation when you can. For example, you might say:

Presenter: *"When you said corrupting your data would be a huge problem, what did you mean?"*

James: *"Losing data would cripple the entire marketing department."*

Presenter: *"Susan, how would data problems affect accounting?"*

Susan: *"We would completely lose track of our assets and liabilities."*

Now that you have identified another need to build value against in your presentation, walk over to the flipchart and write down "Data Integrity." Once again, writing it down confirms that *data integrity* is an important issue, and one that needs to be addressed in the presentation. Data Integrity then becomes the second item on your agenda.

If you repeat this exercise for each of the issues you plan to cover in your presentation, you will end up with a flipchart filled with all the issues your product or service addresses, arranged in the order you plan to present them. I usually complete this process by pointing at the flipchart, and asking, *"Is there anything else you would like me to add to this agenda?"* If you are on target with your questioning, your list will be a comprehensive one.

Congratulations! You have just created an agenda for your presentation. But whose agenda is it? Well, that's the beauty of this technique. The list of issues that you have compiled represents the audience's agenda; because they are the ones who validated the importance of each business issue that was raised.

> *Growth*
> *Data Integrity*
> *Uptime*
> *Network Mgt.*
> *Cost eff.*
> *Upgradability*
> *Support*
> *Performance*

But guess what? This list of issues also represents your agenda for the presentation—after all, you chose which issues to raise and in what order. That's why we call it a Mutual Agenda. You get to present issues that are important to you, and the audience gets to hear about issues that are important to them. This is a far cry from projecting a canned agenda onto the wall and announcing to the audience, *"This is what I plan to cover today."*

Secret #139 The Mutual Agenda is your strategic road map for building value in the Phase II sales presentation.

If you use the Mutual Agenda as a road map for your presentations, you are more likely to get audiences excited about the solutions you present. They will perceive that you are responding to their specific needs as opposed to focusing only on those things that are most important to you.

When It's Time to Knock Their Socks Off

After you have developed a Mutual Agenda for your presentation, it's time to knock the prospect's socks off by showing how your solutions can address their specific business and personal needs. This is the meat of your presentation, where you'll replace all the interest that was generated in Phase I with an even greater sense of value in Phase II.

It's impossible for me to script out your actual sales presentation in this book. I have absolutely no way of knowing what specific value points you have to offer, and I can only hypothesize about what your prospects need. We can, however, identify and outline five specific strategies that you can use to deliver a more effective, question based sales presentation. These five strategies are outlined below.

Divide and Conquer

The Mutual Agenda is a *divide and conquer* strategy. Since we want prospects to have multiple reasons to buy our product or service, we want them to credit us with having accomplished a number of different objectives in the presentation, rather than just one or two. By compiling each of the issues you plan to cover onto a Mutual Agenda, you will expand the prospect's needs and in so doing, increase their sense of urgency for finding a solution.

A divide and conquer strategy also helps to break the larger, more complex decision down into smaller parts. It's easier to educate people when you can focus on the individual components of a decision. Plus, it's easier to accumulate value when you conquer each of the prospect's issues separately.

When you apply this divide and conquer strategy to your own sales presentations, be aware that different people in your audience will gravitate to different issues on the Mutual Agenda. We talked about this in chapter 4 when we introduced the idea that people have different buying motivations. If your Mutual Agenda is comprehensive enough to include something for everyone, don't be surprised if your audience ends up arguing about the different reasons they like your product or service. That's OK!

Stories Get Remembered Long After the Presentation Ends

Your ability to relate to a presentation audience is critical to your success in Phase II. In addition to gaining their buy-in on the key points you make during the presentation, you want your messages to leave a lasting impression. How can you give presentations that audiences will remember? By using stories, anecdotes, and parables that support your value proposition.

Stories get remembered long after your presentation ends. Think about it this way. What do you remember from the seventh grade? Do you remember what was actually taught in the classroom, or are you more likely to remember that Bobbie Schmitt was sent to the principal's office for pulling the fire alarm during study hall? If you're like me, you remember the stories.

I mention this for two reasons. First, your competitors in the account will have an opportunity to present their solutions to the same audience at some point in the process. Your value messages need to stay fresh in the prospect's mind or your probability of success will be significantly reduced. Secondly, strategic purchases often require people in your presentation audience to go out and "sell" others on the idea of buying your solution. Their ability to recall the information you present will most likely determine your success in the sale.

Stories about other prospects and customers are particularly powerful. This is another application of the Herd Theory from chapter 3. During the presentation, be sure to let audiences know how excited other companies are about your offering. That means rattling off a few marquis customer names like Texas Instruments, General Mills, Nike, Owens Corning, Pfizer & Pfizer, IBM, Monsanto, and General Electric. It's valuable to cite stories about prospects who suffered consequences because they elected not to purchase your solution.

Position Gold Medals and German Shepherds

Back in chapter 4, QBS changed the paradigm for positioning benefits. In presentations, prospects will see value in different ways. So, instead of trying to get potential buyers excited about all the wonderful things your product or service offers, you can more effectively motivate prospects if you position your product in terms of both *gold medals* and *German Shepherds*. Remember: *While some people are motivated to run fast toward gold medals, many others run even faster from German Shepherds.* Some prospects will be motivated by reward; others will be motivated more by aversion.

To maximize your effectiveness in the Phase II presentation, you'll want to satisfy both. This means positioning each of your value points both ways—as a *gold medal* and also as a *German Shepherd*. Be sure to let prospects know, for example, that your warranty is the best in the industry *(gold medal)*, which will prevent all those nagging support problems they've been experiencing with their current system *(German Shepherd)*.

Ask Confirmation Questions

Just because you have "the floor" in a presentation doesn't mean that everyone in your audience is always listening. The truth is, it's difficult to get the prospect's attention, and it's sometimes even harder to keep it. This shouldn't surprise us; prospects do have other things on their minds, and if they are not captivated by your presentation, their thoughts will surely drift elsewhere. How can you hold the audience's attention throughout your presentation? One way is to ask *Confirmation Questions.*

A Confirmation Question is a conversational tool presenters use to confirm that everyone is following along with the discussion. I learned this technique from John Van Siclen—one of my early sales mentors.

John was smart enough to recognize that prospects who are responsive in the presentation are emotionally engaged. So when John gave a presentation, whether in a formal setting or one-on-one, he regularly asked confirmation questions to maintain an emotional connection. He wasn't looking for tons of feedback, he was just seeking a subtle confirmation that the presentation audience was following along. *"Does that make sense?"*

Soliciting feedback from your audience is also an effective way to control the pace of a presentation. Since we know that prospects process information differently, going too fast can be just as detrimental as going too slow. Therefore, a few well-placed Confirmation Questions during the presentation give people in your audience a chance to absorb key points before you move on. *"Are you with me?"*

A side benefit of asking confirmation questions happens when you cause gray cells to move. What does this mean? When people in your audience are busy thinking about the questions that you are asking, they won't be thinking about something else. They'll be focused on you and your material. As a result, Confirmation Questions not only solicit the audience's feedback on key points; they also help recapture the audience's time and attention for material you're about to cover, which has the added benefit of increasing the audience's retention rate. *"Do you have any questions?"*

If You Take the Time to Say It, Take the Time to Explain It

One of the best pieces of sales advice I ever received came from another one of my mentors, Barry Gillman. Barry said, *"If you take the time to say it, then take the time to explain it."* This is critical in the sales presentation.

As salespeople, we talk about the same set of issues every day. We are very familiar with how our products provide value and the typical problems prospects face. We're so close that we sometimes fail to recognize that the audience doesn't share the same level of knowledge. Have you ever sat through a presentation where the presenter used an acronym you didn't understand? What about buzzwords? While some people might ask questions to clarify what the presenter is saying, most will remain silent, not wanting to draw attention to themselves. Fortunately, this problem is easy to fix if you, as the presenter, are willing to educate your audience.

> **Secret #140** If you take the time to say it, then take the time to explain it.

Closing Your Sales Presentations

In the QBS model, the end of Phase II (*Presentation*) is also the beginning of Phase III (*Closing Steps*). This is where qualified potential buyers will either want to move forward to investigate the details of a purchase transaction, or they will choose to disengage.

Some people say that the end of a sales presentation is where the real selling begins. They're right. It's an opportunity to summarize how well your product or service matches up to each of the items listed on the Mutual Agenda, and it's also an opportunity for you to start positioning the sale for closure. Consequently, how your presentation ends is just as important as how it begins.

> **Secret #141** How your sales presentation ends is important because the last impression typically leaves a lasting impression.

In smaller sales, where you present to an individual decision maker, the entire sales process can occur within a single sales call. After you understand the prospect's needs, and you have educated them on the value of your solutions, it's time to close. Why wait? If the buyer is on an emotional high after your presentation, you should ask for the order—they might just say, "*Yes.*"

Larger sales are more complex because decision makers, influencers, and executive sponsors all have to weigh the alternatives and come to a decision. With larger sales, the end of a presentation is typically *not* a good time to ask for the order. Most groups don't make decisions without consulting each other first; therefore, putting your audience on the spot usually elicits a stand offish response, which doesn't help you at all.

The end of a sales presentation is also *not* a good time to ask questions like:

Presenter: *"So…what do you think?"*

This vague request for feedback is likely to produce a weak response. People who are not ready to make a commitment, are unlikely to share what they actually think. Instead, they're more likely to say:

Spokesman: *"Thank you for presenting your company's solutions. After we have a chance to carefully consider your proposal, we will get back to you with a decision."*

The value of this response is hardly worth the oxygen required to speak the words. It sounds more like what an unqualified job candidate might hear at the end of a bad interview. Therefore, asking questions like, *"What do you think?"* won't tell you what the audience really thought of your presentation or help you know what to do next.

That doesn't mean you shouldn't ask questions at the end of your sales presentations. Quite the contrary. But if you want to move prospects forward in the sales process, you might try asking a question that will tell you where you stand in the opportunity.

"Do You Like It?"

Here's how I close my sales presentations. First, I summarize each of the points that were made during the presentation. This gives me a chance to reiterate the benefits of my product and show how it will address the issues that were on the Mutual Agenda. Then, I simply say to the audience:

Seller: *"That's pretty much what we had planned to cover today. The question now is, do you like it?"*

Asking audiences if they *like* your solution is a refreshing change from the "same old same old." Instead of asking for a commitment or a dissertation on how they feel about your solution, you are simply asking for their gut reaction. For the presenter, this accomplishes two things. First, it encourages people to put aside the details and focus on how comfortable they are with your solution. Secondly, if the prospect responds favorably and acknowledges that they do "like" what they heard in your presentation, this allows you to easily transition the opportunity into the third phase of the QBS sales process.

There are lots of reasons why prospects might like your solution. Some people will like your product because it's versatile. Other people will like it because it can be upgraded over time, or because they think your solution will increase their productivity and their bottom line. Still others will like your solution because the price can be amortized over the life of the product. Whatever the reason, if prospects like the solution you've just presented, then they will want more information about the details of a purchase—starting with how much it costs. This is your ticket into Phase III.

Your Ticket into Phase III

The transition from the Phase II presentation to the close in Phase III can feel as awkward as having to walk across the dance floor to ask that special someone to dance. It's the moment of truth where sellers will find out if the prospect wishes to continue the relationship.

The good news is the transition between Phase II and Phase III doesn't have to feel awkward. In fact, QBS makes it downright comfortable by making the transition seamless. Rather than finish your presentation and then try to figure out how to move the opportunity forward, we suggest asking transition questions that will make the transition from Phase II to Phase III automatic. Let me show you how this works.

Once the prospect acknowledges that they do *like* what they've just seen in your presentation, you can easily secure the appropriate next steps in the sales process by asking questions like:

Salesperson: *"Would you like me to prepare a detailed proposal that outlines the cost of our solutions?"*

Prospect: *"Yes, please."*

Salesperson: *"Can we schedule a technical meeting so my engineer can assess your existing configuration?"*

Prospect: *"That would be good too."*

I always end my presentations by asking the prospect if they would like to know how much it costs. How can they refuse? If they "liked" your solution, why wouldn't they want to know how much it costs?

In smaller sales, you may have the pricing at your fingertips, but I would still recommend asking the question because it helps transition your conversation without the usual awkwardness. In larger sales, preparing a detailed proposal often creates the need for additional events—in this case, a technical meeting to assess the prospect's existing configuration. It would also make sense to schedule a follow-up meeting to review your proposal.

Some sellers avoid talking about price until the very last minute. We bring it up at the end of the presentation. Besides securing additional events, the best time to cost-justify a purchase is right after the presentation when the value of your offering is fresh in the mind of your prospects. Personally, I want the price to be on the table at the beginning of Phase III because I'd like to know sooner rather than later if price is going to be an obstacle in the sale. This gives me time to overcome objections, and it might spare some wasted effort if the prospect isn't as qualified as I once thought.

> **Secret #142**   Rather than avoid a discussion about price, QBS recommends using price to transition the sale into Phase III.

If the prospect likes your presentation enough to request a proposal, you *earn the right* to suggest all kinds of follow-up events—including site surveys, technical meetings, on-site product demonstrations, executive overviews, even reconvening the committee to review your proposal. Now, you have successfully transitioned the sale into Phase III—*Closing Steps.*

Summary

In the QBS sales presentation, the goal is building enough value to justify a favorable purchase decision. This requires audiences to recognize the existence of a need and listen attentively to the solutions being offered. Presentation skills like voice inflection, facial expressions, and gesturing are definitely important—but even more important is your ability to accomplish the strategic objectives of the presentation, in order to move the opportunity forward into the third and final phase of the QBS sales process. That's what we will focus on next in chapter 15—understanding what must happen to close more sales…faster.

CLOSING MORE SALES...FASTER

With Question Based Selling, closing the sale is just a logical extension of the sales process. Once you have successfully uncovered prospect needs, qualified the opportunity, and presented your solution, it's time to wrap up the business transaction.

You don't have to use high-pressure tactics to be a successful closer, however. QBS simplifies the process by identifying the five prerequisites for closing. Then we focus on the four keys that will enable you to close more sales...faster.

The third and final phase of the QBS sales process is appropriately called *Closing Steps.* As you can see in the diagram, Phase III is represented by the bottom of the sales funnel. This is where all your selling efforts to date will culminate to transform qualified prospect opportunities into valuable customer accounts.

As you saw in the Phase II presentation, your actual closing steps will depend on the product you sell and the audience you are selling to. In smaller sales, where you are face-to-face with a single decision maker, all three phases of the sales process

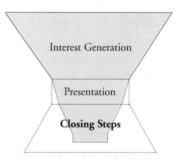

Phase III: Closing Steps

can occur within a single sales call. In this situation, the presentation is followed immediately by the close. After summarizing the value offered by your product or service, you wrap up the sale by securing the prospect's commitment to purchase.

With larger, more strategic sales, however, closing is significantly more complex. Ironically, the reason is simple. When multiple players are involved in a buying decision, it's more difficult to secure the consensus needed to pull the trigger on a decision. Each person involved forms their own impressions about the solutions being offered; and while some people on the committee will favor your offering, others will support an alternative solution. Some might even gravitate to the path of least resistance—wanting to maintain the status quo. So here's the challenge. To close sales, you must succeed in bringing all these people together to make a decision that favors your product or service.

Moving Away from the Old School

Most prospects are nervous in the final stages of a sale. It's a natural reaction—people get nervous whenever they have to make a commitment. We get nervous when we are about to buy a new car; we get nervous when we are about to sign the contract to buy a new house; and many of us have experienced the nervous butterflies that appear on the day of the big wedding. It's understandable then that our prospects may be nervous about making a commitment to purchase our product. What if they make a mistake? What if they make the wrong decision?

The old school of selling tends to view closing as a series of tricks, gimmicks, and schemes designed to manipulate potential buyers into saying yes. In QBS, we think this is a mistake. Prospective customers are smarter and more sophisticated today than ever before, and while most people love to buy, they don't want to be *sold*. Prospects are no longer willing to be pushed, pressured, or otherwise harassed into making a purchase, so there's no point in trying to force a decision. As we said back in chapter 2, the harder you push, the harder your prospects and customers will push back.

Closing shouldn't be a one-sided affair. If you offer valuable solutions at a reasonable price, then you shouldn't have to *dupe* your prospects into buying. Instead, the decision to buy should be a win-win situation—where the salesperson accomplishes his or her goal of completing the sale, and the customer satisfies their own objectives by acquiring a valuable solution.

> **Secret #143** Closing isn't something you do *to* somebody; rather, it's a mutual experience you have *with* them.

QBS's approach to closing sales is an intentional departure from the "old school." Rather than pressing prospects to force a decision, QBS focuses on leading them (via questions) to the desired result. We believe that the key to closing sales is getting buyers to value your product so much that they will *want* to move forward with a purchase.

Closing is by no means easy, however. Phase III of the sales process is filled with risk. Potential buyers are nervous about making a commitment, and salespeople are equally nervous about asking for one. As most of us already know, asking for the order is another one of those moments of truth in the sales process where the seller finds out whether their efforts will result in a successful sale or a missed opportunity.

Hope Is Not a Method

In high school, my tenth grade sex education teacher used to say, "*Hope is not a method.*" Of course, he was talking about birth control. Oddly enough, hope is not a method when it comes to closing sales either.

Some sellers try to avoid the risk of being rejected by plowing forward with different events, activities, and action items, *hoping* that their extra effort will move potential buyers toward a favorable decision. This "hopefulness" can be detrimental to your sales efforts, however. The following story illustrates this point with an important lesson about closing.

A few years ago during the holiday season, I headed off to the mall to do some Christmas shopping. My first stop was Macy's Department Store, where I wanted to purchase some perfume for my wife Laura. If you haven't ever been to Macy's at Christmastime, you have missed quite a spectacle. The displays are beautifully decorated with all the holiday trappings, and the aisles are bustling with people. I headed straight for the cosmetics department, where I noticed several other men who were on similar missions, trying to find that perfect gift for someone special.

When I reached the perfume counter, I was overwhelmed by the number of options from which to choose. There were perfumes, colognes, powders, bath beads, body lotions, and eau de toilette (whatever that is). All kinds of fragrances were on display, from every brand name you could think of. Most of the items were sold separately, but some were also available in holiday gift sets, which seemed like a good option.

One perfume in particular caught my eye, a fragrance by Alfred Sung. I remembered Laura had mentioned this one by name, which reduced my risk of making a bad decision. It smelled nice too. My search was over.

Some People Will Do Anything to Make a Sale

I flagged down one of Macy's finest to complete the transaction—but first, I had a question. I had noticed that Alfred Sung didn't come in a holiday gift set, which was really what I wanted. I shared this concern with the

Macy's clerk, and she offered, *"Would you like me to create a custom gift set by bundling a few items together into a nice basket?"*

"That would be great," I replied.

The Macy's clerk promptly ducked down behind the counter. When she popped back up, she was holding two small bottles; one was a cologne and the other was a scented lotion. She explained that if I bought both, she could include the Alfred Sung body powder at no additional cost.

"That would be wonderful," I said. Then, more out of ignorance than strategy, I asked, *"Can you include anything else?"*

"I'll see what I can do," she said. Once again, she ducked down behind the counter. In thirty or forty seconds, she popped back up and said, *"I can throw in a freshening kit—two smaller fragrance items that would easily fit inside your wife's purse or in a glove compartment."*

"Thank you," I said. Sensing that I was on a roll, I asked, *"What else?"*

She smiled and once again ducked down behind the counter. This time she popped up with a cute little carrying case to add to the pile.

"You're doing a great job!" I said. *"What else?"*

This time, she ducked behind the counter and came back up with a handful of fragrance samplers. *"These make great stocking stuffers."*

To my surprise, we had established a routine. Every time I asked, *"What else?"* my new friend, the Macy's clerk, sweetened the deal. So I continued asking, *"What else?"*

"Hmmm," she said as she disappeared into the back room. After a few moments, she came out holding a neatly wrapped box. *"How about a set of champagne glasses? These were being offered as part of another promotion, but if you like, I can throw them in too."*

"That's terrific…and thank you once again," I said. Even though I sensed the end was drawing near, my curiosity forced me to see just how far this salesperson was willing to go to make a sale. So, once again, I asked, *"What else?"*

After a pause, she smiled and said, *"Isn't that enough?"* I smiled back and nodded. Frankly, it was enough three trips ago, but as long as the clerk was willing to keep making my wife's Christmas present better and better, I had to keep asking, *"What else?"* When I walked out of Macy's that day, I had a shopping bag full of perfume and accessories, all for the price of the first two items. Even though that was several years ago, I think we're still knee-deep in Alfred Sung.

An Important Lesson about Closing

I'm not criticizing Macy's department store. Macy's provides excellent value and their customer service has always been exceptional. That's why I have been a loyal customer for many years. Nonetheless, this scenario does illustrate a valuable lesson about closing—or should I say, how *not* to close.

The Macy's clerk in this story was certainly pleasant, and she provided terrific customer service, but her closing strategy left something to be desired. She made the mistake of assuming that the more value she threw into the deal, the closer she got to making a sale. Her assumption had two problems. First, the only way a salesperson can exceed the customer's expectations is to understand what those expectations are. If the Macy's clerk had simply asked, *"Mr. Freese, if we wrap these three items into a holiday gift set, will that work for you?"* I would have said *"Sure,"* and the sale would have been made. Furthermore, this salesperson's willingness to give away more than was actually required to close the sale was counterproductive. In addition to reducing the company's profit on the transaction, this person's commitment to customer service was actually encouraging me (the buyer) to keep asking for more. In a sense, she was too customer-service oriented—trying to sweeten the deal in the hopes of achieving the desired result. But the more value she was willing to offer, the more my expectations changed, which in this case, actually moved the salesperson farther away from closing the sale.

> **Secret #144** Giving away too much isn't mutually beneficial. Sellers have to know when to add value…and when to stop.

The "kill 'em with customer service" closing mentality isn't restricted to department store clerks. It's alive and well in large account corporate sales, insurance sales, medical sales, technology sales, and many other types of selling. Instead of identifying obstacles in the sale and then addressing the outstanding deficiencies, too many sellers try to close by asking questions like, *"What else can I do?"* This encourages prospects to think up objections or additional action items to keep you busy. In QBS, we want to be effective, not busy. Good intentions and extra effort are only part of the puzzle. If you really want to close more sales, then you must accomplish the five prerequisites for closing.

Five Prerequisites for Closing

It's natural to assume that the most productive salespeople are also the best closers—after all, aren't they the ones who close the most sales? Yes, but there's a catch. Productive salespeople are not successful because they have a secret formula for closing deals. They're successful because they know how to get prospects *ready* to be closed. This is an important distinction.

> **Secret #145** Success in selling hinges less on your ability to close, and more on your ability to get prospects *ready* to be closed.

I have always believed that if the sales process is executed properly, the actual close should be an anticlimactic event. In reality, there are no magical closing phrases that can force a prospect to buy a product or service they don't really want. And if the potential buyer *does* want the solution you offer, you won't need any magic to close the sale.

The only trick is getting your prospects "ready" to be closed, which means satisfying each of the prerequisites for the sale. What do we mean by prerequisites? Just as credibility was a prerequisite for building relationships (in the Conversational Layering Model), there are five prerequisite conditions that must be satisfied before potential buyers will purchase your product or service. These five prerequisites are as follows:

Five Prerequisites to Closing Sales

1. **A Recognized Need**
2. **A Viable Solution**
3. **Value Must Justify the Cost**
4. **A Sense of Urgency**
5. **The Authority to Buy**

Your ability to satisfy each of these prerequisites in Phase III is largely dependent on what happened in Phases I and II of the QBS sales process. For example, prospective customers should recognize needs long before you try to close the sale in Phase III. In fact, by the time you move into the *Closing Steps* phase of the sales process, much of the groundwork for the sale should already be in place. To show you what I mean, let's review each of the prerequisites for closing.

Prerequisite #1   A Recognized Need

Every purchase decision represents a buyer's attempt to satisfy a need. Needs are what initially motivates them to investigate potential solutions, and needs are what ultimately motivates them to buy. Prospects will only want to buy your product or service if they recognize a need for it. Of course, the more needs you uncover in the sales process, the more reasons they will have to make a favorable decision when it's time to close.

Prerequisite #2   A Viable Solution

Once the existence of a need causes prospects to recognize that it's time to change the status quo, the discovery of a viable solution is what motivates them to move forward toward a decision. The best opportunity to showcase the viability of your solution occurs in the Phase II presentation. That's when you get an opportunity to match the benefits of your product or service against the prospect's specific needs.

Prerequisite #3   Value Must Justify the Cost

Cost-justification is the basis for every strategic decision. It's also a prerequisite for closure. By itself, the existence of a need is never enough to justify a purchase. Likewise, just because you offer a viable solution doesn't mean prospects can justify the expense. To purchase your product or service, the perceived value of your solution must exceed its cost. Keep in mind that the greater the value, the easier it is to cost-justify a purchase.

Prerequisite #4   A Sense of Urgency

Without a compelling and discernible reason to make a decision, it's always easier to maintain the status quo. You've heard the phrase, *if it ain't broke, don't fix it.* Well, this phrase applies to closing sales. Until your prospect feels a sense of urgency, he or she is not likely to buy your product.

Creating a sense of urgency is different than cost-justification, however. Even if the value of your solution justifies its cost, some people still won't pull the trigger until they are ready to make an emotional commitment.

Prerequisite #5   The Authority to Buy

Needs, solutions, justification, and a sense of urgency all rolled together still aren't enough to close the sale. Your prospect must also have the authority to make a buying decision. Imagine how rich you would be if you had a nickel for every proposal that was left stranded at the end of the sales process because the prospect did not have the authority to make a decision.

We've said it before, and we'll say it again. Qualifying the opportunity is critical to your success. This includes knowing who will make the actual buying decision. In addition to doing the right things, you also have to be dealing with the right people—those who will make or influence the decision.

QBS Makes Closing Easy

If all five of the prerequisites for closing have been satisfied, meaning prospective buyers recognize the existence of a need *and* the viability of your solution, they have the authority to make a decision *and* the urgency to move forward, *and* the value of your product or service is great enough to justify its cost, then closing sales is a breeze. At that point, all you have to do is offer encouragement and ask for the order.

If one or more of these prerequisite conditions is not in place, however, then the opportunity is not ready to be closed. That's when sellers must either push prospects to try and force a sale, or step back and figure out how to address any outstanding issues. As you might guess, the rest of this chapter is based on the latter.

The Four Keys to Closing More Sales

Some people think the act of closing is a combination of two things: asking prospects for the business and overcoming their objections. That's what the "old school" has been teaching for years—that sellers must be bold enough to ask for the order and aggressive enough to conquer objections when the prospect says no. Essentially, the thinking has always been that a seller's ability to *push* must exceed the prospect's ability to *resist*.

QBS's approach to closing sales is much less pushy and far more productive. Instead of beating potential buyers over the head in the hopes of closing a sale, we base our strategy on mutual benefit and the prevention of conflict. We want prospects to *want* to move forward. That's why QBS focuses our closing efforts on the four keys to closing more sales.

Key #1 Know the Status of the Opportunity

Knowing the status of an opportunity is critical when you are trying to close a sale. Does your buyer like the proposed solution? How does it compare to other solutions? When do they plan to make a decision? How much are they willing to pay? What are their outstanding concerns? The answers to these and other questions are pivotal to understanding the status of your opportunity, and knowing how best to proceed toward completing the sale.

This is an area where sales managers in particular get very frustrated. They know that in order to have an effective strategy for closing a sale, you have to know where you stand in the account. If all five prerequisites for closing have been fully satisfied, then you have a "green light" to ask for the order and wrap up the transaction. Everybody wins. But if the prospect is not ready to be closed, it's critical that you know exactly where you stand, so you can determine what else needs to occur to secure a favorable decision.

Having a complete and accurate status of your prospect opportunities also reduces your risk. If you go all the way back to chapter 1, you will recall how the *Hunt for Red October* anecdote about dating was a risk reduction strategy. The reason it works is because it's a technique that enables you to find out where the other person stands before you ask for a commitment. This is very different from the traditional risk associated with sticking your neck out and hoping that it doesn't get chopped off.

> **Secret #146** Soliciting feedback is important, but it's even more important to solicit complete and accurate feedback.

The real challenge in closing sales is having a complete and accurate status. We've acknowledged that most prospects are naturally cautious of salespeople. Experience has taught them to play it close to the vest, so they are reluctant to share their thoughts, feelings, or concerns. This creates somewhat of a dichotomy—where sellers, who want to know where they stand in their sales opportunities, are facing off against prospects who may not be willing to openly share. Can you see the dilemma?

To Find Out If They're Ready, Ask for the Order

Wayne Gretzky, arguably the greatest professional hockey player of all time, once said, *"You will miss 100 percent of the shots you never take."* The same is true in professional sales—you won't close many sales unless you ask for the order. It's the only way to find out if a sale is *ready* to be closed.

But asking for the order is a high-risk proposition. What if the prospect says no? Then your sale, along with all the resources and effort you've invested thus far, would be lost. Unfortunately, this fear of receiving a negative response causes many salespeople to gravitate to the idea that, *"If I don't ask for the order, the prospect can't say no."*

With Question Based Selling, we believe that asking for the order actually reduces your risk. That's because asking for the order isn't the end of the closing process, it's the beginning. If the prospect *is* ready to move forward, then you simply wrap up the details of the sale. If they are *not* ready, you have still made a valuable step forward because your closing question will help smoke out any obstacles that stand in the way of a deal. If you've satisfied the prerequisites for closing, being "up-front" reduces your risk because you can only overcome those problems and objections that you know about.

To Keep It Simple, Use a Direct Approach

Just as there's more than one way to skin a cat, there's also more than one way to ask for the order. Many salespeople like the direct approach. After each of the prerequisite conditions have been satisfied, they come right out and ask, *"Mr. Prospect, are you ready to make a decision?"* or, *"Is there anything that would prevent you from moving forward on this proposal?"*

The direct approach is remarkably effective, particularly if you invest the time to develop personal relationships with your prospects and customers.

Up Close and Personal

People love to give advice and they love to be asked for their opinion. Since one of our objectives in Phase III is finding out how the prospect feels about your offering, why not get up close and personal to find out where you stand in the sale? Asking for someone's opinion is a terrific way to solicit feedback. Here are some examples of up close and personal questions you might ask:

Seller: *"Ms. Prospect, what are your thoughts about …?"*

"How do you feel about the current status of…?"

"Since you have a great deal of experience, how would you handle …?"

One note: some prospects are cautious about revealing their intentions. This can be a challenge for sellers because cautious prospects tend to limit the quantity and the quality of the information they share. For prospects who are particularly standoffish, try taking your conversations *off the record*. This is a wonderful technique for getting overly prudent prospects to open up. For example, you might ask: *"Mr. Prospect, can I ask you something—off the record? How does your management really feel about the proposal we submitted?"*

> **Secret #147**   It's amazing how many people will suddenly open up when their comments are considered "off the record."

What Are They Expecting?

In addition to knowing how a prospect feels, it's also important to know what they are expecting. For example, suppose one of your prospects raises the issue of cost, saying, "*The price in your proposal seems a little high.*" Many sellers hear this and launch into objection-handling mode. Not so in QBS. We believe that in order to successfully handle an objection, you must first understand the prospect's expectations. Therefore, we encourage sellers to refrain until they probe the issue further—in this case, by saying:

Seller: "*Really? How much did you expect to pay?*"

If you probe an objection and listen carefully to the prospect's response, you will not only know where you stand in the sale, you will also find out what the prospect is expecting.

Another way to ferret out a prospect's expectations is to switch places in the conversation. Ask your prospect what *they* would do if they were in your shoes. Since everyone loves to give advice, this is a good way for prospects to help themselves by helping you.

Seller: "*Mr. Prospect, if you were in my shoes, how would you handle...?*"

"*If you were the salesperson on this account, what would you propose to management?*"

"*If our roles were reversed, what would you be doing differently?*"

Your prospect's insight is a wonderful source of information and ideas. What better way to navigate the sales process than to leverage the experience of those people who are closest to the decision? In fact, most advice is free for the asking...so ask away!

Question Based Trial Closes

If you're uncomfortable with the direct approach, you can still uncover the status of an opportunity by using *trial closes*. Trial closing reduces your risk even further because it allows you to test the waters (to find out if the prospect is ready to be closed), before you jump in with both feet. Here are a few of my favorite question based trial closes.

The Alternate Choice Close

Alternate choice is a popular technique. It's also a very effective closing strategy. Rather than directly asking prospects if they are ready to move forward, you would ask them to choose between two viable alternatives. Hence the name alternate choice. Here are some examples.

Seller: "*Would you rather have a cash discount or attractive financing?*"

"Are you interested in the standard service agreement, or would you like the extended warranty?"

"Is regular mail acceptable, or would you prefer overnight delivery?

If the prospect chooses either option, they are essentially telling you that they are ready to move forward—after all, why would anyone select financial terms, a service agreement, or a delivery preference unless they were planning to purchase your product or service?

Ask about Smaller Components of the Larger Sale

Big decisions are sometimes difficult for prospects to swallow. With larger commitments comes greater risk. This is an emotional hurdle that can stymie the strategic sale. One way to avoid this is by asking questions that cause prospects to focus on smaller components of the larger sale.

Seller: *"Where do you plan to warehouse the product once it arrives?"*

"Have you already talked to your bank about financing?"

"Have you thought about when you'd like to take delivery?"

A real estate agent, for example, might ask a prospective buyer, *"Have you thought about how you would furnish this house?"* If they have, then there's a good chance the prospect is getting ready to make a buying decision.

The Impending Event Close

Some prospects waffle and delay until they are literally forced to make a decision. But rather than allow them to wait until the eleventh hour, I recommend using the impending event close to create a sense of urgency that gives the prospect a reason to move forward.

What's an impending event? It's something that is going to happen in the near future that will impact the price, performance, serviceability, or availability of your goods and services. For example, if your company is planning a price increase on January 1, you have an opportunity to save customers money and pull in orders by leveraging the impending event. To encourage your prospects to focus on completing their business by this date, you might ask:

Seller: *"Mr. Prospect, does it make sense to wrap this sale up by year-end so you can take advantage of our lower price?*

"If so, what needs to happen between now and then?"

Rather than pressuring prospects to close a sale, the salesperson in this example is simply letting the prospect know that there is a significant benefit to be gained by moving forward prior to the impending event. The beauty of this approach is, if a prospect wants to take advantage of the benefit, then they will put pressure on themselves to wrap up the sale.

Neutralize the Disposition of Your Closing Questions

One of the best ways to find out where you stand in the sale is to neutralize the disposition of your questions. We introduced this idea in chapter 10. When it's time to close, sellers start to feel the risk of rejection. As a result, they ask positive questions in the hopes of generating a more positive response. This behavior is counterproductive. Prospects tend to mismatch the hopefulness of positive questions, in which case, salespeople end up receiving cautious, reluctant, or negative responses.

In Question Based Selling, we want prospects to respond openly, honestly, and accurately to our closing questions. If there's bad news lurking somewhere in the deal, we want to know about it. Conversely, if there's good news, we want to know about that too. You can easily accomplish this by neutralizing the disposition of your closing questions.

Seller: *"Ms. Prospect, you look concerned. Something's not right, is it?"*

"Are we in good shape to get the deal, or do you think we're at risk?"

"If there was a problem lurking, one that would negatively impact your decision, would you be willing share it with me?"

By inserting "the negative" into your trial closes, you will be rewarded with more open, honest, and accurate responses. Some sales traditionalists might argue that neutralizing the disposition of your questions gives prospects an easy out. As before, I would argue that prospects already have an out. They don't *have* to buy from you—and many don't, without ever sharing why not.

You Might Try Being Honest

Buyers understand that salespeople have goals and objectives. In fact, most are smart enough to recognize that you probably report to someone who's just as intense and demanding as their boss. This puts you (the salesperson) in a unique position to ask:

Seller: *"Mr. Prospect, can I ask your advice on something? I'm supposed to have a conference call with my sales manager tomorrow. I was*

*originally forecasting this opportunity to close in September,
but I would rather be accurate than optimistic. Do you think
September is still a reasonable target, or should I tell my boss something different?"*

This is a sincere and honest request for help. It reinforces the fact that you
are willing to put accuracy and the prospect's needs ahead of your own goals. If
you have established your credibility with the prospect, and you have provided
value in the sales process thus far, they are usually happy to reciprocate by helping you. If the prospect reassures you that your forecast is indeed accurate, your
probability of closing the sale increases significantly. On the other hand, if they
inform you that your forecasted time frames are not realistic, then you should
ask additional questions to better understand where you stand in the sale.

Key #2 Tit-for-Tat

When an opportunity is not yet ready to be closed, then more selling
needs to occur. So salespeople invest additional time, effort, and resources to
influence the outcome of the decision. When the opportunity still isn't ready,
sellers invest even more effort. After investing even more effort, some opportunities are still not ready to be closed. This can go on and on in what seems
like an endless chase. Some people call it the closing dance.

To avoid falling into this trap, you must realize that a sale represents a
mutual exchange of value. The key word here is mutual. In a mutual
exchange, both parties succeed in accomplishing their own goals. The seller
wins because he completes the sale. The buyer wins because he receives the
equivalent value in products or services. Both parties win.

Tit-for-tat is actually a negotiation strategy that adheres to one simple
principle. If you are going to expend time, effort, and resources working on
a sale, then you should expect something in return—a commitment, or at
least some gesture that lets you know your efforts are accomplishing mutual
goals. Every effective closing strategy is based on tit-for-tat.

> **Secret #148** Salespeople who expend effort and provide value should
> expect to get something in return.

In the Macy's story, the clerk kept throwing more and more value into
the deal in the hopes of closing a sale. But that wasn't mutually beneficial.
She should have secured a commitment first, by saying, *"If I create a holiday*

gift set with these three items, will that work for you?" This one question would have ended the negotiation, and I would have been a satisfied customer.

Asking Prospects for a Commitment

Asking for a commitment is actually easier than it sounds. Rather than be intimidated by the possibility that a potential buyer will say no, sellers can use hypothetical questions to facilitate this concept of tit-for-tat. For example, a salesperson might ask, *"Ms. Prospect, if we do this or that...would you be willing to agree to move forward with a purchase?"*

A hypothetical question like this one will prompt one of two responses. Either the prospect *will* agree to purchase your product or service, or she will back off. If she backs off, then some other obstacle is preventing the sale.

Let's not get hung up on the word commitment, however. With a tit-for-tat strategy, you aren't looking for an absolute guarantee that the prospect will buy, just some indication that your sales efforts will yield a mutual benefit. Using a variation of this technique, you could also ask, *"After we do this or that...what happens next?"* Depending on how the prospect responds, you would then decide how best to proceed.

QBS's tit-for-tat principle applies even when you're not dealing directly with the decision maker. Whether it's a champion, coach, or some other person in the account who doesn't have authority to make a commitment, you can still ask for reciprocal effort. For example, you might say, *"Mr. Champion, if we do this or that...would you be willing to recommend our solution to the rest of the committee?"* Notice that we're still asking for mutual effort.

Is the Business Even Worth Chasing?

Once you know exactly where the prospect stands, you have a decision to make: is the business worth chasing? If the prospect's expectations are reasonable, and the rewards from the sale are worth the invested effort, then it makes sense to continue working toward the sale. But there will be cases where the prospect's expectations are not reasonable. After they ask for the world, they will want you to throw in the moon and the stars. When you are in these situations, you must decide whether to continue chasing the deal or refocus your efforts on other more qualified accounts.

Secret #149 Just because your product or service adds value, doesn't mean every deal is worth chasing.

What should you do when a prospect's expectations are unreasonable? Should you ignore their requests and risk losing the sale, or should you give into their every demand under the theory that the customer is always right?

The answer is neither. Success in today's business environment is based on win-win relationships, and everything's negotiable. Therefore, a request that is unreasonable under one set of conditions might be quite acceptable if those conditions were to change. For example, let's say one of your prospects asked for an extra 10 percent discount off your best price. Would you get upset or indignant and take the position that the customer was being unreasonable? I wouldn't. Instead, it would be wiser to let the customer know what set of conditions would allow you to honor their request. You might say, *"We would be happy to give you an extra 10 percent discount…if you would be willing to double the size of your order."* How's that for a win-win scenario?

Tit-for-tat protects you from having to be the bad guy—the one who ultimately refuses the prospect's request. In that regard, it's a risk reduction strategy. Best of all, you can use tit-for-tat to negotiate just about anything. Here's a little anecdote that illustrates how tit-for-tat can change your perspective.

One night in the middle of supper, Ben Jenkins, a five-year-old boy, asked, *"Can I have a treat?"*

Noticing that Ben hadn't eaten very much, his mother said, *"No, you may not have a treat until you clean your plate."* Ben didn't like his mother's response, so he kicked, pouted, and fussed. Even though his mother was doing the proper thing under the circumstances, she was suddenly the bad guy—the one standing in the way of Ben's request for a treat.

This behavior continued, night after night. Ben would eat a fraction of his dinner and then ask for a treat. And night after night, his mother stuck to her guns and would not allow Ben to have a treat until he finished his supper. Not surprisingly, Ben became increasingly rebellious.

Finally, after more than a week of internal strife, Mr. Jenkins had had enough. He consulted his QBS materials and decided that it was time to invoke a tit-for-tat strategy. From now on, if Ben asked for a treat before finishing his dinner, Mr. Jenkins would handle it.

Sure enough, the very next night, Ben had only eaten a portion of his supper when he turned to his mother and asked, *"Mom, can I have a treat?"*

"Tonight you need to ask your father," Mrs. Jenkins countered.

Surprised, Ben looked at his father and asked, *"Dad, can I have a treat?"*

"Yes," Mr. Jenkins said. *"You may absolutely have a treat…just as soon as you finish your dinner."*

Ben's parents were in agreement on principle, but the way they responded to their son's request was very different. The mother responded based on the current set of conditions. Ben hadn't finished his dinner, therefore, he wasn't entitled to a treat. The father, using a tit-for-tat philosophy, put Ben in control of his own destiny by assuring that he could "absolutely" have a treat as soon as he met the conditions that made his request a reasonable one. The moral to this story is, the next time one of your customers asks for something, rather than dig your heels in and say no, let them know the conditions that would make their request mutually beneficial.

Tit-for-tat is especially valuable once we realize that buyers have been conditioned to ask for more than they actually expect. It's all part of the closing dance. But that certainly doesn't mean you have to bend over backward to close a sale.

Key #3 Reiterate Your Value

Phase III is an appropriate time for review. It's an opportunity for salespeople to help prospects organize their thoughts, and it's also an opportunity to summarize the key points that have been made thus far in the sales process. Ultimately, you want the sale to crescendo and then peak just as prospects are getting ready to make their decision. You want them to be in touch with their own needs and register value in the solutions that were presented. You also want them to feel a sense of urgency. This requires an active effort on your part to summarize needs and reiterate value.

> **Secret #150** Effectively representing a product or service requires salespeople to *re-present* its value prior to closing.

Whether the sales cycle lasts two months or two years, it's easy to look back and assume that if something has already been covered, there's no need to go over it again. *"We've already covered that,"* salespeople sometimes think to themselves. And it's true—through diligence and hard work, they probably have.

Unfortunately, salespeople sometimes fail to recognize is that just because something has already been covered doesn't mean prospects always remember the point. Particularly in larger sales, when prospective buyers are being asked to assimilate lots of information, by the end of the sales process, much of the material that was originally presented has faded over time. This creates a problem. If the information that justifies your solution fades, then the prerequisites for closing that were once satisfied may no longer be intact.

Managing "Half-Life"

In the early 1900s, scientists began studying nuclear particles. During this research, they discovered that the radioactivity in most nuclear substances dissipates naturally over time. They began measuring this phenomenon in units of *half-life*—the time required for a nuclear material to lose half its radioactive energy. Some nuclear substances have a half-life of many years, while others lose half their radiation in a matter of hours.

A similar phenomenon happens in sales. Although we would like to think our prospects and customers remember everything we present, much of the information that gets covered during the sales process also dissipates naturally over time. Case in point, what's the half-life of a typical sales presentation? In other words, how long does it take for someone in your audience to forget a significant portion of what they've heard? Two or three days? Or perhaps only two or three hours?

The human memory is a limited resource—so, when fresh information comes in, older information tends to get pushed to the background. Accordingly, some portion of what was originally stored in memory is lost. For example, if you went to a party one night, soon after the party ended, you would likely be able to name many of the people who were there. You would remember who you talked with and what you talked about. But weeks later, you would likely recall some fraction of the guest list, and only snippets of your conversations. After a few months, you would remember even less...and so on.

> **Secret #151** *Half-life* impacts your sales efforts because it causes information that was once fully intact to fade over time.

During the course of a sale, salespeople provide lots of information to communicate the value of their product or service offering. But as you might expect, some of the points that get made early in the process are subject to this phenomenon of intellectual erosion. As a result, when the end of the sale comes and it's time to close, certain prerequisites that were once intact may no longer be satisfied; in which case, the prospect will *not* be ready to close. That's why one of the keys to closing more sales is reiteration—helping prospects revisit both the problems you solve and the value you bring to the table. If any amount of time has passed since you began the sale, you'll need to remind the prospect of several key issues.

Revisit the Mutual Agenda

If you want prospects to make a decision in your favor, the perceived value of your solution must be great enough to justify its cost. That's one of the prerequisites for closing.

Justification starts with needs. Needs are what originally motivates prospects to investigate potential solutions, and needs will ultimately motivate them to buy. But just like anything else, needs are also subject to this concept of half-life, where a prospect who once had many reasons to buy may only recall some fraction of those needs by the end of the sale.

To rekindle your prospect's sense of urgency, it's always a good idea to revisit the Mutual Agenda—the one you created in Phase II. As a compilation of the prospect's needs, the Mutual Agenda served as a wonderful road map for building value in the presentation. It can also be used to help close the sale. Reviewing each of the items on the Mutual Agenda is an excellent way to bring the prospect's needs back to the forefront of the decision.

> **Secret #152** As a prospect's hot buttons get hotter, the corresponding value of your solutions will increase significantly.

In addition to revisiting the prospect's needs, you should also reiterate the value of your product or service. But since people are motivated differently, be sure to revisit your *gold medal* and *German Shepherd* benefits. Since reward and aversion can each weigh heavily on a purchase decision, QBS recommends that you reiterate both.

This brings us to an interesting point about cost justification. Most sellers try to cost-justify the purchase with *gold medal* benefits—by pointing out all the wonderful things the prospect will get from choosing their solution. But what about the cost of *not* selecting your solution? Perhaps we should take a lesson from Charlie Simms, one of the largest contractors in the Southeast.

Whenever Charlie is asked to provide a price estimate on a roofing job, for example, he inspects the job site and then gives the homeowner a two-part quote. At the top of the quote, he details the specifications for the job—square footage, estimated materials, and labor. These line items are subtotaled into a cost estimate for installing a new roof.

The bottom of the estimate is reserved for a second quote. There, Charlie details how much the job will cost if the homeowner chooses to ignore the current problems, and the existing roof is exposed to further weather damage, leakage, or rot. Essentially, he gives prospective customers a chance to realize that while fixing the current problem isn't cheap, it's significantly less expensive than doing nothing and letting the problem get progressively worse.

Charlie is an excellent salesman, and his two-part quote has helped him close lots of business. This same concept can be applied in almost any sale. For example, what's the cost of *not* having life insurance? What's the cost of *not* keeping pace with technology or *not* updating the service contract? What's the cost of downtime? With a little effort on your part, you can help prospects realize that *not* buying your product or service might be their most expensive option.

> **Secret #153** For prospects who have pressing needs, not buying your product or service might be their most expensive option.

Key #4 Emotional Reassurance

The fourth and final key to closing more sales is providing emotional reassurance. Most purchases are highly emotional. After all, the analysis has been completed and the committee has issued its recommendation, the actual decision usually boils down to how the decision maker *feels* about the solution being offered, and whether they are comfortable enough to pull the trigger on a purchase.

Consequently, decision making is very subjective. It's also laced with a tremendous amount of uncertainty and risk. On one hand, decision makers want to make the right decision for themselves and the organizations they represent. On the other hand, they want to avoid making a mistake. They get particularly nervous as the end of the sale approaches; as I've said before, the larger the purchase, the greater their risk.

To offset this risk, sellers must offer support at the end of the sales process—analytical support to justify the cost of the decision, and emotional reassurance to make prospects feel more comfortable.

> **Secret #154** Spending a few minutes to make customers feel special is more significant than spending hours to make them feel average.

There are lots of ways to reassure your prospects. Some of this might be common sense, but much of it is strategic positioning. In either case, the net effect is the same. The more comfortable your prospects are, the more likely they are to make a favorable buying decision.

Empathy is a Powerful Bonding Tool

When a prospect is facing the pressure of a difficult decision, they don't need to be pushed. What they really need is a friend—someone who can empathize with the challenges of the decision, rather than caring only about the status of the sale. Your ability to show this kind of emotional support will help you bond with prospects and close more sales. Here are some sample questions that sellers can use to empathize with their prospects.

Seller: *"I understand this is a difficult decision. How can I help?"*

"Obviously you've been thinking long and hard about this decision. Would you feel better if...?"

"Are you comfortable with...?"

Another way to empathize with a prospective buyer is to walk a mile in their shoes. This is accomplished by offering to participate in the decision. You simply adjust your questions by replacing the word "you" with the more inclusive pronoun, "we." Here are some examples.

Seller: *"What can we do to convince the rest of the committee?"*

"How should we position this proposal to your vice president?"

"Is there anything we should be doing differently?"

Sincere empathy is very reassuring to a prospect who is about to make a decision. It shows that you can appreciate the importance of the purchase and it also lets them know that you are interested in their success.

Safety in Numbers

The Herd Theory is a powerful strategy for engaging new prospects in productive sales conversation. But it's also a good technique for making prospects feel comfortable at the end of the sales process. Knowing that "everyone else" seems to be moving in the same direction is very reassuring to prospects. It lets them know that they are indeed making the right decision. You can use this sense of momentum to bolster the prospect's confidence as an opportunity gets closer to closing. If your prospect raises a question or concern about price, for example, you can easily leverage the rest of the herd by saying:

Seller: *"Mr. Prospect, I'm not surprised to hear you ask about price. Do you know why? It's because I've had this same discussion with US West, Southern Company, NationsBank, General Motors, United*

> *Healthcare, Hewlett Packard, BellSouth, Sun Microsystems, British Telecom…and many others. Would you like to know what finally pushed their decision over the top? They found that…"*

The Herd Theory is not only a momentum play, it's also an effective objection-handling strategy. By giving potential buyers the sense that other customers have already blazed the trail to success, you increase your own credibility while reducing the prospect's risk. Everybody wins!

Ask Solution Questions to Develop Internal Champions

In decisions that involve multiple players, salespeople can gain tremendous leverage from an internal champion who is willing to "go to bat" for their product or service. Particularly in large corporate sales, you probably won't have the luxury of personally engaging every person who will influence the decision. That's why it's so important to develop internal champions—people who are willing to carry your flag when you can't.

> **Secret #155** A champion who understands *how to sell* your product or service is worth their weight in commission checks.

For an internal champion to be effective, they must be emotionally involved. They must *like* what you are selling and they must be willing to tell others why they should like it too. You can help develop these internal champions, and their sense of loyalty, by asking Solution Questions.

We first talked about Solution Questions in chapter 9, when we were probing for needs. Now, as we near the end of the sale, these same questions are excellent tools for grooming potential champions, and making sure they know how to effectively position the value of your product or service. To find out how effective your internal champions are, you should make it a point to ask questions like:

Seller: *"Mr. Champion, how do you think this product will benefit your specific environment?"*

"How would you compare our solution to other alternatives?"

"What will you do if your boss, or someone on the committee, objects to our proposal?"

Prospects who can thoughtfully articulate the benefits of your solution will respond by "selling you" on why their needs are important and how your solutions add value. This gives you an opportunity to coach them if they need help or cheer them on if they can articulate a robust message.

Summary: Wrapping Up the Sale

Once the prerequisites for closing have been satisfied, it's time to wrap up the business transaction. That means working through the details of the purchase and providing prompt and excellent service. If the sales process is executed properly, the actual close should be an anticlimactic event.

But there's a larger lesson to be learned. If you want to close more sales, then you need to have more opportunities coming into the top of the sales funnel. This means using the Question Based Selling methodology to penetrate more new accounts, uncover more needs, present more value, and differentiate yourself from the competition. At the end of the day, there is no substitute for hard work. If you are committed to excellence, and you achieve each of these goals, you will accomplish the larger objective of doubling your sales results.

FOR SALES MANAGERS ONLY

Salespeople who read *Secrets of Question Based Selling* are trying to increase their own sales effectiveness. They want to penetrate more new accounts, uncover more needs, create a greater sense of urgency, and move qualified opportunities forward toward closure. Sales managers, on the other hand, are tasked with increasing the effectiveness of the sales team as a whole.

Sales managers definitely have the bigger challenge. They have to deal with many different selling styles and they are usually managing a broad range of sales experience. Salespeople who are just starting out often need lots of attention. But experienced sellers need attention too, even if it's just a kick in the pants to fix some bad habits that have crept into their daily routine. Ultimately, sales managers want to boost productivity by getting the entire sales organization to execute on a consistent and proven strategy.

Implementing a strategic sales methodology is *not* as easy as it sounds, however. With so many different philosophies to choose from, sales managers are discovering that while some sales methods are overly simplistic, others are so incredibly complex that their implementation in the real world is impractical.

Too much hype is another problem. An enthusiastic approach may succeed in making some salespeople more excited, but it has been my experience that being "super-positive" rarely makes up for poor technique. High-pressure sales tactics are equally ineffective, as today's prospects are no longer willing to endure the constant hammering from a steady stream of overzealous salespeople.

Not surprisingly, salespeople and sales managers have grown tired of the same old sales training. Experienced sellers have heard it all before, and brand-new salespeople are applying traditional methods with limited success. What they want is something different—something that works.

> **Secret #156** In today's business culture, there is an *overwhelming* demand for proven sales talent, but there is an *underwhelming* infrastructure for teaching salespeople how to succeed.

Question Based Selling is a refreshing change from traditional sales methodologies. We don't use "hype" to get salespeople excited in the hopes that they will sell more. Instead, we show them how to become more effective, knowing that salespeople who are more effective will get excited and, therefore, will get their prospects excited.

Question Based Selling is easy to implement and salespeople no longer have to wait weeks or months to see results. Results come immediately. The realization that buyers are motivated by *gold medals* and *German Shepherds,* for example, will instantly double the number of benefits your salespeople can present. It will also double the number of needs they can uncover. Salespeople will receive similarly impressive results when they implement the Conversational Layering Model, the Herd Theory, lukewarm sales calls, and the Mutual Agenda. They will also discover how to leverage the most powerful tool in sales as they learn how to effectively manage the *scope, focus,* and *disposition* of their questions. Each of the QBS strategies and techniques outlined in this book is designed to be implemented right away, perhaps in your very next sales opportunity.

This brings us to a very important question. What's the best way to introduce Question Based Selling to your sales organization? Actually, there are several ways. Each sales organization has different needs, and every Question Based Selling client is unique; therefore, we offer a variety of options from which you can choose to implement the QBS methodology. These options include:

This Book

Secrets of Question Based Selling is a unique book because it was written with a dual purpose. In addition to explaining the QBS methodology, this book also serves as a reference guide that salespeople can use over time. Whether people read the book from cover to cover or go directly to those sections that speak to their specific needs, salespeople will learn how positioning themselves differently will uncover more needs, communicate more value, and significantly increase their sales results.

This book is not just for salespeople, however. It's for everyone who touches the sales process, including product specialists, sales engineers, managers, marketing, telesales, and customer service personnel.

QBS Methodology Training

QBS Research, Inc., offers a complete menu of sales training programs that focus on every aspect of the strategic sale. In our two- and three-day classes, salespeople learn how to more effectively penetrate new accounts, move opportunities forward in the sales process, overcome objections, justify the proposed solution, and close more sales. QBS training is an interactive experience, and each program is customized to meet the specific needs of the QBS client. We encourage clients to broaden the scope of their sales training to include telesales, sales engineers, product managers, and marketing.

QBS Sales Talk

Salespeople who are highly motivated tend to be more productive. One of the best ways to motivate your sales organization is by giving them a taste of Question Based Selling at your next regional or national sales meeting. Using the QBS methodology as a backdrop, certified QBS instructors will deliver a powerful sales talk that will inspire your salespeople and transform your speaking engagement into a real learning experience. QBS sales talks are one to four hours in length.

One-Day QBS Sales Training "Blitz"

The One-Day QBS Sales Training Blitz is a hybrid solution. Some clients want more than a sales talk, but they can only carve a single day out of their regional or national sales meeting for strategic training. For these clients, we have created a condensed version of the full QBS sales training. In a single day, we cover large portions of the QBS methodology at a very aggressive pace. While many salespeople are accustomed to getting only one or two things out of a full day of sales training, the One-Day QBS Sales Training Blitz offers a thought-provoking program packed with new ideas and strategic techniques.

QBS Continuing Education

Some sales training is a one-time shot. You educate the sales force, and then hope they remember enough to successfully implement the material. To maximize our client's return on investment, QBS Research, Inc., offers several options for ongoing training. Once your salespeople understand the methodology, periodic refresher courses can be scheduled to reinforce the original QBS training and tune specific skill sets, including curiosity and credibility strategies, objection handling, presentation skills, and closing.

Train the Trainers

Salespeople who implement Question Based Selling can also learn how to teach it. "Train the trainers" and mentoring are concepts that have been in practice for a long time, and have proven themselves to be very effective. Any major roll-out of the QBS methodology can be significantly enhanced by developing in-house trainers and mentors. We can help you accomplish this.

QBS Research, Inc., will also host periodic "train the trainer" conferences. At these conferences, sales managers and QBS mentors will receive advanced QBS materials that they can bring back to their sales organizations. We will have skill-specific break-out sessions where attendees from different companies and industries can share their ideas and experiences with other people who have successfully implemented the QBS methodology.

Contact Information

If you enjoyed reading *Secrets of Question Based Selling*, then you will really enjoy putting the QBS methodology to work in your business. Success is contagious and selling is exciting when prospective buyers *want* to hear more about the solutions you offer. To get started with QBS, all you need is a commitment to excellence and a willingness to step outside the box of traditional sales thinking. Please let us know how we can help.

For more information about QBS Research, Inc., or QBS Sales Training Programs, please contact:

QBS Research, Inc.
P.O. Box 922933
Atlanta, GA 30010-2933
Office: (770) 394-0727
Fax: (770) 394-3222
Email: admin@QBSresearch.com

...or visit our website at QBSResearch.com

Notes

Index

About the Author

The first time Tom Freese oversold his sales quota by 200 percent, everyone thought it was a fluke. When he did it again, they assumed it was just some sort of freak accident. Over and over for seven consecutive years, Tom not only exceeded his sales quota, he doubled it. Suddenly, his success in selling was more than a trend. It was a business phenomennon!

With more than seventeen years' experience in the corporate sales and management trenches, Tom packaged his unique approach into a highly proven strategic sales methodology called Question Based Selling. Now, he works with sales organizations all over the world to show salespeople how a question-based approach can significantly increase their sales results. As founder and president of QBS Research, Inc., Tom is considered one of the foremost authorities on sales methodology, buyer motivation, and business strategy.

Tom Freese lives in Atlanta, Georgia, with his wife and two daughters. Between speaking events, Tom is working on his next book—a collection of strategic tools and selling techniques that will give salespeople the edge they need to compete in an increasingly tumultuous sales marketplace.

Visit our website at: www.QBSresearch.com

"As a salesperson, I was bored with traditional methods. I had been through all the standard 101 training, and I had already endured all the hype I could stand. What I really wanted was a methodology that would increase my effectiveness and differentiate my value in every aspect of the sales process. That's why I created Question Based Selling."

—Thomas A. Freese, President, QBS Research, Inc.